Waiting for Antichrist

Waiting for Antichrist

*Charisma and Apocalypse
in a Pentecostal Church*

DAMIAN THOMPSON

OXFORD
UNIVERSITY PRESS

2005

OXFORD
UNIVERSITY PRESS

Oxford University Press, Inc., publishes works that further
Oxford University's objective of excellence
in research, scholarship, and education.

Oxford   New York
Auckland   Cape Town   Dar es Salaam   Hong Kong   Karachi
Kuala Lumpur   Madrid   Melbourne   Mexico City   Nairobi
New Delhi   Shanghai   Taipei   Toronto

With offices in
Argentina   Austria   Brazil   Chile   Czech Republic   France   Greece
Guatemala   Hungary   Italy   Japan   Poland   Portugal   Singapore
South Korea   Switzerland   Thailand   Turkey   Ukraine   Vietnam

Published by Oxford University Press, Inc.
198 Madison Avenue, New York, New York 10016
www.oup.com

Oxford is a registered trademark of Oxford University Press

Library of Congress Cataloging-in-Publication Data
Thompson, Damian, 1962—
Waiting for antichrist: charisma and apocalypse in a Pentecostal church / Damian Thompson
p. cm.
Includes bibliographical references and index.
ISBN-13 978-0-19-517856-2
ISBN 0-19-517856-4
1. Millennialism.   2. Pentecostal Churches—Doctrines.   I. Title
BT892.T46 2005
236'.9'08828994—dc22   2004012518

9   8   7   6   5   4   3   2   1

Printed in the United States of America
on acid-free paper

Acknowledgments

I owe a huge debt of gratitude to two scholars. First, to Professor Eileen Barker, my wonderful academic supervisor at the London School of Economics, who showed me how to derive my theory from my findings and not the other way round. Eileen taught me how to think systematically; she made me weed out the colorful but lazy generalizations that have proved so difficult to resist in my career as a newspaper journalist. Second, to Professor Stephen O'Leary of the University of Southern California, whose study of apocalyptic discourse is the most important contribution to millennial studies in recent years. My intellectual debt to Stephen is obvious from this book; but he is also a dear friend and has been a gracious host to me on many occasions. Other scholars have been generous with their time and advice: I am thinking especially of Professor Richard Landes, founder of the Center for Millennial Studies at Boston University; the Rev. Dr. Martyn Percy of the Lincoln Theological Institute; Dr. Judith Fox; and Professor Norman Cohn, the world's leading historian of millenarianism. I am grateful, too, to my fellow students at the LSE, Amanda van Eck, David V. Barrett, and Dr. Marat Shterin, who took time off from their own work to read early drafts of this book. Thank you for your patience; it must be a relief to know that you will no longer have to listen to me drone on about the finer points of apocalyptic belief. I must also thank San Kim for his invaluable assistance with the processing of survey data. Finally, I am grateful to all the staff and members of Kensington Temple who welcomed me into their community: to Pastor Colin Dye, Sunil Choti, Larry Grant, Andrew Kenworthy, and Dr. Chris Shell; and, above all, to Will Napier, an interviewee who became an intellectual sparring partner and indispensable friend.

Contents

Waiting for Antichrist

I

Introduction

Theories of Millenarianism

How can people believe that the supernatural end of the world lies just around the corner when, so far, every such prediction has been proved wrong? Some scholars argue that millenarians are psychologically disturbed; others maintain that their dreams of paradise on earth reflect a nascent political awareness. This study looks at how members of one religious group with a strong apocalyptic tradition—Kensington Temple, a large Pentecostal church in London—reconciled doctrines of the end of the world with the demands of their everyday lives. As we shall see, they subjected these doctrines to a process of scrutiny, moderating and marginalizing them in response to what I call the "Problem of the End," the tendency of apocalyptic discourse to predict things that do not happen. In doing so, they employed the same subjective rationality that they applied to all manner of risky religious claims, such as those relating to miraculous healing. In effect, they were testing hypotheses: not in a scientific fashion, but according to the dictates of common sense. These findings are difficult to reconcile with the notion that there is a single psychological or material *cause* of millenarianism.

This study arose out of a conviction that various academic theories of millenarianism, like the popular image of apocalyptic believers, oversimplify a complicated reality. I was not alone in thinking this: much of the theoretical groundwork for my ideas was laid by the communications scholar Stephen O'Leary, whose book *Arguing the Apocalypse* (1994) suggests that millenarianism is best analyzed as a form of rhetoric. In this approach, the key to millenarianism is an understanding of how its arguments are framed, circulated, and managed, rather than (mostly untestable) speculation about the deep-seated attitudes it represents. But O'Leary's work was text-based; my aim has been to produce an ethnographic study of the operation of apocalyptic ideas in one setting, based on interviews and survey data. In the event, my findings led me well beyond the area of belief in the end of the world. It soon became clear that a study of the management of millenarianism could throw light on a wider social process: the management of deviant or "high-tension" ideas by religious groups in general. My main theoretical chapter, chapter 2, therefore introduces the broader sociological concepts of tension, rational choice, and charismatic authority before applying them to millenarianism. First, however, I want to underline the need for this study by examining the existing academic theories of millenarianism, some of which reflect, and may even help shape, popular misconceptions of apocalyptic believers.

Millenarian belief tends to be regarded by modern society as either sinister or silly. So-called "millennial fever" is associated with terrifying extremes of behavior—understandably so, since the history of millenarianism is scarred by upsurges of violence. Apocalyptic prophecies typically assure the faithful that only God's people will survive the coming crisis; the rest of the world is controlled by dark forces whose ultimate defeat will be accompanied by warfare and convulsions of the natural order. From time to time, the imagined violence of these scenarios has helped to inspire real-life tragedies: the murderous sorties of medieval sectarians, the siege of Münster, the slaughter of the Ghost Dancers, the twentieth-century tragedies of Jonestown, Waco, Tokyo, and Heaven's Gate (see Cohn [1957] 1993; Hall, 2000; Wessinger, 2000). In some of these cases, apocalyptic believers have sought to bring on the End by their own violent acts, occasionally directed against themselves; in others, they have been more or less gratuitously assaulted by the forces of the state; often, a pattern of mutual misunderstanding means that it is not clear who bears the ultimate responsibility for the bloodshed. But the stigmatization of apocalyptic belief is not purely the result of its association with violence. The prophet wearing a sandwich board announcing that "The End is Nigh" is an enduring comic stereotype; the setting and passing of apocalyptic deadlines is seen as intrinsically humorous. As early as 1844, newspapers made fun of the Millerites, American prophecy enthusiasts who predicted that Jesus would return on the night of October 12 that year. According to one account, once the deadline had passed, "the taunts and sneers of the scoffers were well-nigh unbearable. If any of Miller's followers walked abroad, they ran the gauntlet of merciless ridicule. 'What! Not gone up yet? We thought you'd gone up! Wife left you behind to burn, did she?' " (Alnor 1989: 58).

Although scholars of millenarianism avoid value-laden adjectives such as "sinister" or "silly," much of their work gravitates toward either millennial violence or the peaceful but painful failure of doomsday prophecies. This emphasis reflects the enormous influence of two books published in the 1950s: Norman Cohn's *The Pursuit of the Millennium* ([1957] 1993), a study of revolutionary and mystical millenarians in the later Middle Ages, and *When Prophecy Fails* ([1956] 1964) by Leon Festinger, Henry Riecken, and Stanley Schachter,[1] a frequently hilarious ethnographic account of a UFO cult confronted by the nonfulfillment of its prophecy of a catastrophic flood. Both these classic studies have initiated scholarly debates: Cohn's about the causes of millenarianism and Festinger's about the reactions of apocalyptic believers to the disconfirmation of prophecy.

The Pursuit of the Millennium has provided us with one of the most authoritative definitions of millenarianism. According to Cohn, millenarians always picture salvation as collective, terrestrial, imminent, total, and miraculous ([1957] 1993: 13). This formulation is widely accepted,[2] but the book's explanation of the causes of millenarianism is more contentious. Cohn emphasizes the desperate situation of the people who joined medieval sectarian movements: landless peasants, beggars, journeymen—"people who were not simply poor but who could find no assured and recognized place in society at all." Lacking their own kinship groups, they turned to prophets whose eschatological fantasies offered an escape from their atomized condition and "emotional compensation for their abject status" (282). Cohn's stress on psychological rather than material factors is in contrast to the work of scholars in the Marxist tradition such as Peter Worsley (1957) and E. J. Hobsbawm ([1959] 1965), for whom millenarianism marks the early stages of political consciousness. For Hobsbawm, millenarians are social revolutionaries who can "readily exchange their primitive costume in which they dress their aspirations for the modern costume of Socialist and Communist politics" (1959: 64). Few scholars would now defend this interpretation of apocalypticism as political or economic aspirations in disguise: the whole trend in the sociology of knowledge has been away from the conception of ideas as the simple product of material circumstances toward recognition of the power of symbols (see McCarthy 1996: 11–26). Cohn's ideas have worn rather better: according to the sociologist Malcolm Hamilton, Cohn "seems to be right concerning the importance of social displacement, insecurity and emotional anxiety in these movements and their essentially fantastical character." But he adds that "it is less easy to accept that they were the product of mass psychological disturbance or pathological mental states. The social character of them refutes such a claim" (1995: 92).

In recent years, the most influential explanation for millenarianism has involved the concept of *relative deprivation*, which utilizes psychological and political arguments and can be reconciled with the perspectives of Cohn and the Marxists. Ted Gurr (1970: 23–24) defines relative deprivation as "the tension that develops from a discrepancy between the 'ought' and the 'is' of collective value satisfaction." It arises not from some absolute level of poverty, but from poverty relative to expectations. Millenarianism identifies the source of deprivation and legitimates the use of violence to achieve a desired end; it is a natural outgrowth of relative deprivation. There are, however, significant problems with this theory. Despite its subtlety, it remains preoccupied with material factors. Millenarians are often, but not always, poor: what are we to make of middle-class American fundamentalists who believe that Jesus will return in their lifetimes but do not think of themselves as deprived in any sense, relative or absolute? The concept of relative deprivation might fit the wandering brigands described by Cohn or the Melanesian cargo cults studied by Worsley, but it is of dubious value to an analysis of, say, the Jehovah's Witnesses: James Beckford, in his study of the British Watch Tower movement, reported that his interviewees "gave no indication . . . that they felt economically or socially deprived, nor were any objective indicators of such deprivation prominent in their reported backgrounds" (1975: 156).[3] Beckford adds that the concept of relative deprivation is "too gross and undiscriminating; it clearly applies to so many people that it cannot possibly succeed in distinguishing between those who are motivated by it and those who are not" (1975: 157–58). Methodologically, too, it is suspect. Relative deprivation tends to be identified *after* a millenarian outbreak; it has yet to establish itself as a way of predicting such outbreaks. The same objection applies to many explanations for the phenomenon, such as, for example, Mary Douglas's theory that millenarianism arises in societies in which group identity is low but where people are subjected to impersonal rules (1973: 171).

If the debate about the causes of millenarianism has focused disproportionately on violent and exotic movements, that initiated by *When Prophecy Fails* is open to the charge that it caricatures belief in the end of the world. The group studied—one might almost say infiltrated—by Festinger and his colleagues was led by a prophet they called "Mrs. Keech" (her real name was Dorothy Martin), who claimed to have received warning from extraterrestrial spirits of a flood that would submerge most of North America; before this happened, however, flying saucers would rescue her and her followers. *When Prophecy Fails* tells the story of the disappointment felt by the group when the spaceships and flood failed to come, after which many of its members, instead of abandoning their beliefs, sought to promulgate them even more vigorously through the media. This surprising development led Festinger to claim that, under the right circumstances, apocalyptic believers in general react to prophetic disconfirmation by stepping up their efforts to spread their message ([1956] 1964: 3–6). In the decades since the book's publication, several scholars have sought to refine Festinger's thesis or to prove it wrong. Jane Hardyck and Marcia Braden (1962) interviewed a group of Pentecostal Christians who hid in a bunker awaiting a nuclear attack; after disconfirmation, members of the group avoided proselytizing. Richard Singelenberg ([1989] 2000) studied the reaction of Dutch Jehovah's Witnesses to the failed apocalyptic deadline of 1975; he found that evangelization decreased after disconfirmation. The consensus is that apocalyptic groups rarely react to disconfirmation in the manner described by *When Prophecy Fails*. Instead, they are more likely to try to reinterpret the original prophecy in ways that allow them to claim that it has been fulfilled; many of them fall apart in the process.[4] Yet Festinger's thesis is too valuable to be discarded in its entirety. It may be wrong about the likely behavior of millenarians after disconfirmation, but its recognition that they act to reduce "cognitive dissonance" recognizes the essential rationality of people who are often written off by society as irrational.

Put simply, cognitive dissonance is the tension between belief and experience. According to Festinger, people act to reduce this tension by changing their beliefs or behavior, by acquiring new information or beliefs, or by trying to forget or reduce the importance of dissonance-causing cognitions ([1956] 1964: 25–26). This is a convincing argument; but I would suggest that, rather than prompting disappointed apocalyptic believers to proselytize further, as Festinger states, the instinct to reduce cognitive dissonance leads most members of millenarian religions to steer clear of time-specific, dissonance-inviting doomsday prophecies—or, at the very least, to treat them with caution. This fact is overlooked by Festinger and many of his critics, who, while disagreeing about how people react to prophetic disappointment, between them give the impression that the history of millenarianism is dominated by failed deadlines. It has been left to the American scholar of religion, J. Gordon Melton, to point out that millenarian groups are not necessarily obsessed with prophecy:

> Though one or more prophecies may be important to a group, they will be set within a complex set of beliefs and interpersonal relationships. They may serve as one of several important sources determining group activity, but the prediction is only one support device for the group, not the essential rafter. The belief that prophecy is the organizing or determining principle for millennial groups is common among media representatives, nonmillennial religious rivals, and scholars. In their eagerness to isolate what they see as a decisive or interesting fact, they ignore or pay only passing attention to the larger belief structure of the group and the role that structure plays in the life of believers. ([1985] 2000: 147)

Melton's argument, which is based on ethnographic observation of dozens of groups, effectively pulls the rug out from under several theoretical explanations of millenarianism. If prophecy belief is only part of a theological system, and not necessarily the most important part, how confident can we be of isolating its cause? If, as Melton implies (and my own fieldwork at Kensington Temple suggests), many millenarians spend most of their time thinking about subjects other than the coming end of the world, this suggests that they are neither psychologically disturbed nor tormented by relative deprivation. No doubt the scholars criticized by Melton would reply that the people he is describing are not really millenarians. But what *is* a millenarian, anyway, and who decides?

Cohn's celebrated formulation tells us how millenarians conceive of salvation, but does not define them by their behavior. *The Pursuit of the Millennium* demonstrates that the actions of certain groups were inspired by millenarian teachings, but wisely refrains from claiming that millenarianism always leads to revolution and bloodshed. (In fact, as we know from the work of Bernard McGinn [(1979) 1998], medieval ideas about the end of the world were often peacefully expressed and exploited by the religious and political elite of the day.) Festinger and his colleagues thought they knew what millenarians did in certain circumstances, but their theory has failed most of its empirical tests. The truth is that it is no easier to generalize about millenarian behavior than it is to discover the causes of millenarianism. We can agree that the phenomenon is characterized by belief in the imminent end of the world, but we must also come to terms with the fact that millions of people subscribe to this radical and counter-intuitive idea without allowing it to influence their daily lives too much. Again, one could reply that they are not really millenarians; but that objection implies that people cannot be classified according to their beliefs unless they act on them in some conspicuous way.

We need to find a more flexible way of thinking about millenarianism, one that avoids defining it as pure belief or, alternatively, a set of extreme actions inspired by belief. One solution is to focus on its operation as rhetoric. In O'Leary's view, apocalyptic discourse is a dynamic process, the outcome of which depends on many more factors than predisposing economic status. As he points out, "expectations can be fostered and legitimated only through discourse, and social systems of status, behavior, and worth have their origins in language and symbolic communication" (1994: 10). People must be *persuaded* that the world is coming to an end:

> It comes as no surprise that sociologists and historians, lacking the perspective of rhetorical studies, should expend so much energy in trying to explain the appeal of apocalyptic discourse by discovering audience predispositions based in conditions of social and economic class, in experience of calamity, or in psychological anomie. It is curious, however, that even those rhetorical scholars who attempt to account for the appeal of apocalyptic never seriously entertain the hypothesis that people are actually persuaded by apocalyptic arguments; that is, that the nature of apocalyptic's appeal should be sought in transactions of texts and audiences. (1994: 11)

The advantage of O'Leary's analytical framework is that it encompasses much more than the classic (and relatively rare) millenarian movements in which a single prophet whips up his or her followers into a state of hysterical expectation. We can apply it, for example, to the medieval literature collected by McGinn ([1979] 1998) and the 3,000 documents surveyed in Tom McIver's apocalyptic bibliography (1999). These are millenarian texts, in the sense that their visions of the future fit the criteria set out by Cohn. But, crucially, the vast majority of them do not attempt to incorporate the audience into a sect; what they seek to do is to persuade people that the end of the world is coming—not necessarily as a spur to action, but as a way of explaining troubling features of contemporary society. As O'Leary points out, the apocalyptic genre holds out the promise of a remarkably effective theodicy: it demonstrates that the action of sinister forces in the world forms part of a divine master plan that is just about to come to fruition, thereby offering its audience a mythical and rhetorical solution to the problem of evil itself (1994: 32–44). People who are persuaded by the millenarian argument to the extent that they expect, or think it likely, that the end of the world will happen before they have a chance to die can legitimately be described as millenarians.

One obvious objection to this broad definition of millenarianism is that it is fuzzy at the edges. Not all transactions between a text or speaker and an audience have lasting effects; many fail because the audience is not persuaded. Plenty of people merely toy with millenarian ideas, and it is difficult to know how to categorize them. But recognizing this difficulty is, I would argue, an important insight in itself. Millenarianism *is* fuzzy at the edges. Too much of the academic literature assumes that either you believe firmly that the world is about to end or you do not. One of the findings of this study is that members of an apocalyptic religion can slip in and out of a prophetic paradigm, or reject it altogether; and this is consistent with Melton's observation that members of "millennial cults" are often preoccupied with other matters.

A more serious objection to a wide definition of millenarianism is that it lumps together the extraordinary and the ordinary, fanatics and mild-mannered churchgoers. This is a problem that also confronts those scholars who, conceiving of millenarianism as essentially neurotic or bellicose, are not sure what to make of large bodies of law-abiding apocalyptic believers, such as American fundamentalists.[5] The solution in some cases has been to suggest, misleadingly, that the latter are separated by only the thinnest of membranes from those who seek the violent fulfillment of their fantasies.[6] Other scholars have rightly stressed the difference between extreme and moderate varieties of millenarianism, and have adjusted their terminology accordingly. J.F.C. Harrison (1979), in his study of apocalyptic ideas in England from 1780 to 1850, employed the word *millennialism* to distinguish the sophisticated eschatology of the Anglican clergy from the crude millenarianism of self-educated Adventists. But the use of a near-synonym in this context strikes me as potentially confusing, particularly as some authorities do not distinguish between millennialism and millenarianism. In a previous study, I made a distinction between the "hard" apocalypticism of classic millenarianism, in which the wicked of the earth will perish, and the "soft" apocalypticism of the New Age, in which the world is renewed by the spiritual transformation of enlightened individuals (Thompson, 1996: 196). Catherine Wessinger (1997) offers a similar dichotomy, between "catastrophic" and "progressive" varieties of millenarianism. One criticism of these categories is that most millenarian scenarios incorporate both catastrophic and progressive elements: it is interesting to note how many apparently peaceful transitions prophesied by the New Age movement feature geographical convulsions in which a large number of unenlightened people die. This study will suggest that the most important factor distinguishing extreme from moderate millenarianism is the imminence of the End, not its violent character. Chapter 2 sets out a distinction between *predictive* millenarianism, in which the prophet nails his or her colors to the mast by announcing when the apocalypse is coming, and *explanatory* millenarianism, which is organized around the identification of "signs of the times." These signs (which might, for example, point to the imminent emergence of the Antichrist) suggest that the end of the world is not far off; but their main function is to account for the persistence of evil in contemporary society. As I shall argue, the shift from predictive to explanatory millenarianism that has occurred so often in the past is the result of rational choices: most millenarians are not psychologically disturbed, and their usual reaction to the threatened or actual failure of apocalyptic prophecies is to adopt the safer, explanatory style of millenarian discourse.

Unfortunately, almost every specialist term in this field has more than one meaning. The word *Millennium*, with a capital "M," refers specifically to the concept of the thousand-year reign of Jesus and the saints derived from the Book of Revelation (20:4). In its lower-case form, it usually means a calendar unit of 1,000 years; it can also refer to the earthly paradise envisaged by any millenarian believers, Christian or otherwise. *Apocalypse* comes from the Greek word meaning "to unveil"; its nuances are many and varied. The word will be used here to mean both the sudden end of the world and a literary genre. There have been a number of attempts to distinguish apocalypticism from millenarianism, but they point in different directions; in this study, the word *apocalyptic* is synonymous with millenarian (see glossary).

The Outline of This Study

The analysis of apocalyptic transactions raises questions that are more modest, but intrinsically more answerable, than those about the causes of millenarianism. Who is making the argument that the world is about to end, and on whose authority? How is it communicated? Which members of the intended audience are persuaded by it? What are the practical consequences for them? How do they rationalize their position? Do they customize the argument in some way? O'Leary's discourse-centered approach cries out for ethnographic research into how millenarian ideas operate in a specific setting. An important study by the psychologist Charles Strozier (1994), into the apocalyptic beliefs of born-again Christians in New York City, goes some way to providing this; but its focus is on the relationship of those beliefs to the individual psyche rather than the means by which they were acquired. It also contains generalizations: Strozier states that fundamentalists (a term he employs loosely, to incorporate evangelicals and Pentecostalists) "feel the dangers of the signs of the end acutely, and their lives alter accordingly" (145). My study takes members of a British church that Strozier would certainly classify as fundamentalist and, in effect, uses them to test this dangerously sweeping hypothesis. First, however, it sets out a theoretical framework that extends beyond apocalypticism to take into account the acquisition of religious ideas in general.

Chapter 2 argues that religious movements and individual believers are faced with rational choices that have the effect of increasing or decreasing tension with society. Tension (or subcultural deviance) rises when charismatic claims are accepted by an audience. Some organizations and people choose a higher degree of tension than others; many find themselves pulled simultaneously toward and away from the societal consensus. Predictive millenarianism involves ambitious charismatic claims that, because they are so easily proved wrong, are hard to translate into lasting authority—the Problem of the End. The history of millenarianism is littered with disappointment, and the lesson has largely been learned: most apocalyptic believers are comfortable with lower-cost explanatory narratives that do not require them to sell their houses and head for the hills. Slowly, prophecy belief has been pushed to the margins of intellectual life. It has become a mark of eccentricity, the preserve of the individual who enjoys knowing secret information about the fate of the world that is denied to others.

Chapter 3 shows how Pentecostalism deals with the double pressure to resist and conform to society's norms, in respect of both its own tradition of miracles and the End Times beliefs it has inherited from Christian fundamentalism. Chapter 4 introduces Kensington Temple and its senior pastor, Colin Dye, a truly charismatic leader who pushes the church's level of subcultural deviance up or down according to his perception of risk. Chapter 5 explores the different strategies employed by leaders and members of Kensington Temple with regard to the troublesome subject of the End Times. Most interviewees were extremely wary of being seen as apocalyptic fanatics, and this finding is reinforced by data from a survey of nearly 3,000 church members carried out in October 1998, in which apocalyptic ideas were given a very low priority and most respondents declined to speculate about the return of Christ. Chapter 6 focuses on the small number of textbook millenarians in the congregation—people who were confident that Jesus would return in their lifetimes. It concludes that their beliefs were influenced by their conversion experiences, individual psychology, and degree of subcultural immersion, but finds no evidence for a simple cause of millenarianism.

Chapter 7 discusses the significance of the year 2000 for secular society, evangelical Christianity, and Kensington Temple. It argues that, in all three arenas, the looming deadline raised hopes that had already been disappointed by the time it dawned. At Kensington Temple, a scheme to create a network of 2,000 churches by 2000, heavy with apocalyptic resonances, had to be abandoned in 1999; the theological maneuvering that followed illustrates what can happen when a charismatic strategy fails. Finally, chapter 8 considers the parallels between the management of apocalyptic belief in this one setting and trends in the wider society. It attempts to answer one of the central questions to arise from this study: is the marginalization of millenarian theology at Kensington a response to its inherent weakness, or does it reflect the emergence of a secularized, utilitarian mindset that is peculiar to modernity?

2

The Problem of the End

The first half of this chapter introduces the sociological concepts underlying this study. It suggests that people make rational choices about religion, weighing costs and benefits: they seek to avoid conflicts between belief and reality; they work on ideas until they make sense; and they are influenced by the degree of social support available for a particular belief. Sometimes, these choices lead organizations and individuals in a direction that raises the degree of tension between themselves and society. More often, the gravitational pull of the societal consensus leads to an easing of tension. In cases where people or groups choose to increase their subcultural deviance, the crucial factor is usually the attribution of charismatic powers to a leader, community, or doctrine. But the authority created by the recognition of these powers is hard to sustain, since it is dependent on outcome and vulnerable to disconfirmation. Holders of traditional or bureaucratic authority are particularly wary of charisma, associating it with deviance and instability: they therefore tend to marginalize the people who make or recognize charismatic claims.

The second half of the chapter applies these ideas to millenarianism, perhaps the quintessential charismatic belief system. Predictive millenarianism offers a classic illustration of the fragility of charismatic authority: the threat of disconfirmation is so great that people are reluctant to invest in it. A more attractive option, for many believers, is explanatory millenarianism, in which the rhetoric of apocalypse is used to explain the state of contemporary society. Finally, the chapter examines the association of apocalyptic belief with a broader corpus of deviant ideas, the "cultic milieu." It argues that the status of millenarianism as secret knowledge lies at the heart of its appeal, but also contributes to its stigmatization and helps account for the suspicion with which it is regarded by the authorities.

Key Sociological Concepts

Rational Choice

In recent decades, sociologists have moved away from the idea that religion is an essentially irrational response to the problems of mortality toward recognition that religious activity is governed by rational choice. In doing so, they have been influenced by the work of Max Weber, who, although he subscribed to the notion that religion in the West was being by progressively eroded by secularization, also argued that religious behavior followed rules of experience and was "relatively rational" ([1922] 1993: 1). Recent sociological perspectives tend to avoid judgments about whether it is reasonable to espouse particular doctrines; that is more the preserve of the theologian and philosopher. What they emphasize instead is that, in making religious choices, people do not abandon their "ordinary procedures for weighing alternatives and evaluating explanations" (Neitz 1987: 79). Much of the ground for this approach was laid by Peter L. Berger and Thomas Luckmann in *The Social Construction of Reality* ([1966] 1971), an influential treatise in the sociology of knowledge by two scholars of religion. This suggested that the acquisition of religious knowledge is not very different from the acquisition of other forms of knowledge; the mental and social processes involved are broadly the same. It was not until the 1980s, however, that scholars began to apply "rational choice theory"—until then, chiefly a tool for analyzing economic activity—to religion. Laurence Iannaccone, an economist who pioneered this approach to religious studies, sets out its basic assumptions as follows:

> Rational choice theorists assume that people approach all actions in the same way, evaluating costs and benefits and acting so as to maximise their net benefits. Hence people choose what religion, if any, they will accept and how extensively they will participate in it. Over time, most people modify their religious choices in significant ways, varying their rates of religious participation and modifying its character, or even switching religions altogether. (1997: 27)

In other words, the world of religious activity operates like a marketplace; it is governed by such factors as the quality of the spiritual products on offer, consumer loyalty, and the level of regulation in the market. The analysis of costs and benefits helps us to understand religion at both an organizational and an individual level: once we grasp that people are constantly modifying their choices in order to derive maximum benefits from them, then it becomes easier to understand why neat "top-down" models of spiritual leaders dictating doctrines to the faithful oversimplify reality. There are, however, serious limitations to the rational choice model that need to be acknowledged right at the beginning. Some scholars feel that the analogy between religious and economic activity can be pushed too far, since so many of the "products" of religion are intangible.[1] The rationality that people employ in everyday life is not that of science or philosophy; it is a *subjective rationality* that combines elements of logic with a whole range of factors: personal taste and convictions, the limits of the available information, the circumstances of the moment.[2] The word "subjective" is particularly apt where religious choices are concerned, since the extra-empirical nature of many spiritual claims makes them difficult to assess objectively according to scientific criteria. One might ask, therefore, in what sense such subjective choices are rational at all. The answer is that, as we suggested earlier, religious believers make use of ordinary mental procedures for weighing evidence; as Mary Jo Neitz points out, drawing on the work of Harold Garfinkel (1967), they use their common sense in working out strategies, analyzing consequences, and assessing "the goodness of fit between an item and an explanation" (1987: 79).

Theodicy, Cognitive Dissonance, and Ideological Work

How do people go about assessing the benefits and costs of religion? Any attempt to answer this question must consider the appeal of religion in general. Most scholars agree that one of the chief benefits of religion is its operation as a theodicy—that is, its ability to explain the existence of suffering and death, something that Max Weber saw as central to the development of most world faiths ([1948] 1970: 275). Malcolm Hamilton summarizes this perspective as follows:

> Religion is fundamentally a response to the difficulties and injustices of life which attempts to make sense of them and thereby enables people to cope with them and feel more confident when faced by them. Religious conceptions arise as a result of the fact that life is fundamentally precarious and uncertain. . . . There is always a discrepancy between what we think ought to be and what actually is. It is the tension generated by this discrepancy which is the source of the religious outlook. (1995: 138)

There are, of course, many benefits that arise out of religious activity, some of which are more social than spiritual: many people join a church to find a partner or because they like its music. But religion's ability to make sense of suffering and death, to provide meaning where it is most needed, remains the source of its enduring appeal. Indeed, there is not necessarily a big gap between the small-scale benefits of religion, such as singing in the choir or making cakes for the bazaar, and the large-scale benefit of theodicy. As Berger observes, society itself acts as a sort of theodicy by providing a meaningful context for the experience of anomic events ([1967] 1969: 58); seen in this light, religious groups are doubly effective, in that they provide both the implicit theodicy of social order and the explicit one of a religious cosmology.

The costs of religious activity can range from mild boredom during a sermon to martyrdom; but, whatever their magnitude, they are likely to outweigh the benefits of religion only if they frustrate the search for meaning that lies at the heart of its appeal. If the source of the religious outlook is the discrepancy between what we think ought to be and what actually is, then religion must undermine itself when, as often happens, it *creates* such a discrepancy. Believers who encounter such a cost will not necessarily abandon their faith; they may not even reject the doctrine that led to the discrepancy. But they will usually act to reduce the tension, thereby restoring the integrity of the overarching theodicy. In psychological language, they will attempt to remove the cognitive dissonance that is troubling them. As we saw in the Introduction, Festinger and his colleagues derived this term from their study of a 1950s UFO cult that expected the end of the world. But its usefulness is not confined to the study of millennial disappointment. The theory of cognitive dissonance seeks to explain what all human beings do when ideas contradict each other, or when there is a mismatch between ideas and behavior. According to Festinger, this "dissonance" makes people feel uncomfortable, and so they act to remove or reduce it in one of three ways: by modifying their existing ideas or behavior; by acquiring new information or beliefs; or by forgetting or reducing the importance of the ideas that caused the dissonance ([1956] 1964: 25–26).

The sociologist Bennett Berger has also written about the tension that is created when ideas and real life are in conflict:

> When beliefs do not seem to be very effective in serving the interests of believers (from their own point of view) or when routine behaviour is in apparent contradiction with professed belief, tensions are added to that relationship that constrain people to resolve or reduce them by some alteration in their ideas or their circumstances or both. (1981: 15–16)

This process of alteration, which is necessary to keep people's convictions in a viable relationship with their interests and circumstances, is what Berger calls *ideological work*. He also uses the phrase "remedial ideological work" to describe alterations forced on individuals or groups by discrepancies between ideology and practice (114). As he admits, he is effectively restating Festinger's thesis that humans act to reduce cognitive dissonance; but the concept of ideological work is still a useful one because it reminds us that, throughout history, ideologies have been worked on until they fit circumstances better.

Tension and Plausibility Structures

It is one thing to state that people will act to reduce cognitive dissonance; it is another to predict what those actions will be. Some believers react to a dissonance between a controversial religious teaching and the beliefs of the wider society by deciding to embrace the former more intensely; others, however, will move in the other direction, adjusting the teaching or their behavior until they conflict less sharply with societal norms. This idea that there are two directions in which a believer can move—toward and away from society's standards—is consonant with the influential sociological theory that religious groups can be distinguished by the degree of *tension* between themselves and their environment. According to Stark and Finke (2000: 143), drawing on the earlier work of Stark and Bainbridge (1985), all groups can be located along an axis of tension, at one end of which serious antagonism exists between a group and society, sometimes erupting into bloody conflict, and at the other end of which there is such compatibility between a group and its environment that it is hard to distinguish between the two. Sects and cults are high-tension groups; churches and denominations are low-tension groups. Stark and Finke also state that tension is equivalent to *subcultural deviance*, subcultures being defined as "cultures within a culture, groups having norms and values different from that of the surrounding society" (144).

The extent of the tension between a group and society influences the balance of costs and benefits available to members. High-tension groups tend to be more "expensive," in that the material, social, and psychic costs of belonging to them are higher. But there is also a reciprocal relationship between expense and the rewards of membership: groups that demand a lot from their members offer substantial levels of certainty, emotional support, and even material security (150). Several researchers have concluded that "strict" churches in higher tension with their environment tend to grow more quickly than others (Kelley 1972; Iannaccone 1997). But it is, of course, possible for a group to demand too much from its members; there is an optimum level of tension or strictness above which costs outweigh benefits.

In practice, these observations are not quite as useful as they sound: religious choices are notoriously hard to anticipate, and no one has devised a model that allows us to predict the degree of tension that an individual or group will opt for. But certain patterns are observable in the way groups act to decrease and, less often, increase the degree of tension between themselves and society. Many religious movements begin life as high-tension sects. Over time, however, sects often develop a more comfortable relationship with their environment. Society itself may moderate its objections to the original teachings; but it is just as likely that a sect will moderate or even abandon the deviant elements in its cosmology. H. Richard Niebuhr (1929) coined the term *denominationalism* for the slow accommodation of sectarian groups to their surroundings; he had in mind groups such as the Methodists and the Quakers, which are today almost unrecognizable as the high-tension sects that they once were. There is, however, nothing inevitable about the process of tension-reduction or denominationalism.[3] Just as cognitive dissonance is sometimes resolved by an intensification of the dissonance-creating belief, so some groups and individuals respond to the gravitational pull of societal norms by increasing their degree of subcultural deviance (Stark and Finke 2000: 154). One common pattern of tension-increase can be observed in the behavior of purists who break away from a movement because it is becoming too "soft" or denominationalized and found a new sect. A slightly different pattern emerges when revivalist preachers, working from within, try to recapture the original spirit of a movement. Sometimes the founder or leader of a group will increase its level of subcultural deviance in order to discourage uncommitted members and to consolidate his own authority (Wallis 1984: 103–18).

In reality, many religious groups are pulled in both directions—toward and away from societal norms. The imaginary needle pointing to the degree of tension between a group and society is constantly flickering as teachings are developed or modified through the interaction of leaders, members, and non-members. For many groups, the secret of success seems to lie in sustaining a degree of *medium* tension with their environment. This can be achieved with different combinations of high- and low-tension beliefs and practices. The Jehovah's Witnesses and the Mormons, for example, combine novel doctrines with sober respectability (Bainbridge 1997: 118). In Pentecostalism, the mixture is different: the theology is close to Christian orthodoxy, but aspects of group behavior are seen as exotic. What these medium-tension groups have in common is that they maintain a significant degree of subcultural deviance while operating in the world: they are what Marc Galanter ([1989] 1999) calls "open systems" whose distinctive belief systems are inevitably influenced by the secular consensus. These groups know that it is hard to muster social support for deviant beliefs—or, to put it another way, that the group can sustain only a certain degree of subcultural deviance before people start falling away (which is much the same thing as saying that churches tend to work toward an optimum level of "strictness"). Certain questions present themselves again and again. How much commitment is it reasonable to demand from the membership? What are limits of acceptable theological discussion within the group? What weight, if any, should be attached to criticism from the outside world? The answers to these questions help determine a group's position on an axis of subcultural deviance. As we noted earlier, there is no reliable way of predicting the choices people will make. We can, however, extract one useful guideline from our assumption that religious activity is, in Weber's phrase, "relatively rational." People will subscribe to ideas—doctrines, directives, ritual formulae—that they find *plausible*. They do not have to give them their unqualified approval, but they must find them broadly acceptable (the original meaning of the word "plausible" is "deserving of applause").

A crucial factor in determining whether a proposition is plausible is the degree of social support that is available for it—what Berger and Luckmann ([1966] 1971) call its *plausibility structure*. As Berger explains, "With the possible exception of a few areas of direct personal experience, human beings require social confirmation for the beliefs about reality. Thus the individual does not require others to convince him that he has a toothache, but he does require such social support for the whole range of his moral beliefs" ([1979] 1980: 17–18). Some ideas are made plausible by the support of Western society in general and can be classed as belonging to intellectual orthodoxy. These include certain basic moral beliefs, such as those relating to the sanctity of human life; and the findings of science—knowledge certified by agreed methods of empirical inquiry (Ben-Yehuda [1985] 1987: 107). In contrast, other ideas are considered to be deviant: their plausibility is not recognized by society in general, though of course the degree to which it regards them as implausible will vary. Examples of mildly deviant ideas (from a secular Western perspective) include the Roman Catholic doctrine of transubstantiation, belief in UFOs, and the claims of faith healers; more sharply deviant ideas might include advocacy of sex between adults and minors, a commitment to armed struggle against the state, and a belief that the world is about to end on a specified date.

The more deviant an idea, the more difficult it is to muster social support for it. There is a certain circularity to this statement, since it is hard to define deviance except in terms of lack of social support; [4] nevertheless, it is important to note that certain ideas, lacking a plausibility structure supplied by the wider society, call for special reinforcement if they are to seem credible to people who are used to judging things according to common sense rationality. Admittedly, it is possible to entertain bizarre ideas without attaching any weight to them; ideas encountered in this way do not require robust social support, since they can be easily discarded. But if strongly deviant claims—those that can be demolished by empirical investigation or are morally offensive in society's eyes—are to take on the status of belief, then they require a strong plausibility structure supplied by people who accept those claims. An extreme example of this is the cult that protects its members from ideological contamination by shutting them away in a compound: Galanter ([1989] 1999: 105) calls this *boundary control*. (It is worth noting that groups in this situation frequently combine a number of ultra-deviant beliefs: many isolated apocalyptic cults have indulged in what society regards as immoral sexual practices. The affinity between apparently unrelated deviant ideas is an important subject to which we shall return.)

We should not underestimate the powerful attraction of the societal consensus. The strength of society's plausibility structures helps to explain why most minority religions drift in the direction of lower rather than higher tension with society. The exercise of common sense relies heavily on consensus; even members of stigmatized groups derive most of their ideas about the world from information held in common with the rest of society. Religious believers instinctively follow the rules of evidence like everyone else. For the societal consensus to be successfully challenged, it is necessary to produce compelling evidence and arguments, often reinforced by new social ties. A fresh plausibility structure must emerge, sustained by a special—and notably fragile—type of authority.

Charisma and Routinization

It is not easy to manage a deviant organization. It usually requires the exercise of what Weber termed *charismatic authority*, rooted in "specific gifts of the body and spirit" ([1948] 1970: 245). In its simplest form, Weber's concept of charisma revolves around a great personality, a prophet, magician, or war leader whose special powers, often regarded as divine in origin, persuade others to grant them authority. This authority is different in quality from traditional or rational forms of domination; those who hold it and those who acknowledge it "must stand outside the ties of this world, outside of routine occupations, as well as outside the routine obligations of family life" (248). At least, this is true of charismatic authority in its "ideal" form; but, as Weber acknowledged, over time it becomes mixed with traditional and bureaucratic authority. It becomes *routinized*, accommodated to the routines of everyday life.

A crucial feature of charismatic authority is its fragility. In Weber's words:

> The charismatic leader gains and maintains authority solely by prov-
> ing his strength in life. If he wants to be a prophet, he must per-
> form miracles; if he wants to be a war lord, he must perform heroic
> deeds. Above all, however, his divine mission must "prove" itself in
> that those who faithfully surrender to him must fare well. If they do
> not fare well, he is obviously not the master sent by the gods.
> ([1948] 1970: 249)

This tells us two important things: that charismatic authority is outcome-dependent, and that it is bestowed by others, who judge its claims according to subjectively rational criteria. In Ian Craib's words, charisma can be seen "not as a quality of a leader but as a quality projected onto a leader by virtue of situation, opportunity and events" (1997: 134); when it fails, creating cognitive dissonance, the authority can quickly evaporate. In the above passage, charisma is created by the leader's personal power to win battles or work magic; but Weber implies elsewhere that charisma can also repose in *ideas*, and that these, like the cult of the leader, are subject to routinization. According to Ralph Schroeder, we can derive from Weber's writings an understanding of charisma as "the novel impact of a belief-system on social life." This sort of charisma is routinized not so much by the transmission of a leader's special powers to his followers as by "the systematisation of a belief-system by a stratum of religious virtuosi, or through the accommodation of this belief-system to the predispositions of a certain strata of believers" (1992: 17–18). The anthropologist Thomas Csordas (1997: 138–39) suggests that the real locus of charisma is *among* participants in a religious movement: it is "a product of the rhetorical apparatus in use of which leader and follower alike convince themselves that the world is constituted in a certain way." Understood in this way, charisma is an active process of attribution and imputation that ebbs and flows according to situational exigencies.

Weber's concepts of charisma and routinization can help us understand what happens when religious groups raise or lower their degree of tension with society. Charisma is what makes the raising of tension possible; it creates extraordinary conditions in which the cost of deviant activity or the deviant label is worth bearing. Charismatic claims challenge the societal consensus, and, once they are accepted, become translated into an authority that supersedes it. Yet charisma in its raw form rarely retains its original force for long: its claims to be able to control the future—through the production of miracles, the winning of battles, or the transformation of society—are frequently modified in response to disconfirmation or the encroachment of more stable forms of authority; and, as this routinization takes place, tension falls. This is the point at which institutions develop, often according to a pattern that combines the development of bureaucracy and the rationalization of belief patterns (O'Dea 1966: 36–44).

Although the origins of charisma are not always directly traceable to one person, and its operation is dependent on complex social interaction, as a form of authority it is strongly marked by individualism: charismatic movements are typically centered on leaders, prophets, and revelations granted to individuals. Sharp rises in a group's degree of tension with society can often be traced back to the actions of people acting on their own initiative. But this individualism is a weakness, too: those aspiring to charisma rarely earn society-wide support for their claims, and only occasionally manage to win over the institutions—churches, political parties, or whatever—to which their appeal is directed. If they are granted authority, it will probably be by limited numbers of people in a restricted arena. In effect, would-be charismatic leaders face a vicious circle: they find themselves marginalized because they advance deviant claims, and their claims are judged to be deviant because they originate from the margins.

Any assessment of the costs and benefits of high-tension religion will be influenced by one's vantage point: for example, a charismatic claim that excites people on the fringes of an organization may strike those in authority as ludicrous and threatening. Often, pressure to lower subcultural deviance comes from the routinizing administrative center of a group, while pressure to raise it comes from the margins. Sometimes, however, precisely the opposite is the case. Csordas has coined the term "radicalisation of charisma" to describe the cranking up of tension that occurs in groups that decide to suspend the security of routine in favor of a grander ideological striving (1997: 101). In these circumstances, the administrative center of a movement may prove more radical than its fringes. Leaders may take steps to increase their own charismatic aura, or they may welcome evidence of charismatic excitement within the membership, recognizing its potential for institutional rejuvenation.

Underlying all these calculations is the organizational dilemma described by the sociologist Donald Swenson:

> In order for a religious organisation to be effective it needs some
> sort of organisational structure. However, if the routinisation pro-
> cesses increase, the original charisma is lost and what is left is an
> over-elaborate organisation or bureaucracy that tends to be self-
> perpetuating. The key seems to be some sort of balance. The object
> is to have enough routine to make effective the religious organisa-
> tion but also to maintain a certain element of the charisma as well.
> (1999: 248)

This balance is, of course, essentially the same as that between high- and low-tension religion. The question facing many religious bodies can be stated very simply: how deviant should we be? Or, to put it another way: how much risk should we take?

The Benefits and Costs of Millenarianism

In the first half of this chapter, we have considered a number of concepts: subjective rationality, cognitive dissonance, ideological work, subcultural deviance, charisma, and routinization. These are all useful tools for analyzing the changing dynamics of a system of religious belief. The second half of this chapter explores the operation of one such system, millenarianism. Its basic assumption remains the one outlined earlier: that people make religious choices in the way they make other choices—they seek to maximize benefits and minimize costs. But we need to bear in mind that "benefit" and "cost" are not scientific categories. What looks like a benefit to one person can look like a cost to someone else (or to the same person under different circumstances).

Predictive Millenarianism: The New World and Its Non-Arrival

A doomsday prophecy is the ultimate high-tension doctrine, especially if it is attached to a looming deadline. A clear prediction of the timing of the apocalypse can raise expectations to a point where believers feel impelled to take action (such as, for example, selling their possessions or leaving their homes); likewise, the disappointment caused by disconfirmation can produce a violent reaction. Predictive millenarianism is an extreme manifestation of the radicalization of charisma, in which an escalation of rhetoric leads a group to abandon security in favor of a greater goal—in this case, surviving the apocalypse. It is not, however, a common phenomenon. Christian churches with an apocalyptic heritage tend to draw back from explicit anticipation of the end of the world; and, as Melton observes, even some "millennial cults" turn out on closer examination to be less apocalyptic than one might imagine ([1985] 2000: 147). To understand why, it is worth examining the balance of benefits and costs associated with classic millenarian beliefs.

The most obvious attraction of millenarianism is the promise of paradise on earth, and it forms the basis of textbook definitions of the phenomenon. Norman Cohn ([1957] 1993: 13) writes that millenarian movements picture salvation as collective (to be enjoyed by the faithful as a collectivity); terrestrial (to be realized on the earth, not in heaven); imminent (to arrive soon and suddenly); total (in the sense that nothing will be left unchanged); and miraculous (to be accomplished by, or with the help of, supernatural agencies). This definition encompasses countless ways of imagining the millennium, whose imagined specifications have varied enormously throughout history. For the ancient Zoroastrians, it consisted of a "making wonderful" in which the world would become a single fertile plain and no one would be older than 40 (Cohn 1993: 98–99). For the fourteenth-century Franciscan Spirituals, it was a society miraculously purged of the evils of private property and the Roman Church

(McGinn [1979] 1998: 221). For the contemporary new religious movement known as the Raelians, it will be a sexually liberated utopia presided over by benevolent aliens (Barrett 2001: 390–95). In every case, the most striking feature of the millennial theodicy is the contrast between present misery and the glory to come: the latter justifies and makes tolerable the former. It is like the promise of heaven, but with the added attraction that the believer does not necessarily have to die to experience the post-apocalyptic paradise and may even pass unharmed through the dreadful events that lead up to it. Millenarian narratives typically envisage the destruction of civilization by wars and natural disasters: in the Book of Revelation, for example, the prophesied horrors include plagues, famine, poisoned water, hailstones mixed with blood, and flesh-devouring birds, to say nothing of the carnage of Armageddon. Yet the anticipation of violence does not constitute a cost of millenarianism, since the blood being shed will be that of the unsaved: in most predictive millenarian discourse, it is strongly implied that true believers will escape not only harm but mortality. The Jehovah's Witnesses put it succinctly with their slogan, "Millions now living will never die" (Barrett 2001: 190). In effect, this rhetorical abolition of death creates the ultimate theodicy: death can have no sting if it is not going happen.

Moreover, the coming millennial kingdom will be a place where all the injustices of the old world will be put right. The yearning for social justice looms so large in much apocalyptic rhetoric that some scholars have concluded that the prime cause of millenarianism must be social and economic (Hamilton 1995: 89). Whatever flaws this has as a catchall explanation, there is no doubt that, for many millenarians throughout history, the egalitarian features of the millennium have provided a good reason to believe in it. Millenarian movements themselves have the potential to redistribute power: once accepted by an audience, apocalyptic claims create an especially potent form of charismatic authority, one that rubs off on ordinary believers as well as the prophet. The possession of foreknowledge about one of the most important subjects imaginable—the fate of the planet—creates a special, even intimate, bond between those who share it. In the pure millenarian scenario, after all, they are destined to enter the new world together. Knowing this can have an extraordinary effect on behavior, producing a sense of purpose that can lead to increased proselytizing, religious ecstasy, and (occasionally) violent confrontation with the state.

Such things can happen, however, only when people really believe that the transformation of society is about to occur. The problem is that it is not an easy thing to believe. Since the emergence of the apocalyptic genre 2,000 years ago, every prophecy of the end of the world has been proved false. Peter Berger describes vulnerability to disconfirmation as millenarianism's great weakness:

> There are, to be sure, various cognitive and psychological mechanisms to rationalise empirical counter-evidence. All the same, there remains a theoretical problem in accounting for the fact that Yahweh has *not* brought the rain, that the parousia is delayed longer

and longer, that the alleged Mahdi turns out to be another all too
mundane ruler, and so on. ([1967] 1969: 70)

Note that Berger lists the absence of rain alongside the delay in the Second
Coming of Jesus. Dismay at the failure of the world to end is related to other
forms of prophetic disappointment. The non-arrival of the millennial kingdom
is an extreme example of disconfirmation; it might be regarded as the biggest
single cost that a millenarian can incur, necessitating radical and often unsuccessful ideological work, but it is certainly not the only one to arise from a lack
of correspondence between prophecy and the real world.

The history of millenarianism is overshadowed by disappointment. The
emotional and social cost of failed prophecy leaps out from the historical record
and is particularly acute where predictions of the end of the world have been
date-specific. The first extant millenarian document, the Book of Daniel, dating
from the second century B.C., appears to have been altered soon after it was
written, extending the period of time before the end of the old world and the
supernatural triumph of the Jewish people, presumably in response to prophetic failure (Hartman and Di Lella 1990: 419). The writings of St. Paul hint
at the frustration of the early Christians at the delay in the Second Coming,
though it was not until many centuries later that Christian millenarians began
to write about the experience of disappointment. "Take heed of computing
[apocalyptic calculation]," lamented one seventeenth-century millenarian after
the eschatological excitement of the English Commonwealth came to nothing.
"How woefully and wretchedly have we been mistaken by this" (Hill 1980: 58).
An even more acute sense of failure emerges from the so-called "Great Disappointment" of October 22, 1844, when thousands of followers of the American preacher William Miller waited in vain for the Second Coming. "Our
fondest hopes and expectations were blasted," wrote one Millerite, "and such
a spirit of weeping came over us as I never experienced before. It seemed that
the loss of all earthly friends could have been no comparison. We wept and
wept until the day dawn" (quoted in O'Leary 1994: 108). The same misery was
experienced in the UFO cult described by Festinger when neither the prophesied flood nor the rescue of the faithful by spacemen took place. Mrs. Keech,
the group's leader, "broke down and cried bitterly," while the other members
suffered agonies of disappointment ([1956] 1964: 168).

There are numerous strategies for reducing the cognitive dissonance
caused by millennial disappointment: a prophet can claim that he miscalcu-
lated the date; that the apocalypse has been delayed through the power of prayer
or as punishment for lack of faith; or that a form of apocalypse did occur but
has been revealed only to the faithful. Jon R. Stone (2000: 25) argues that most
prophets, when a prediction fails, retreat to more ideologically defensible positions, concentrating instead on nonempirical understandings of their original
prophecy. But such strategies are rarely completely successful: many former
believers are unwilling to shoulder the heavy burden of remedial ideological
work involved in explaining away disconfirmation; the disappointed movements usually collapse—and with them the charismatic authority of their lead-

ers. Those that do not collapse, meanwhile, usually find ways of moving away from their millenarian origins, of directing religious zeal toward institutional ends. Just as millenarianism represents perhaps the ultimate charismatic claim, so the slow absorption of apocalyptic theology by religious bodies offers a classic example of the routinization of charisma (a quality which, as we saw earlier, can repose in ideas as well as in the aura of an extraordinary leader). Many well-known movements—mainstream Christianity, Mormonism, the Baha'i faith, the Unification Church—have apocalyptic roots that have become progressively obscured in the aftermath of millennial disappointment and as their leaders have worked to reduce the degree of tension between themselves and the surrounding society. Even movements that retain a strong millenarian inheritance, such as Seventh-day Adventism and Pentecostalism, have attempted to reduce the overall importance of apocalyptic themes as they have moved toward denominational status. They have not repudiated millenarianism, exactly; but they have discovered that there are varieties of belief in the end of the world that, because they are less likely to lead to crippling disappointment, are more cost-effective.

The disruptive power of predictive millenarianism is indirectly revealed by the many campaigns against dating the apocalypse that have been waged across the centuries by religious authorities. Gershom Scholem reports that Jewish teachers repudiated attempts to calculate the End "again and again, not without reason, though with little success" ([1971] 1995: 11); St. Augustine implored millennial mathematicians to "relax your fingers" (City of God, 1972: book 18: chapter 54); the sixth-century Paschal List of Campania described date-setters as "arrogant fools" (ignari praesumptores) and "crazies" (deliri) (McGinn 1995: 63); and there is compelling evidence that the medieval Church twice changed its dating system rather than allow it to reach the year 6000, traditionally associated with the apocalypse (Landes 1988). Since then, Church authorities have repeatedly moved against what McGinn calls "predictive imminence" (1995: 63). Date-setting is essentially incompatible with traditional authority, though it can form a powerful tool for the creation of charismatic authority. If established leaders endorse a prediction of Christ's imminent return (or any apocalyptic event), their authority will be undermined by its disconfirmation. They will have pointlessly raised the degree of tension between themselves and the outside world; at the very least they will be forced to engage in ideological work in order to undo the damage to morale and their credibility. Even if they condemn predictive millenarianism, however, they may be forced to deal with its consequences: waves of expectation and disappointment in which apparently rational people become swept up, creating problems of discipline and (sometimes) public order. Again, what we observe here is the quintessentially charismatic nature of millenarian claims: the clash of interests between religious or secular institutions and the millennial prophet and his followers illustrates in a concentrated form the incipient tension between traditional and charismatic authority.

There are few quicker routes to subcultural deviance than the issuing of doomsday prophecies. One reason for this is the association between predictive millenarianism and violence (see Robbins and Palmer 1997; Hall 2000; Wessinger 2000). Date-setting has played a role in numerous apocalyptic tragedies; although not necessarily the crucial factor in generating disorder, it often concentrates expectations to the point where armed conflict is possible. The subject of millennial violence impinges on this study because the period of my fieldwork, the late 1990s, coincided with public anxiety about "Pre-Millennial Tension": the tragedies of Waco, Aum Shinrikyo, the Solar Temple, and Heaven's Gate led many people to conclude—wrongly—that the arrival of the year 2000 would lead to a worldwide upsurge in millennial violence (see Thompson 1996; Wojcik 1997; Abanes 1998).

But, as I noted in the Introduction, apocalyptic movements can inspire ridicule as well as fear. The danger of being laughed at has often formed part of the social cost of millenarianism. As early as the fifth century, St. Augustine warned his listeners to be cautious in evaluating apocalyptic claims, so that "when we fall into a panic over present happenings as if they were the ultimate and extreme of all things, we may not be laughed at by those who have read of more and worse things in the history of the world" (1955: 387). One could cite many other examples, such as the Venerable Bede's good-humored criticism of the *rustici* who were forever asking him the date of the Millennium (Landes 1988: 176) or the discovery by a seventeenth-century English wit that the name of an apocalyptic prophet of the day, Dame Eleanor Davis, was an anagram of "never so mad a ladie" (Thomas [1971] 1973: 163). The effect of this sort of stigmatization was clearly visible during my fieldwork at Kensington Temple: many of my interviewees were at pains to distance themselves from what they saw as the comic absurdity of over-the-top prophecy belief. Such reactions remind us of the power of labeling in society. As Richard Jenkins argues, once a label is applied to an individual, his or her behavior and biography becomes organized with reference to an identification that is now internal as well as external (1996: 75). But *fear* of labeling is also significant. The popular identification of millenarianism with the silly or sinister may discourage someone from investing in the concept of the end of the world; it greatly increases the social cost of such a belief—even for those people who are otherwise attracted by it.

To sum up: the costs of predictive millenarianism usually outweigh the benefits; its charismatic claims are unsustainable in the long term, and for this reason people's rational choices will tend to move in the direction of accommodation with society—toward an acknowledgment that the world is not about to end. There are, of course, circumstances in which quite large numbers of people can suddenly be led in the other direction, and scholars are still divided as to what these are: the most convincing explanation remains that of Cohn ([1957] 1993: 281–88), whose analysis of radical medieval millenarianism combines material factors (a background of social disaster) with psychological ones (the relief of psychological disorientation provided by apocalyptic fantasies). This analysis is not incompatible with a rational choice perspective: people who have been disorientated by extraordinary circumstances can still make subjectively rational decisions; unless we recognize this, we are unlikely to be able to account for the breadth of the appeal of the classic millenarian movements that occasionally spring up. From our point of view, however, what matters is the rarity of such movements. This can be ascribed to predictive millenarianism's extreme vulnerability to disconfirmation and its challenge to established authority, leading to an almost automatic presumption against it on the part of risk-averse religious and secular leaders.

Explanatory Millenarianism: Making Sense of the Present

If millenarianism existed only in its most extreme form—as belief in an imminent, time-specific apocalypse, expressed in a discourse that inspires radical social action—it would probably be confined to isolated eccentrics or ultra-deviant cults. There is, however, a more routinized version of millenarianism that does not create such a high degree of tension with society. This is explanatory millenarianism, in which the main function of apocalyptic prophecy is not to provoke action but to make sense of the present moment in terms of an overarching scheme of history. Before elaborating on this concept, however, I should make it clear that my categories of predictive and explanatory millenarianism are dynamic, not static. The difference between the two often lies in the tone and balance of the argument rather than in questions of doctrine, and one mode can easily develop into the other: explanatory rhetoric is sometimes radicalized by the introduction of date-specific predictions, while predictive millenarianism has often become routinized through the removal of such risk-inducing details.

The historian Hillel Schwartz hints at the existence of explanatory millenarianism when he observes that, in practice, millenarians seem less interested in the features of the world they are waiting for—the millennium—than in the circumstances that will give birth to it. He suggests that this is because the millennium is "a time of instant and perfect communication whose seamlessness makes anatomical detail unnecessary. Millenarians are, rather, diagnosticians of bodies in metastasis" (1987: 525)—the body in question being the doomed pre-apocalyptic modern world. My own experience of apocalyptic religions in London, California, and Peru (Thompson 1996, 1999b, 2001b) bears this out. In conversation, members of such religions rarely volunteer descriptions of a radiant post-apocalyptic order. Instead, they are more likely to analyze current affairs in terms of sacred prophecy: a recent earthquake, a terrorist bomb, the spread of homosexuality, or even an international trade agreement shows that the End is not far off. Quite often, people using prophecy in this way will say that they think it "likely" that the world will end in their lifetime. Or they may decline to speculate about when the End will come, but will nonetheless espouse a conspiracy theory whose basic premise is that mankind is living in its last generation. A further complication is that the strength of people's millenarian convictions appears to rise and fall according to the circumstances of the moment, so that during a crisis in international relations they are more interested than usual in biblical prophecy but tend to forget about the subject when the situation returns to normal.

As we have already noted, the difficulty of drawing the line between millenarians and non-millenarians tends to be glossed over in the academic literature, which too often implies that anyone who subscribes to apocalyptic
doctrines has become a predictive millenarian whose whole life is lived in
expectation of the End. This is not the case. Once we accept O'Leary's argument
that millenarianism is best understood as a form of rhetoric, we can see more
clearly how people are free to make use of it as they see fit. The category of
explanatory millenarianism helps to fill the gap between classic millenarianism
and the rest of society. It can be viewed as a routinized form of predictive
millenarianism, in so far as its vision of the end of the world is derived from
that of intensely expectant apocalyptic believers: thus, the explanatory, mostly
non-predictive End Times discourse of modern evangelical Christians draws
heavily on the ideas of early Christians who expected the Second Coming of
Jesus within their lifetimes. Explanatory millenarianism is, however, more than
a watered-down version of the predictive variety. Its emphasis on the contemporary world highlights an important function of millenarianism. The urge to
make sense of contemporary society has been present in apocalyptic thinking
since the emergence of the genre; it is part of its broader operation as a theodicy. A historical perspective is helpful here: we need to remember that millenarianism as an ideology did not appear suddenly, but grew slowly out of the
ancient human project to locate the present moment within an overarching
divine plan. Models of time that organize history into ages or cycles pre-date
the notion of the sudden end of the world by many centuries.[5] The Book of
Daniel, written during the Seleucid occupation of Jerusalem between 168 and
164 B.C., divides history into a sequence of four kingdoms that is related to the
Greek sequence of ages of gold, silver, iron, and bronze and may have its
origins in the Mesopotamian concept of history as a "Great Year" of four seasons (Campion 1994). Like so many apocalyptic texts, it has a political subtext:
Daniel's visions are replete with many-headed beasts that, in passages of almost
impenetrable allegory, are made to represent the military enemies of the Jewish
people. The Book of Daniel is, among other things, the first extant conspiracy
theory, demonstrating that, from the birth of the apocalyptic genre, explanatory
narrative was at least as important as predictive imminence.

There is a remarkable consistency to the way societies separated by vast
stretches of time and geography have used prophecy to explain otherwise in-
comprehensible events. For example, Daniel provides us with an early demonstration of the technique known as *vaticinium ex eventu*, history disguised
as prophecy (McGinn [1979] 1998: 7): the close match between certain of its
images and the invasion of Jerusalem is attributable to the fact that the invasion
was already history. More than 2,100 years later, in the days after September
11, 2001, an anonymous Internet author played the same trick, rewriting the
famous Nostradamus quatrain prophesying the arrival of a "king of terror" to
make it look as if it predicted the destruction of the World Trade Center by
Osama bin Laden (Thompson 2001a). Likewise, the search for the true identity
of the Antichrist, a demonic world ruler derived from the Beast of the Book of
Revelation, has continued for nearly 2,000 years, throwing up hundreds of

nominations from the Emperor Nero to Bill Gates (see Boyer 1992; McGinn 1994; Fuller 1995). According to most versions of the Antichrist legend, the appearance of a great warrior or statesman who later reveals himself to be the Beast will be the first sign that the Last Days have arrived. But, given the difficulty of interpreting the complex prophecies of Revelation, and the fact that Antichrist's true nature will initially be hidden, it may not be easy for Christians to identify him. Speculation about Antichrist often has a tentative quality that sits more comfortably with explanatory than with predictive millenarianism.

The real significance of such ideas lies in the way they place the present moment, with all its ugliness and chaos, in the all-embracing context of divine history. As O'Leary argues, apocalyptic eschatology simultaneously addresses the problems of evil and time, offering "the perfection (which is to say the annulment) of time as the redemptive solution to the problem of evil" (1994: 33). It anticipates an apocalypse that will justify everything that has ever happened. The story of humanity is understood as a progressive conflict between absolute good and absolute evil that is only now reaching its climax, and whose contours can be discerned behind the machinations of today's evil men; hence the centrality of conspiratorial themes in millenarian tradition. Framed on either side by the predetermined working out of history, the present is replete with cosmic significance; no turn of events is too anomalous to be absorbed into a foreshortened future. The desecration of the Temple in Jerusalem, the Mongol invasions, the Reformation, the French Revolution, Hiroshima: all of these dissonance-creating threats to the reality of everyday life—many of them appearing with little warning—have at various times been neutralized by incorporation into an apocalyptic framework.[6] At the same time, however, millenarianism itself is partly neutralized by being confined to the (mostly harmless) identification of "signs of the End." On rare occasions, a perceived correspondence between current events and prophecy can have dramatic consequences: an apocalyptic sect might take up arms because it believes that the government has begun the persecution prophesied in the Book of Revelation. It is far more likely, however, that the recognition of "signs" will be confined to the level of rhetoric, reflecting a desire on the part of the believer to reduce the threat posed by anomic events. Apocalyptic ideas, particularly in a routinized form, can be comforting and occasionally even a source of social stability. As McGinn observes, throughout the Middle Ages apocalyptic traditions "were used to *support* the institutions of medieval Christianity rather than to serve as a critique, either mild or violent" ([1979] 1998: 29); many apocalyptic texts were "attempts of the educated clerks to make sense of major changes in society within the universal scheme of history provided by apocalypticism" (35).

Today, although the major institutions in society no longer make use of apocalyptic ideas in this way, something of the same, routinized, millenarianism can be found in religious movements for whom apocalyptic belief is essentially a matter of cultural identity or of sustaining (but not increasing) their traditional degree of tension with society. The social costs of such beliefs need not be high. It is easier to sustain a plausibility structure for a vague anticipation of the end of the world in the next few years than it is to create one for an imminent apocalypse that requires urgent action, such as retreating to the wilderness. In many cases, the only action arising from explanatory millenarianism is the deployment of certain images in speech and texts; this does not mean that we should not take such images seriously as expressions of belief, but it does suggest that in these cases millenarianism resembles mainstream, uncontroversial religious doctrines in operating mainly on the level of rhetoric.

The contrast between the two styles of millenarianism becomes clearer if we consider the ways they conceive of the future. A distinction is sometimes made in the anthropology of time between the long-term future (in French, *le futur*) and the short-term future (*l'avenir*, the forthcoming). The former is distant, a world imagined in opposition to this one; its landscape has a fictional or dreamlike quality. The latter is easy to visualize: it is the day after tomorrow, an extension of the present peopled with familiar characters and situations.[7] Predictive millenarianism inserts a mythical apocalypse into the immediate horizon; it tells us that an incredible event, whether it be the Second Coming or the arrival of a spaceship, will occur so soon that we might as well enter it in our appointments diaries. Such a claim is, under normal conditions, hard to believe—and, even where it is accepted, carries with it formidable costs. Explanatory millenarianism, in contrast, makes only relatively modest claims about the immediate future and relegates the strange events of the apocalypse to the medium-term future. The apocalyptic audience may live long enough to experience the End, but there is still a comforting degree of doubt about when it will occur. In the meantime, life can be lived according to everyday rhythms, secure in the knowledge that otherwise baffling current events correspond to sacred prophecy. The theodicy that this knowledge creates is less comprehensive than that of predictive millenarianism, but it is also more subtle and, to many people, intrinsically more believable.

It is not completely risk-free, however. The main cost of explanatory millenarianism is essentially the same as that attached to doomsday eschatology: the threat of empirical disconfirmation. In practice, explanatory prophecy always contains a predictive element, offering its audience clues as to what will happen next. The problem is that even the most careful predictions tend to be proved wrong over time; and the more detailed the prediction, the more likely this is to happen. In short, the most important quality of explanatory prophecy—its willingness to address the fast-changing details of contemporary life— also constitutes its Achilles' heel. Thus, countless Christian prophecy books of the 1970s and 1980s, having analyzed the Cold War in terms of Bible prophecy, went on to tell their readers to watch out for a Soviet invasion of the Middle East, or the signing of a peace treaty between Israel and the nations of the EEC, whose number—ten—corresponded to the ten horns of the Beast in Daniel (Boyer 1992: 276). Like predictions of the end of the world, however, these more modest forecasts were overtaken by events: the Soviet Union, instead of invading Israel, fell apart; the EEC grew to more than ten nations. Explanatory millenarianism, like doomsday millenarianism, contains a claim

to charismatic authority, since it depends on recognition of the special illu-
minative powers of a prophet or prophetic document, and it shares in the
weakness of such authority—that is, its constant need to prove itself to its
audience. This fragility is not necessarily fatal, but in the long term it imposes
a burden of ideological work on the person making the claim. The ability of
the apocalyptic paradigm to explain the details of the contemporary world
quickly breaks down when the details change; therefore the prophet or exegete
can only preserve the match between prophecy and real life by constantly shifting his or her ground. The more detailed the material demonstrating the alignment between prophecy and real life, the more ideological work is required.[8]

That said, the sheer proliferation of explanatory apocalyptic texts, compared to the rarity of the full-scale dramas of the type described by Festinger,
tells us something about the respective benefits and costs of the different levels
of millenarianism. Put simply, explanatory apocalyptic rhetoric is a safer option
than the time-specific doomsday prophecy. The reward it offers is more accessible, and less disturbing, than the world-shattering prospect of an immediate
End, and the dissonance created by disconfirmation is more manageable. Explanatory millenarianism does not usually make great demands of its audience,
since it postpones an apocalyptic crisis that demands urgent action to an in-
determinate date. Its claim to charisma is of a limited variety. Often, all it
requires of its consumers is that they entertain its propositions; indeed, more
than any other form of religious argumentation, it has functioned historically
as a sort of entertainment—notably during the Middle Ages, when eschatological prophecies were a popular form of folklore (Lerner 1976, 1983; Taithe and
Thornton 1997; McGinn [1979] 1998), and in the prophecy subculture of modern fundamentalist Christianity (Boyer 1992; Wojcik 1997). The amusement
value of "soft" millenarian rhetoric constitutes one of its benefits; it is no accident that, since the dawn of the genre, so many apocalyptic texts have been
packaged in a way that might appeal to the general reader.

Secret Knowledge and the Cultic Milieu

In this section our focus shifts away from the distinction between types of
millenarianism toward its status as secret knowledge and its similarity to other
deviant ideas. The word "apocalypse" comes from the Greek verb meaning "to
unveil." Apocalyptic information is something that was once hidden and remains hidden from nonbelievers. This fact is crucial to its appeal, constituting
a benefit in itself. Seen from another angle, however, it is one of the great costs
of millenarianism. The family resemblance between apocalyptic theology and
other ideas rejected by society—conspiracy theory, the occult, "alternative" history and science—has tarred millenarianism with guilt by association. Religious institutions, in particular, are reluctant to endorse apocalyptic ideas that
seem to belong in a wider category of bizarre beliefs. Not only are they worried
by the damage to their reputations that might result but they also recognize
the disruptive potential of an epistemology in which the ultimate judge of truth
is the individual.

Hidden knowledge is often deviant knowledge: its premises are rejected by society, usually on moral or empirical grounds, and this rejection only adds to its importance in the eyes of believers. Furthermore, people who subscribe to one rejected idea are more likely to entertain others: the fact of knowing secret things counts for more than the actual content of the secrets themselves. The mixing and merging of deviant knowledge is not a recent phenomenon: in an essay on the roots of the New Age, Robert Ellwood writes of "a western alternative spirituality tradition going back at least to the Greco-Roman world. The current flows like an underground river through the Christian centuries, breaking into high visibility in the Renaissance occultism of the so-called 'Rosicrucian Enlightenment', eighteenth-century Freemasonry, and nineteenth-century Spiritualism and Theosophy" (1992: 59). The sociologist Colin Campbell ([1972] 2002: 14) has coined the phrase *cultic milieu* to describe the "cultural underground of society," incorporating all deviant belief systems and their associated practices. The cultic milieu is characterized by a common consciousness of deviance, says Campbell; indeed, one of its most pronounced features is syncretistic sharing of deviant ideas by groups that, at first glance, have little in common with each other. Thus, many modern-day witches make use of the Jewish number-mysticism of the Kabbalah (Luhrmann 1989: 60); believers in "lost civilisations" argue for life on Mars (Hancock 1998); ultra-traditionalist Catholics flirt with the ideology of the survivalist Right (Cuneo 1997); and the neo-Buddhist Japanese sect Aum Shinrikyo found room in its cosmology for UFOs, "earthquake weapons," Masonic conspiracies, and the Catholic apocalyptic folklore known as the Prophecies of St. Malachi (Thompson 1996; Barkun 2003).[9]

It is hard to define deviance beyond stating that it involves the violation of norms (Ben-Yehuda [1985] 1987: 3); it is socially constructed and therefore always culturally relative. We can, however, identify one feature common to most of the deviant ideas in the cultic milieu, and that is their appeal to the authority of the individual. Roy Wallis (quoted in Lewis 1992: 7) noted that "there prevails in the [cultic] milieu an attitude of 'epistemological individualism', that is, a belief that the individual is the ultimate locus for the determination . . . no individual or collectivity possesses a monopoly of the truth." Such an attitude implies a rejection of traditional plausibility structures. In the cultic milieu, the very implausibility of an idea, in society's terms, may be a reason for taking it seriously; indeed, in the absence of shared procedures for evaluating evidence, there are really no limits as to what might be considered plausible.[10] This state of affairs is hard to reconcile with the stable power relations operating within established institutions, since every heterodox or secret idea can be regarded as a potential claim to charismatic authority. The possession of hidden knowledge is not translated into authority until it is communicated to and accepted by others; but, once this happens, it raises the prospect of a redistribution of spiritual or political power.

It is true, of course, that there are such things as deviant institutions: in terms of our earlier discussion, these are high-tension groups whose subcultural deviance is preserved by their own plausibility structures. Even here, however, the individualism of the cultic milieu sits uneasily with established authority. Many religious movements have, in their sectarian early days, flirted with conspiracy theories, sexual experimentation, and the occult—but it is interesting to note that the same groups have, over time, tended to move away from deviant ideas, or reduced the range of such ideas that they endorse. In rational choice terms, the social cost of public identification with these ideas has been too great.[11] The cost for the individual, on the other hand, need not be anything like as high. One can explore bizarre or dangerous ideas in private without being branded deviant by society; indeed, engaging with these ideas behind closed doors, or within a closed circle of friends, may be an essential part of the experience. The fact that, in Wallis's phrase, the individual is the "locus of determination" does not imply unwavering commitment to a set of ideas. In the cultic milieu, the audience is under little pressure to pronounce on the validity of the charismatic claims being made by, say, an esoteric author or a conspiracy theorist. On the contrary: they are often asked only to consider whether something *might* be true. The authors of deviant claims tend to tailor their rhetoric to the tastes of individuals whose commitment to ideas is tentative and transitory. Those authors are themselves usually acting as individuals unencumbered by official responsibilities. Even where they belong to a religious tradition, their productions have a freelance and freewheeling quality to them: in the modern cultic milieu, it is noticeable that many authors move promiscuously from one "mystery" to another in search of an audience.

Popular millenarianism—"prophecy belief"—forms an almost inescapable part of the cultic milieu: a great many deviant beliefs have millenarian overtones or exist in a millenarian version. Secrecy and individualism have permeated the apocalyptic genre from the very beginning. The Book of Daniel and the other early apocalypses, although they envisage the collective salvation of the Jewish nation, do not address the people in the straightforward manner of the earlier prophets: in Gershom Scholem's words, "what reached the prophets as knowledge which could hardly be proclaimed with sufficient loudness and publicity, in the apocalypses becomes secret" ([1971] 1995: 6). In Jewish literature, the moment at which the coming redemption of God's people takes on the status of a millenarian event, leading to the resurrection of the dead and the Last Judgment, is also the moment at which knowledge of the future becomes a mystery to be penetrated by the individual. Moreover, the appeal of apocalypticism was strongest among those Jews who emphasized other forms of esoteric knowledge, such as Kabbalah and gnostic throne-mysticism. Many scholars have pointed out the family resemblance between millenarianism and gnosticism. Both systems are radically pessimistic about the present order of society and assume that a special class of people—the chosen ones—will survive its inevitable destruction. They also tend to frame their arguments in ways that repose authority in the individual: people choose themselves, as it were, by penetrating mysteries that are insoluble by the unenlightened.[12]

In the apocalyptic genre, the pre-eminent mystery is the timing of the End—yet, we have seen, the history of attempts to uncover this information is one of humiliating failure. Many apocalyptic documents tackle this problem by hiding the date of doomsday behind a firewall of millennial arithmetic and other ciphers (the Book of Daniel being the first example). They provide clues rather than a clear answer, thereby protecting themselves from disconfirmation and placing the responsibility for solving the puzzle onto the reader. There is little sense that their authors intend this knowledge to be uncovered collectively, by members of an institution; indeed, as we have seen, institutional hostility to apocalyptic calculation is one of the leitmotifs of millennial history. The reasons given for such condemnations include the biblical injunction against calculating Christ's return and the fact that such theories have been proved disastrously wrong in the past. Often, however, something else lies behind this official disapproval: an intense mistrust of the do-it-yourself epistemology described by Wallis and a suspicion that people who indulge in date-setting will prove dangerously suggestible in other areas.

For centuries, the anxieties of the religious authorities concentrated on millenarianism's links to heresy and superstitious folk belief. The significance of the latter is often overlooked: as J.F.C. Harrison argues, folklore, with its belief in omens and the significance of dreams, "provided a matrix in which millenarian yearnings could be nourished"; the authority of local prophets was acknowledged alongside that of conjurers, magicians, and astrologers (1979: 39–41). Increasingly, however, the intellectual establishment rejected empirically disprovable claims. In the early modern era, European governments began to treat millenarianism as a threat to public order rather than as heresy; there was a growing awareness that people claiming to be prophets or the Messiah might be mentally disturbed. By the eighteenth century, few educated Europeans made use of Bible prophecy as an analytical tool, though in England apocalyptic calculation remained "an indoor sport for eccentric clergymen" (Thomas [1971] 1973: 172). Millenarianism was seen as the preserve of sectarians, mystics, the deranged, and their uneducated followers; and it was associated with a range of "enthusiastic" attitudes and behaviors, such as speaking in tongues or public displays of nudity.

In America, millenarianism was closer to the intellectual mainstream, but even here it was recognized that prophecy belief could lead the gullible into error. William Miller himself was worried that his prediction of the Second Coming had opened the floodgates of fanaticism. In a letter of 1843, he wrote: "My heart was deeply pained during my tour east, to see in some few of my former friends [i.e., followers], a proneness to the wild and foolish extremes of some vain delusions, such as working miracles, discerning of spirits, vague and loose views on sanctification, &c" (quoted in O'Leary 1994: 115). There could hardly be a clearer demonstration of the instability of charismatic legitimation: having succeeded in persuading an audience of his own authority, Miller provoked a whole new set of charismatic claims and was soon forced to engage in boundary maintenance. He would have been horrified to learn that, within a few years, a Millerite remnant would become the heterodox Seventh-day Adventist Church, and that this, in turn, would give birth to a twentieth-century cult, the Branch Davidians, whose messianic leader claimed to have traveled to heaven in a spaceship (Reavis 1995: 94).

Modern prophecy material offers extensive evidence of millenarianism's ability to open up a shortcut between conventional religious belief and the furthest reaches of the cultic milieu. McIver's survey of nearly 1,500 apocalyptic documents published in English since 1970 demonstrates how receptive millenarians are to heterodox notions in general. Among the ideas put forward are: the alien authorship of Mayan prophecies (1999: 199); a Satanic conspiracy involving the British Royal Family (220); pollution of the atmosphere by flying saucers (229); an ancient civilization in Antarctica (245); interplanetary body-snatching (251); talking animals (256); telepathy and time travel (264); cyber-electronic mind control (277); and Caucasian racial superiority (290). The political scientist Michael Barkun, in his study of recent conspiracy theories, argues that the indiscriminate combination of themes from science fiction, occultism, and radical politics in contemporary apocalyptic scenarios, especially on the Internet, constitutes a new style of millenarianism—"improvisational millennialism" (2003: 18–21). It is certainly true that many Christian apocalyptic authors are increasingly influenced by secular conspiracy theories of a dawning New World Order. The affinity between Christian millenarianism and conspiracy theories goes back many centuries and can partly be explained by the similar explanations they offer for the operation of evil. But Barkun makes the interesting point that, while in the past Christian millenarianism has normally adopted only those conspiracy motifs grounded in biblical tradition, the increasingly improvisational style of apocalyptic fantasies is blurring the boundary between Christian and non-Christian themes, so that some fundamentalist preachers feature aliens in their conspiracy narratives while UFO writers insert the Antichrist into their visions of a New World Order. This is an age of "millenarian entrepreneurs," says Barkun, in which conspiracy ideas have become the ideological glue binding together an ever more disparate array of elements (184).

To sum up: it is hard to disentangle the benefits from the costs of millenarianism's status as secret knowledge. For some people, the fact that an apocalyptic argument is rejected by society counts in its favor; others will conclude that it has been rejected for good reasons. Likewise, the association of apocalypticism with other ideas from the cultic milieu can be regarded as a benefit, pointing the way to a universe of hidden secrets, or as a cost, demonstrating that millenarianism belongs in a wider category of foolish and bizarre beliefs. Different people will reach different conclusions, and for unpredictable reasons; but what we can say is that the balance of benefits and costs is different for individuals and institutions. Individual believers enjoy the advantage of being able to explore millenarian or other deviant ideas without investing heavily in them. The curious consumer can follow the trail of "alternative" wisdom wherever it leads—toward millenarianism, secular conspiracy theory, the occult, or gnostic self-knowledge. He or she is unlikely to be held to account for this exploration, and there is no need to establish a robust plausibility structure for every deviant idea, since many will be presented as a form of entertainment. Cognitive dissonance can easily be brushed aside. As Campbell notes, "individuals who 'enter' the cultic milieu at any one point frequently travel rapidly through a wide variety of movements and beliefs and by doing so constitute yet another unifying force within the milieu" ([1972] 2002: 15).

For an institution, in contrast, any engagement with secret knowledge raises awkward questions. If hidden information acquires the status of official doctrine, not only does it cease to be secret, but the organization can be held responsible when the information is discredited. Often, a religious institution will compromise by allowing various ideas that are mildly deviant in its own terms (and more so in society's terms) to circulate under its umbrella without explicitly endorsing them. In theory, this strategy poses a double threat to institutions, since the extremist or eccentric figures who hold these ideas can damage the reputation of the organization in the outside world while also disrupting its internal stability by their claims to charismatic authority. It is, however, a very common dynamic, and probably unavoidable in large institutions where doctrinal orthodoxy is unenforceable. All the major religions and many minor ones have a millenarian/esoteric fringe whose claims have to be managed in some way: Judaism has a long history of false messiahs and revolutionist movements; Islam has mystical millenarian sects; Roman Catholicism has its Marian apocalyptic traditionalists; conservative evangelical churches have their End Times conspiracy theorists. In each case, religious institutions have had to make decisions about boundary control, which affect the degree of tension that exists between themselves and society.

Conclusion

Let us quickly glance over the balance sheet of apocalyptic belief. In textbook or predictive millenarianism, the most obvious benefit is the promise that paradise is about to materialize on earth. This belief is, however, difficult to sustain under ordinary circumstances; a more accessible benefit is provided by the ability of apocalyptic rhetoric to explain the operation of evil in the world. This creates an unusual and effective theodicy that can be exploited by individuals and institutions; while it presumes that history is drawing to a close, it is not dependent on the accuracy of a specific doomsday deadline. Moreover, for those people who are persuaded by millenarian arguments, there is the extra thrill of possessing secret knowledge denied to the vast majority of humanity.

For each benefit, however, there is a corresponding entry on the debit side of the ledger. Indeed, the costs of millenarian belief are tied in so closely to its benefits that one could say that the apocalyptic discourse subverts itself. The glorious new world fails to materialize, giving rise to disappointment, humiliation, and sometimes violence. The ability of explanatory millenarianism to account for the shape of the modern world is continually being tested and breaking down, forcing its proponents to perform laborious ideological work. And even the possession of secret knowledge has its drawbacks, for one man's secret is another's bizarre conspiracy theory. Millenarianism has historically been associated with other bodies of knowledge that society regards as deviant;

those who invest in it run the risk of being labeled fanatics or eccentrics—even within religious institutions that take the notion of the end of the world seriously.

Do the costs of millenarian belief outweigh the benefits? There can be no definitive answer to this question because the balance sheet varies from person to person and group to group. What we can say is that groups and individuals work toward a *level* of apocalyptic belief at which, according to their subjective assessment, benefits outweigh costs. On the whole, the effect of this work is to accommodate millenarian ideas to the conditions of everyday life, though the degree of such accommodation varies enormously. For many members of apocalyptic religions, the status of the millennial tradition as a discourse, as opposed to nonnegotiable dogma, is crucial: it means they are free to move in and out of an apocalyptic paradigm in response to their perception of benefits and costs. The whole area remains an unusually sensitive one: millenarianism is so stigmatized in the public imagination that any decision to embrace apocalyptic theology is likely to be fraught with difficulties. The same could be said, however, of many controversial beliefs: the presence of millenarian ideas within a religious tradition raises questions about charismatic authority, subcultural deviance, and boundary maintenance that frequently surface in non-apocalyptic contexts. This point is illustrated in the next chapter, which discusses Pentecostalism and its fascination with the End Times.

3

Pentecostalism and the End Times

The previous chapter suggested that the central assertion of mille-narianism—"the End is coming, and here is the proof"—has much in common with other charismatic claims: it undermines traditional authority, increases subcultural deviance, and is threatened by empirical investigation. Pentecostal churches offer an ideal environment in which to observe this shared dynamic. Pentecostalists not only claim to be able to harness divine power in order to work miracles of healing, tongue-speaking, and personal prophecy; they are also taught that mankind is living in the End Times. The first half of this chapter shows how Pentecostal churches are pulled toward and away from accommodation with society as they seek to exercise ministries of miraculous healing and non-eschatological prophecy. The second half describes the millenarian traditions that Pentecostalism has inherited from fundamentalism. Here, too, we can observe opposing forces at work: on the one hand, self-styled "prophecy experts" who seek to increase subcultural deviance by offering secret knowledge from the cultic milieu; and, on the other, critics who regard such ideas as "unbiblical" and dangerous. Finally, the chapter discusses specifically Pentecostal attitudes to the End Times, which range from enthusiastic participation in the prophecy subculture to a complete lack of interest in it, and also include a more recent, optimistic belief in the coming restoration of God's kingdom.

Pentecostalism and Charisma

Tension versus Accommodation

Pentecostalism began, in David Martin's phrase, as "a fusion of the faith of culturally despised blacks with that of culturally despised whites" (2001: 5). At the start of the twentieth century, evangelical revivals broke out in Kansas, Wales, and Los Angeles. Their theology drew heavily on the traditions of Methodism and the American holiness movement; but this time the respectable poor who attended the meetings made unusually explicit claims for themselves. They believed that, as a result of being baptized in the Holy Spirit, they had received the miraculous gifts (*charismata*) bestowed on the disciples at Pentecost (Acts 2:1–4). Chief of these was the ability to speak in tongues, usually producing a glossolalia that only the enlightened could translate, but sometimes also—it was claimed—the instant acquisition of foreign languages. Other gifts included faith healing, the casting out of demons, and prophecy (see Hollenweger 1972; Cox 1994; Kay 2000a). Pentecostalists emphasized spiritual experience over reflection: at their meetings people clapped, shouted, fainted, and were apparently cured of illnesses. Dozens of "classic Pentecostal" denominations arose on both sides of the Atlantic. The movement spread to Africa, then to Latin America. In the 1960s, white middle-class congregations in the house churches and mainstream denominations began to adopt a similar "Charismatic" theology and worship, speaking in tongues, exorcising demons, and issuing prophecies. Some Pentecostals did not welcome this competition; but gradually the movements overlapped. Recently, members of both traditions have found themselves swept along by the so-called "Third Wave," a vigorous Charismatic spirituality emphasizing miracles and spiritual warfare, which emerged from America in the late 1980s (Smail, Walker, and Wright 1995a; Percy 1996; Coleman 2000). Pentecostal churches are today among the fastest growing in the world: a recent survey estimates that the number of their adherents will rise from 12 million in 1960 to 154 million by 2010 (Brierley 1999: 1.5).[1]

Pentecostalism is a charismatic religion according to several definitions of the word.[2] In the Pentecostal tradition, everyone who is "born again in the Holy Spirit" theoretically possesses one or more of the *charismata*, such as the ability to speak in unknown tongues. In practice, however, the more spectacular gifts of the Spirit tend to be channeled through senior figures who, in a circular dynamic typical of Weber's charismatic authority, owe their positions to their ability to manifest these gifts. Most Pentecostal leaders aspire to perform miraculous healings and to prophesy. Although they are careful to attribute these powers to Jesus and the Holy Spirit, they are, in fact, making classic charismatic claims which, once accepted by the faithful, translate into a potent form of authority. Moreover, the charismatic nature of Pentecostal leadership extends beyond the purely religious sphere. Pentecostal leaders are often expected to manifest the charisma of the inspired business leader, achieving phenomenal levels of church growth. For Pentecostals, there is no great distinction between actual miracles and "miracles" of evangelization: the two blend together in what Roland Howard (1997: 126) describes as the Pentecostal and Charismatic obsession with success. From a sociological perspective, too, they have much in common. Forecasts of supernatural healing and church expansion both imply an ability to manipulate the future—and therefore run the risk of being invalidated by the turn of events. Disconfirmation of a charismatic claim, whether it relates to a cancer prognosis or attendance at a revival meeting, is destructive of authority. Admittedly, disconfirmation is partly a question of perspective: the audiences at Pentecostal rallies do not judge reports of miracles by the rigorous standards of medical science. But it would be wrong to conclude that Pentecostalists and Charismatics suspend their common sense: religious claims *are* evaluated. Evangelists who predict that revival will break out at a certain place and time will be expected to explain themselves if nothing happens; faith healers whose "miracles" are dismissed as fraudulent by the outside world may also arouse suspicion within the religious community. In a tradition that demands proof of spiritual success, and in which congregational allegiances tend to be fluid, failure is swiftly punished.

As we saw in chapter 2, religions often find themselves confronted by the question of how deviant they should be. High-tension religion is associated with more substantial benefits and costs than low-tension religion: the greater the risk one is prepared to take in terms of dissonance-inviting claims, the greater the reward if those claims are accepted by one's chosen audience—and the bigger the disaster if they cannot be sustained. The demonstration of special powers is a dangerous business. That is one reason why charisma becomes routinized: it is an exercise in risk management. But, as Swenson observes (1999: 248), it is not in the interests of a religious tradition to extinguish the exciting, unpredictable spirit that provided the impetus for its growth. Religious movements are often pulled in two directions: toward accommodation with society by risk-averse routinizers, and away from it by charismatic risk-takers. Few traditions offer a clearer example of these opposing forces than Pentecostalism, a movement built around the belief—highly vulnerable to disconfirmation—that modern Christians possess the same miraculous powers as their New Testament forebears.

Almost from the moment it emerged, Pentecostalism found itself under pressure to scale down its Charismatic claims. The two gifts that caused the most trouble were prophecy and healing. The concept of prophecy is a loose one: the gift can be exercised through tongues, or in a biblical "word of knowledge," or in dreams and visions; and the scale of its subject matter ranges from the domestic (a church member's search for the right job) to full-blown eschatology (the coming of the Antichrist). The sociologist Margaret Poloma describes prophecy as one of the most problematic Charisms:

> What is to be done about the person who disrupts religious drama
> and institutions in the name of being a spokesperson for the divine?
> How can the damage that private prophecy may pose for the undis-
> cerning believer be controlled by those more aware of its dysfunc-
> tional uses? What about its use to promote a position of power and
> prestige by leaders who are at best naïve and at worst unscrupulous?
> (2001: 177)

The leaders of Pentecostal churches were acutely aware of these questions. Within a few years of the first revivals, mechanisms were put in place to distinguish between authorized and unauthorized prophetic messages, and also between types of prophecy: local and eschatological, private and public. As early as 1908, there was an attempt to ward off disconfirmation by steering the gift of prophecy away from anticipation of the future: at a conference that year, the Rev A. A. Boddy, a leader in the Welsh revival, condemned the idea that New Testament prophecy was a recital of future events. A move by the Apostolic Faith Church to place its ministers' prophetic utterances on a par with Scripture was quickly repudiated by the other denominations. The Apostolic Church declared that prophecy was not infallible and should only take place "when the local church is assembled with its presbytery in charge"; the use of this gift in making appointments was abandoned (Kay 2000a: 60–66). This is typical routinization: an attempt to control the exercise of charisma by setting out increasingly restrictive boundaries of belief and behavior. Much the same could be said of the changes to Pentecostalism's theology of healing, a potent source of disconfirmation and disillusion. The founder of Elim Pentecostalism, George Jeffreys, originally taught that Christians could expect to enjoy perpetual freedom from illness. By 1934, the denomination's position had softened: it stated that "we believe that our Lord Jesus Christ is the healer of the body and that all who will walk in obedience to his will can claim Divine Healing for their bodies." Today, Elim talks about the Gospel embracing "the needs of the whole man" and says only that the Church is commissioned "to fulfil a ministry of healing and deliverance to the spiritual and physical needs of mankind" (Kay 2000a: 86).

This progressive restriction of the scope of Pentecostalism's prophetic and healing claims can be seen as a specific form of routinization arising from its quasi-magical theology. At the same time, moreover, it was undergoing a more general routinization of the sort experienced by most religious movements when they put down roots—a process of institutionalization. Thomas O'Dea, expanding on Weber, describes the components of institutionalization: they include the emergence of myth, the development of religious bureaucracy, and the rationalization of belief patterns (1966: 36–44). The history of twentieth-century Pentecostalism provides evidence of this process. Poloma, in her study of the Assemblies of God (1989), found that, in its growth from 300 members to two million members and 22,000 ordained ministers, it had become less like a sect and more like any other American denomination. The same could be said of Elim, which was one of the subjects of Bryan Wilson's book *Sects and Society*, published in 1961, but is now far less sectarian in character.

But what the story of Pentecostalism also shows is that there is nothing inevitable about tension reduction: the impulse toward greater accommodation with society has frequently been offset by an exuberant, dissonance-inviting revivalism that has attempted to drag the movement back in the direction of the cultic milieu. One example of this was the ministry of the American healing evangelist William Branham (1909–65), a Baptist who talked with angels, argued with demons, and diagnosed illnesses through the colors of the aura, and whose followers expected him to be raised from the dead.[3] Impressed by Branham's popular following, Pentecostalists initially welcomed his claims; but, as Walter Hollenweger notes, this friendly reception "turned into an almost unanimous rejection when [he] announced that the Millennium would begin in 1977" (1972: 355). It is interesting that the Pentecostalists should have used this excursion into predictive millenarianism to mark the boundary of acceptable belief. During my fieldwork, a Kensington Temple pastor offered the story of "Brother Branham" as an example of what happens when a Spirit-filled individual goes off the rails.

If Branham's crude attempts to raise subcultural deviance were easily resisted, the same cannot be said of the tension-raising miraculous claims that have swept through the Pentecostal and Charismatic world in recent years. This development dates back to the 1980s, when American Charismatics began to speak of a Third Wave of the Holy Spirit, manifested in powerful healings and unprecedented church growth. (The first two waves were the founding of the classic Pentecostal churches at the turn of the century and the emergence of the house churches in the 1960s.) A key figure in this movement was the late John Wimber, a former Quaker whose international ministry was preoccupied with the power of God (Percy 1996: 16). Wimber helped to produce a renewed interest in prophecy: he was associated with a group of preachers called the "Kansas City prophets" who forecast that full-scale revival would break out, beginning in Great Britain, at the beginning of the 1990s (Wright 1995a). This failed to happen, but something unusual did emerge from the Vineyard: the so-called Toronto Blessing, in which whole congregations would be "slain in the Spirit" or burst into "holy laughter" (Percy 1996). Meanwhile, in a separate but related development, worldwide Pentecostalism, especially in Africa, increasingly came under the influence of "health and wealth" ministries, which promised that faith would bring material rewards (Coleman 2000).

Faced with an upsurge in reports of miracles, the structures of Pentecostalism responded with characteristic ambiguity. Some leaders reveled in the possibilities of the Toronto Blessing and mass healing services; others worried that things were getting out of hand. The concerns of the more cautious Pentecostals and Charismatics are encapsulated in *Charismatic Renewal* (1995), a collection of essays by Tom Smail, Andrew Walker, and Nigel Wright, three British theologians sympathetic to the movement. The book gives us a clear idea of the areas of disagreement between proponents of low-tension and high-tension Charismatic Christianity. In an essay entitled "The Rise of the Prophetic," Wright criticizes the American evangelist Paul Cain for prophesying that a revival would break out in Britain in 1990, and Wimber for supporting him: "It is evident in retrospect that this claim did not materialise in the way anticipated, and that the outcome was a great disappointment" (Wright 1995c: 118). Wright calls for greater restraint in the exercise of prophecy and suggests that it should focus on society rather than on risky anticipation of the future: "A prophetic ministry which addresses the issues of an unjust world is less likely to become in-house entertainment for the saints" (122). He also criticizes Wimber's theology of Charismatic healing, in which illness was regarded as essentially Satanic. For Wright, sickness is part of the disorder of the natural world, and it is more dignified for Christians to recognize it as such (1995b: 75). It is also less damaging to charismatic authority: if illness can be natural as well as demonic, then the healer does not need to engage in elaborate ideological work to explain why the person prayed for has died.

An essay by Andrew Walker, entitled "Miracles, Strange Phenomena and Holiness," tackles the problem of Pentecostalism's uncritical evaluation of claims of the miraculous:

> It is precisely at the level of rigorous investigation into the miraculous that the Pentecostal movements, since their earliest days, have let themselves down. In the euphoria and excitement of revival, miracles have been testified to in abundance, but rarely verified. . . . Congregations awash with the emotion of enthusiasm feed off rumour, conjecture and hearsay. When you know that God heals, what you look for is not empirical evidence but tacit confirmation of your belief, in the form of positive reports, reconstructions of events, or books replete with amazing stories. (1995b: 125)

Walker, a former Elim Pentecostalist who has converted to Eastern Orthodoxy, emphasizes that he is open to the possibility of real miracles. But, in his opinion, silly and exaggerated claims bring the Charismatic movement into disrepute: "Nothing convinces people more that miracles do not occur than endless claims of bogus prophecies, unsubstantiated healings, and the sanctification of trivial supernatural happenings. . . . Today I still shudder at the 'God found me a parking place' kind of testimony" (126). Like Wright, Walker is troubled by some Charismatics' extreme emphasis on the demonic. Certain contemporary preachers and authors have created a "paranoid universe," he says, infested by demons of abortion, masturbation, and witchcraft, which supposedly have the ability to enter fetuses or cling like flies to the back of a person's head. Such doctrines breed fear and sow dissent, says Walker; and they are unbiblical, since they are ultimately derived not from Scripture but from "inside information" granted to an elite few (1995a: 86–105).

The dangers of secret knowledge are elaborated on in the book's final essay, in which Smail, Walker, and Wright jointly denounce the Faith movement, a loose network of Pentecostal ministries, which teach that a believer has a right to the blessings of health and wealth won by Christ, and that he or she can obtain these blessings merely by a positive confession of faith (Gifford 1998: 39; Coleman 2000: 27). Emanating originally from America, Faith ministries have attracted a vast following in Africa, where the promise of freedom from sickness and poverty has a particular resonance; African members of Kensington Temple tend to be heavily influenced by it. Smail, Walker, and Wright quote one of the original Faith authors, E. W. Kenyon, to the effect that "when these truths [of the Faith Gospel] really gain the ascendancy in us, they will make us spiritual supermen, masters of demons and disease" (1995b: 137). The essay argues that such claims are not only ridiculous: the "truths" on which they are based are heretical. The "revealed knowledge" offered by present-day Faith leaders such as Kenneth Hagin and Kenneth Copeland is really gnosticism, since it teaches that Satan is in control of the world and that Christians can only defeat him by taking upon themselves the divine nature of God (142). It even invokes a sort of magic—and not a beneficent magic, either: the essay's final quotation is from a taped message by Copeland in which he says that several people who criticized the Faith movement "are dead right today in an early grave because of it, and there's more than one of them got cancer" (151). The excesses identified by Smail, Walker, and Wright are important because they are so similar to those associated with apocalyptic belief. Like millenarianism, "signs and wonders" theology is vulnerable to unanticipated events: disconfirmation strikes simultaneously at the personal authority of the prophet or healer and at the credibility of the belief system. Furthermore, the implicit gnosticism of the Pentecostal fringe opens doors to the cultic milieu: as Walker points out, Charismatic demonology is not far removed from the world of Dungeons and Dragons (1995a: 96) and flirts with the occult in much the same way as gnostic eschatology.

The Pentecostal world, therefore, is one in which there is a constant struggle for equilibrium: between exotic beliefs and behavior that conflict with the values and scientific methodology of Western society, and a respectability that brings in its wake a dangerously comfortable accommodation with the secular world. Yet, judging by its worldwide growth, Pentecostalism has achieved a remarkably successful balance between the high- and low-tension elements in its cosmology. What is it about Pentecostal and Charismatic Christianity that modern people find so appealing?

Personal Experience and Consumer Choice

Most Pentecostalists enjoy a greater degree of religious freedom than one might gather from examining the movement's uncompromising spiritual claims. This is not a religion of self-contained sects. Writing in 1970, Luther Gerlach and Virginia Hine observed that the organization of Pentecostalism tended to be "reticulate and acephalous," characterized by interacting networks with no single clearly identifiable leader. Since then, the globalization of conservative evangelical Christianity has further reduced the level of ideological control exercised by leaders. The flow of books and broadcast material across national and denominational boundaries means that the typical Pentecostal pastor enjoys limited influence over the degree of tension that exists between his church members and society at large. He may wish to distance the congregation from certain controversial ideas or phenomena, such as the Toronto Blessing; but it is difficult to stop individual worshippers from absorbing such influences from other sources and promulgating them informally. The free-market ethos of Pentecostal religion permits a greater degree of specialization than one encounters in mainstream Christianity. Careful selection of religious material allows the believer to "get into" particular fields such as spiritual warfare, evangelization, faith healing, or millenarianism. The level of subcultural deviance among Pentecostals or Charismatics therefore tends to fluctuate to a greater extent than in more self-contained movements: it is not only a question of which churches believers attend, but of what material they consume and where they position themselves in relation to a variety of spiritual fads and charismatic claims. In the words of Thomas J. Csordas, "the multiple reinterpretations, reflections, backwashes, anchorings, hybridizations, and discontinuities of the Charismatic Renewal in its global manifestations [form] an ideal showplace of the postmodern condition of culture (1997: 58).

One need not, however, invoke the language of postmodernism to analyze the social forces that have given Pentecostalism its competitive, self-referential qualities. Peter Berger, in his book *The Heretical Imperative* ([1979] 1980), showed how religious allegiance in general is taking on some of these characteristics. For Berger, the development of modern consciousness entails a movement "from fate to choice." Modernity (not postmodernity) has disrupted taken-for-granted explanations of how the world works and opened up an unthinkable range of choices, so that society is now characterized by "unstable, incohesive, unreliable plausibility structures" (19). With this has come a strong accentuation of the subjective style of human experience. In the religious sphere as in many others, people are forced to pick and choose between alternatives, using their own experience as a reference point: they ask themselves, "Does this feel right to me?" and "How can I know what is true?" Berger's study does not mention Pentecostalism, but its appeal to this mindset is obvious: Charismatic worship provides immediate, validating experiences for consumers looking for a quick return on their investment; and, by offering "proof" of the operation of the Holy Spirit, it addresses epistemological doubts.

All of this makes it difficult to assess the doctrinal stance of Pentecostalists. In theory, at least, most of them are theologically conservative. They believe that the secular world is the province of Satan. Most Pentecostal churches, including Kensington Temple, teach that every word of the Bible is divinely inspired and inerrant; they expect believers to observe the Commandments and refrain from all sexual activity outside marriage. They are firmly Protestant in their theology and, together with non-Charismatic fundamentalist Christians, are usually fitted into the category of conservative evangelical churches.[4] Some scholars maintain that Pentecostalism is itself a version of Christian fundamentalism. The Anglican theologian Martyn Percy argues that Pentecostals and Charismatics should be included in a "wide" definition of fundamentalism as a set of doctrines, linguistic practices, assumptions, and behaviors. Pentecostals are just as anti-liberal as other fundamentalists; they "simply construct their remedial programme differently" (1996: 11). The anthropologist Simon Coleman describes Pentecostals and Charismatics as "fundamentalistic": he reports that the traditional disagreements between Pentecostals and fundamentalists over miracles and tongue-speaking have become less intense in recent years as the two constituencies have fought side by side against the common enemy of diabolical atheism (2000: 26).

The sociologist Bernice Martin, in contrast, rejects the term "fundamentalist." Pentecostalism may be highly disciplined and literal in its reading of the Bible, she says, but the authoritarian tone of its pastors is chiefly designed to protect boundaries and reinforce participation. Moreover, the Pentecostal belief in biblical inerrancy does not produce uniformity because it is accompanied by an extreme form of the Protestant insistence on the right of each believer to read the Bible and become his or her own theological authority:

> Latin American Pentecostals certainly read the Bible literally, though they do so less as a matter of settled principle than because they actually share the mental world of the writers of the New Testament. . . . They regard the Apostles as their own familiar friends, people like themselves with whom they converse on intimate terms in their prayers. . . . It is important, too, to remember that narrative is a far more common usage than generalised theological or dogmatic formulae among the new Pentecostals: telling and retelling the stories of their own, personal, individual salvation is at the heart of their evangelism, their worship and their self-understanding. (1998: 131)

It is the cognitive style of modern Pentecostals and Charismatics, rather than the fine print of doctrine, that distinguishes them from fundamentalists or their own sectarian predecessors. According to Russell Spittler (1994: 108), where fundamentalists mount arguments, Pentecostals give testimonies: "The one goes for theological precision, the other for experiential joy. There is a profound difference between the cognitive fundamentalist and the experiential Pentecostal."[5] To a much greater extent than traditional Protestantism, Pentecostalism mobilizes the senses, manipulating images, feelings, and ideas in a way designed to integrate the self—mind and body—into a global Charismatic culture (Coleman 2000: 66–71). In this culture, ideology is often subordinated to personal experience, and this has implications for the way people relate to a range of "difficult," tension-inducing doctrines—including those relating to the end of the world.

Pentecostalism's Apocalyptic Heritage

Expectation of the Second Coming of Jesus is an important theme in Pentecostalism. The early Pentecostalists were in no doubt that the rediscovery of the Charismatic gifts was a sign of the approaching end of the world: their early documents spoke of the "Soon-Coming of the Lord in the air" (Kay 2000a: 132), while the first general council of the Assemblies of God proclaimed that the message "predominant . . . in all this great outpouring . . . is 'Jesus is coming soon.' " Virtually every written interpretation of a message in tongues mentioned the approaching apocalypse. Indeed, the appearance of glossolalia was described as a "reverse Babel": Christ would return when all Christians were united by speaking in tongues (Prosser 1999: 254). In the century that followed, apocalyptic expectation faded somewhat, but was revived from time to time in conjunction with the high-tension claims of the miraculous: many of the most controversial Pentecostalist healers, such as Morris Cerullo, have stressed the imminence of Christ's return.

Pentecostalists have always been familiar with the notion of the End Times, in other words; but a feature of their eschatology is that it is not distinctly Pentecostal. Rather, they have tended to borrow it wholesale from two related traditions, both of them rooted in non-Charismatic American Protestantism. The first is what one might call the "official" millenarianism of conservative evangelicals and fundamentalists, enshrined in complicated premillennial models of history, of which the best known is dispensationalism. The second is the "unofficial" millenarianism of American prophecy belief, in which free-lance variations on dispensationalism blend into conspiracy theory and other ideas from the cultic milieu. The categories of "official" and "unofficial" are not the same as the distinction between explanatory and predictive millenarianism made in chapter 2; there is some correspondence between them, however, since one of the aims of the official sponsors of dispensationalism was to discourage Christians from indulging in date-setting. In this, as we shall see, they were only partly successful.

Official Millenarianism: Dispensationalism

It is not surprising that the first Pentecostalists should have looked forward to the Second Coming: the conservative Protestantism from which the new move-ment sprang was strongly flavored by apocalyptic expectation, albeit of a re-spectable, undemonstrative variety. In the early years of the twentieth century, millions of evangelicals and fundamentalists believed that Jesus would return soon, before the thousand-year reign of the saints prophesied in the Book of Revelation: hence the name of this position, *premillennialism*. Many of them also subscribed to dispensationalism, an ingenious variety of premillennialism that acquired a huge following in America thanks to the best-selling Scofield *Reference Bible* (1909), which incorporated dispensationalist ideas in its mar-ginal notes. The Scofield Bible was the Pentecostalists' favorite edition of Scrip-ture, and most Pentecostal denominations adopted its eschatology (Prosser 1999: 253; Kay 2000a: 129–33).

Dispensationalism, whose adherents still number in the tens of millions, draws heavily on the ideas of John Nelson Darby (1800–92), an Anglican min-ister who left the Church of England to found the Plymouth Brethren. Darby divided human history into a structure of divine ages or dispensations not dissimilar to those constructed by medieval exegetes (McGinn [1979] 1998). According to dispensationalists, mankind currently lives in the "Church Age" in which Bible prophecy is not being fulfilled. But, at any moment, Christ could return for his Church, lifting all true believers into the clouds in the manner prophesied by Paul (1 Thess. 4:16–17), leaving everyone else behind. After this "secret Rapture," the world will come under the sway of a seductive leader. Initially welcomed as a peacemaker, this man will soon reveal himself to be the Antichrist, a Satanic tyrant who will desecrate the Temple at Jerusalem and order everyone to worship him. After seven terrible years of chaos and tyranny, the so-called Great Tribulation, Satanic forces will converge on Israel in order to destroy the Jews. As the armies gather at Armageddon, Christ and his saints will descend from the skies and destroy the enemy. King Jesus will reign from Jerusalem for 1,000 years. At the end of this period, Satan will mount one last rebellion. After it is defeated, the resurrection of the dead and the last judgment will take place; God will create a new heaven and a new earth for his people (T. Weber 1979: 23).

The theologian James Barr, in his study of Protestant fundamentalism, describes dispensationalism as "a remarkable achievement of the mythopoetic fantasy," adding that "as a feat of the imagination it might well compare with the apocalyptic poems of Blake, and indeed these latter may have done something to influence its origin" (1977: 195). From our perspective, its most interesting feature is the compromise it represents between high- and low-tension religious belief. On the one hand, dispensationalism focuses unwaveringly on the Bible's apocalyptic passages, interpreting them literally wherever possible. It assures Christians that the apocalypse could come at any moment and seeks to capitalize on the sense of urgency this creates by urging them to evangelize as many people as possible before the End. On the other hand, it incorporates a safety valve to protect against apocalyptic panic or disappointment. The pioneers of dispensationalism were determined not to witness a repeat of the Millerite fiasco; therefore they insisted that God's prophetic clock had stopped for the duration of the Church Age and that any attempt to guess the date of the apocalypse was fruitless. In addition to this ban on predictive millenarianism, they also placed restrictions on the explanatory variety: while it was permissible to interpret the state of the world as evidence of mankind's pre-ordained slide into wickedness, nothing that happened in the contemporary world could be presented as the fulfillment of prophecy.

Given these restraints, both the benefits and the costs of dispensationalism tended to be relatively modest. James Snowden, one of the movement's early critics, was struck by its limited impact on the lives of believers:

> What do they [the dispensationalists] do that is different from what other Christians . . . do on this subject? . . . As far as we can make out, they do not differ in their practice from other Christians, unless it be that they hold "prophetic conferences"; and carry on a propaganda to convert other Christians to their view. They do not engage in any distinctive or special kind of Christian service that fulfils their doctrine. . . . On pragmatic principles, if this doctrine is true, it should "make a difference." (quoted in T. Weber 1979: 44)

Arguably, however, the whole point of dispensationalism is that it does *not* make too much of a difference. A scholarly theory about the End Times that forbids risky speculation is unlikely to inspire extremes of belief or behavior. Dispensationalism is a routinized form of apocalypticism, compatible with the exercise of denominational authority. Admittedly, its status in modern society has always been mildly deviant, in the sense that, even in the late nineteenth century, mainstream Christianity and secular orthodoxy rejected its premises; but, paradoxically, it was informed by the same sort of rationality that drove the Victorians to create systematic models of the development of civilization or the evolution of species (quite an irony, given that dispensationalists were in the vanguard of the battle against the theory of evolution). For literal-minded Protestants, for whom Biblical verses possessed the status of hard data, the organization of the contradictory texts of Ezekiel, Daniel, the Gospels, Thessalonians, and Revelation into a single scheme served to strengthen the empirical basis of their beliefs.[6] In Weberian terms, this is an example of the development of the "rational theology" that accompanies the routinization of charisma in Western society (M. Weber [1948] 1970: 327; O'Dea 1966: 43–45). Dispensationalism and other varieties of premillennialism, such as covenant theology, are complex theories, difficult to master; but this can be seen as an advantage, since they place the troublesome subject of the end of the world in the hands of what Weber called religious virtuosi—experts who have mastered a specialist eschatological discourse. This is reassuring for many ordinary believers, who can leave the burden of understanding apocalyptic prophecy to seminary-trained individuals who have "gone into" the relevant texts. In Festinger's terms, the existence of a specialist discourse permits them to reduce the importance of a cognition—knowledge of an imminent End—that might otherwise make life unbearable. For those in authority, meanwhile, qualified prophecy commentators are supposed to act as border guards on the frontiers of doctrine, using their professional skills to repel "crazy" ideas from the cultic milieu. We can draw an analogy between the official millenarianism of dispensationalism and the scaled-down theology of healing adopted by the Pentecostal denominations. In both cases, those in religious authority have routinized a message that has the potential to channel power to the wrong people— doomsday prophets and bogus healers—and to damage the integrity of the belief system by exposing various charismatic claims to public ridicule.

Yet by any standards they have been only partly successful. In a religious tradition lacking a settled hierarchy, there can be no definitive map of the boundaries of acceptable belief and behavior. Just as the Pentecostal world still struggles with disruptive prophets and dubious signs and wonders, so the conservative evangelical community plays host to innumerable tension-raising millenarian claims. As Barr points out, Christian fundamentalism lacks any conceptual mechanism capable of controlling eschatological speculation; it "is unable to discipline its own millenarian offspring" (1977: 206). Many "prophecy experts" have dubious qualifications and use dispensationalism as a jumping off point for their own heterodox theories, happily ignoring the prohibition against measuring contemporary events against Bible prophecy. The next section considers the place of their ideas in conservative evangelicalism as a whole.

Unofficial Millenarianism: Popular Prophecy Belief

When an evangelical Christian is described as being "into the End Times," it is unlikely to mean that he or she is a specialist in dispensationalist theory. It is more likely to signal an appetite for popular material emanating from a prophecy subculture heavily influenced by American fundamentalism.[7] This subculture straddles the respectable and the bizarre, theology and conspiracy, revivalism and survivalism. It influences the content of Sunday sermons, Right-wing websites, and the tabloid magazines sold in American supermarkets, in which predictions of the return of Christ alternate with sightings of Elvis Presley. The basic framework of this prophecy belief is Protestant, premillennial, and usually dispensationalist; a majority of its exponents expect the Second Coming to be preceded by the rise of Antichrist and the Great Tribulation. But, in its endlessly resourceful improvisations on biblical texts, and in its determination to unmask the Satanic conspirators leading the world to perdition, it strongly resembles the medieval and early modern prophetic texts described by Cohn ([1970] 1993), McGinn ([1979] 1998), and McIver (1999). In the apocalyptic subculture, the specialist discourse of seminary professors shades imperceptibly into conspiracy theory, urban myth, and the popular beliefs and practices of what Hornsby-Smith (1991) calls "common religion." As the folklorist Daniel Wojcik points out, apocalyptic ideas have often operated outside the sanction of religious institutions and tend to be founded in personal experience rather than doctrine:

> Today, many of the leading proponents of apocalyptic worldviews are not formally trained theologians associated with mainstream religious denominations . . . but visionaries or prophecy interpreters who derive their apocalyptic authority from their charisma, predictive abilities, or divinely inspired revelations attained outside the formal sanction of dominant social institutions. (1997: 16)

The anthropologist Susan Harding has depicted the consequences of this eschatological free market:

> The old-fashioned dispensationalist scheme is still spoken in sermons on the Rapture, the Tribulation, and the Second Coming, in self-declared pretribulational, premillennial churches (see ads in the Yellow Pages), and in books by (older) Dallas Theological Seminary professors. But believers are routinely exposed to an undifferentiated array of variations—in other sermons by their preachers, in other books (the prophecy sections in most Christian bookstores contain a hodgepodge of millennial texts), in television, audio and video tapes, in conversations among Christian friends from other churches. (1994: 66)

On the face of it, the popularity of this sort of improvised prophecy belief within conservative evangelicalism represents a failure of boundary maintenance by the proponents of official millenarian schemes. Yet such a failure was inevitable, given the unstable nature of millenarianism and its usefulness as an analytical tool. It was unrealistic of strict dispensationalists to expect that the faithful, while being assured that Christ could return at any time, would refrain from looking for signs of the End in the world around them. The twentieth century offered too many clues that the Last Days were about to begin, the most striking of which were the 1917 Balfour Declaration and the foundation of the state of Israel in 1948. Since the Middle Ages, apocalyptic believers had looked forward to the return of the Jews to the Holy Land, and the fulfillment of the prophecy so soon after the invention of nuclear weapons that promised a literal Armageddon was enough to persuade many dispensationalists that God's prophetic clock had started ticking again.[8]

The full explanatory power of popular premillennialism was revealed after Israel's victory in the Six-Day War of 1967, which seemed to provide further evidence of the fulfillment of prophecy. In 1970 Hal Lindsey published *The Late Great Planet Earth* ([1970] 1971), a fundamentalist Christian analysis of the Cold War, which was to become the best-selling American non-fiction title of the decade (Boyer 1992: 5). Lindsey, a former Mississippi tug boat captain, offered his audience a brilliant contemporary spin on dispensationalism that showed how the emerging crisis in the Middle East would soon lead to the emergence of a diabolical "Future Führer." This figure was, of course, the Antichrist; initially charismatic, he would soon initiate a persecution that would make the regimes of Hitler, Mao, and Stalin "look like Girl Scouts weaving a daisy chain" ([1970] 1971: 110). But the book's real originality lay in its detail and in particular its depiction of the post-Tribulation nuclear war. Biblical descriptions of lightning, hailstones, beasts, and "locusts with scorpion tails" were identified as, respectively, missiles, ICBMs, armored tanks, and Cobra helicopters spraying nerve gas from their tails. Lindsey produced the testimony of engineers and scientists to demonstrate the divine prescience of biblical texts—and all within a framework of God's unalterable plan for mankind.[9]

The Late Great Planet Earth introduced premillennialism to millions of people and breathed new life into prophecy literature. The influence of such material on born-again Christianity has been considerable—yet it has not been welcomed by everyone in the community. There are a number of vociferous evangelical opponents of the prophecy subculture, whose reservations are shared by many ordinary church members. Books such as William Alnor's *Soothsayers of the Second Advent* (1989), B. J. Oropeza's *99 Reasons Why No One Knows When Christ Will Return* (1994), and Richard Abanes's *End-Time Visions* (1998) roundly mock the prophetic pretensions of Lindsey and his imitators. Alnor, Oropeza, and Abanes are Bible-believing Christians who object to what they regard as the prophecy genre's frivolous interpretations of Scripture. They are not writing from a secular perspective; but they do employ reason and scientific data in an attempt to demolish what they regard as demonstrably wrong empirical assertions. Their criticisms resemble those leveled at the "signs and wonders" movement in the essays by Smail, Walker, and Wright that we considered earlier: in both cases, the authors are trying to protect the religious tradition from damage to its reputation caused by dubious and disconfirmable ideas.

One of the major charges laid against popular prophecy by its evangelical opponents is that, by issuing false predictions of the Rapture or the return of Christ, it invites the ultimate disconfirmation. According to Oropeza (1994), date-setting can "ruin a believer's faith," "ruin a teacher's reputation," and "make a mockery of Christianity." It is certainly true that many prophecy authors have crossed the line from explanatory to predictive millenarianism. In the last quarter of the twentieth century, commentators such as Harold Campling and Jack Van Impe issued a series of "possible" deadlines for the Rapture. Perhaps because they were so careful to open up rhetorical escape routes for themselves ("I could be wrong, but . . .") they were rarely taken seriously; but from time to time a prediction would gain sufficient currency to alarm church leaders. In 1988 Edgar Whisenant, a former NASA engineer, published a book entitled *88 Reasons Why the Rapture Will Be in 1988* that caused a considerable stir in conservative evangelical circles; 4.5 million copies were printed. "Nearly every evangelical Christian in America was at least aware of Whisenant's predictions," writes Alnor. "Some laughed. Others dared not" (1989: 29). Better known authors, such as Hal Lindsey and the Canadian evangelist Grant Jeffrey, flirted with millennial arithmetic in more subtle ways: Lindsey suggested that the apocalypse might occur within a biblical generation (40 years) of the founding of Israel in 1948. Abanes quotes a prophecy teacher reminiscing about the early days of Calvary Chapel, a network of mildly Charismatic congregations founded by Chuck Smith in the 1970s:

> How excited we were. Oh, some of the prophecy preachers got a little out of hand and those plagues like Revelation 9 were Vietnam helicopters and you know we sort of started dating things and we were even told that a generation is 40 years, and when Israel became a nation in 1948 it would be 40 years and the Lord would come. So we back it up [advance the deadline] seven. So the Rapture's coming in 1981. I've met people all over this country who believed that, followed that, and anticipated that. It did not come and as a result many of them bombed out, dropped out, copped out— they're not around anymore. (1998: 327)

Today, Calvary Chapel is a hugely successful operation, celebrated by the sociologist Donald Miller in his book *Reinventing American Protestantism* (1997) as an example of culturally innovative "new paradigm" evangelicalism. Calvary congregations offer a relaxed, informal style of worship that can be seen as a calculated attempt to lower subcultural deviance; one would never guess from Miller's admiring portrait that they had engaged in anything as deviant and risky as date-setting. The quotation from the prophecy teacher suggests that, although predictive millenarianism might be stigmatized in respectable evangelical churches, it can sometimes be found lurking beneath the surface.

Explanatory millenarianism is as vulnerable to disconfirmation as the predictive variety, albeit on a smaller scale. Evangelical opponents of the genre are well aware of this, and rarely miss an opportunity to stress the all-round unreliability of unofficial apocalyptic ideas as a guide to the future. As Abanes puts it:

> If God reveals every detail before it happens, then why didn't he reveal the date of the Jews' 1948 return to Palestine, the date of the

Six-Day War in Jerusalem, the date of the fall of communism and so forth? Virtually all doomsday-setters consider such events prophetically significant, yet we have no evidence that anyone predicted the date—not even the month or year—of these events. (1998: 26–27)

What worries these critics even more, however, is the association of prophecy belief with other forms of deviant secret knowledge. Oropeza's 99 Reasons Why No One Knows When Christ Will Return—the title an obvious send-up of Whisenant—provides a tour d'horizon of the "unbiblical ideas" that have been generated by Christian prophecy belief or have become grafted onto it in the cultic milieu. The book's "reasons" include: "Discerning the signs of the times does not warrant date suggestions"; "Humans lived on earth prior to 4004 BC"; "Scripture does not say that Christ will return by AD 2000"; "Current earthquakes do not tell us the time of the End"; "The fact that Israel has returned to Palestine does not necessarily mean that Christ will return in our generation"; "We do not know that the European Union is the revived Roman Empire"; "We do not know that the Roman Catholic Church is the Whore of Babylon"; "UFO enthusiasts do not know the date of the End"; "The prophecies of Nostradamus are not accurate"; "The Procter & Gamble company is not Satanist"; and "The current Universal Product Code is not the Mark of the Beast." Oropeza's list provides a useful map of the boundaries of Christian prophecy belief and what lies just beyond them: motifs from the occult, the New Age, and secular conspiracy theory. His book shows how the prophecy genre brings together different types of deviant knowledge. These include empirically questionable data from Christian and secular sources, such as claims that the earth is 6,000 years old and dubious statistics relating to earthquakes; religious statements that are thought morally unacceptable in a pluralist society, such as anti-Catholic rhetoric; the disconfirmable predictions of astrologers and psychics, cited with surprising frequency by Christian prophecy authors; obvious urban myths; and conspiracy theories current on the Far Right.

What Oropeza and the others are saying, in effect, is that unofficial millenarianism carries with it crippling costs. So why, then, do so many conservative evangelical churches—themselves cautious in their pronouncements about the End Times—help to circulate the works of freelance prophecy writers, including outright date-setters and conspiracy theorists? Why is the boundary with the cultic milieu not policed with more vigilance? Barr makes the point that fundamentalism lacks a conceptual instrument that is capable of controlling millennialism; and there is not much of a will to do so, judging by the shelves of colorful prophecy material to be found in church bookshops in America and Britain. The basic explanation for this lack of concern, I would suggest, is that the theoretical costs of unofficial millenarianism rarely translate into actual social costs; its disruptive potential remains unfulfilled. There are two major reasons for this. The first is that only a minority of born-again Christians are "into the End Times"—and those who are find themselves occupying a mildly deviant and not particularly influential position within the community. The second is that popular prophecy does not require its consumers to engage in socially disruptive activity: it is in many ways a form of entertainment.

Some born-again Christians are fascinated by the End Times, but many others either have no interest in it or only occasionally read a book devoted to the subject. The level of prophecy belief—official and unofficial—varies between and across congregations. The historian Paul Boyer offers this topography of the subculture:

> I have found it helpful to visualise the world of prophecy belief as a series of concentric circles, at the centre of which is a core of devotees who spend much time thinking about the Bible's apocalyptic passages and trying to organise them into a coherent scenario. These are the men and women who attend prophecy conferences; raise the topic in Sunday school classes and Bible study groups; and avidly devour the prophecy paperbacks, cassette tapes and study aids that annually pour into the market. . . . Next in this concentric series one finds those believers who may be hazy about the details of biblical eschatology, but who nevertheless believe that the Bible provides clues to future events. . . . In the outer circle there are those superficially secular individuals who exhibit little overt prophecy interest, but whose worldview is nevertheless shaped to some degree by residual or latent concepts of eschatology. (1992: 2–3)

Boyer is right to emphasize that there are different levels of prophecy belief, but his notion of a "core" of devotees is potentially misleading. Many of the people who attend official, church-sponsored prophecy conferences are also enthusiasts for conspiracy theories and other forms of rejected knowledge from the cultic milieu—often to the dismay of other believers. They are sometimes known by fellow worshippers as "prophecy nuts" or some similar dismissive term. Far from making up the core of congregations, such people can find themselves pushed to the fringes, relegated to an outer circle alongside other "difficult" types, such as people who issue unorthodox personal prophecies (with whom they may in any case overlap). They are, however, unlikely to find themselves excluded from the wider religious community. Partly this is because born-again Christianity has such permeable borders; someone whose millenarianism is too intense for one congregation can easily switch allegiance to another. But the fact remains that even pastors who play down the subject of prophecy in their sermons are prepared to sell conspiracy-flavored material to "prophecy nuts" and other interested parties. They feel free to do so because they regard it as essentially harmless: with the exception of the occasional date-setting embarrassment, the practical consequences of unofficial millenarianism are limited. Just as Snowden wondered what difference dispensationalism made to the lives of believers, so one might ask what prophecy fans actually *do* with the knowledge that the European Union is controlled by a Satanic computer in Brussels or that supermarket barcodes conceal the Number of the

Beast. The answer is that they do little, since the terms of this particular apoc-alyptic discourse rarely require any action other than the consumption of more prophecy material.

In theory, the claims made by prophecy experts might seem to pose a threat to the holders of religious authority within the conservative evangelical denom-inations. Sometimes problems do arise—for example, when someone invokes a personal message from God in support of an apocalyptic argument.[10] For the most part, however, prophecy authors do not pose a significant threat to church order. Hal Lindsey and his imitators are not interested in attracting disciples or founding their own sects: their prime concern seems to be to carve out a paying audience for their message and to hold on to it. They are constantly updating their material to take account of new trends in the marketplace, and to disguise the disconfirmation of earlier prophecies: the Canadian fundamen-talist Grant Jeffrey, for example, was quick to exploit the mid-1990s fad for discovering hidden codes in the Bible and the later panic over the Y2K com-puter bug. The most obvious question raised by such material is the one that was raised in chapter 2: to what extent is it a form of entertainment?

In 1995, a quarter of a century after *The Late Great Planet Earth*, premil-lennialism once again crossed over into the best-seller lists—but this time as fiction. The novel *Left Behind* and its many sequels, written by veteran prophecy author Tim LaHaye and journalist Jerry Jenkins, are set during the worldwide Tribulation that follows the Rapture: the first book observes this event from the vantage point of an international flight on which many passengers sud-denly disappear, leaving behind their socks, shoes and clothes (LaHaye and Jenkins 1995: 16). By 2002 the novels had sold 50 million copies (McCain 2002). Like Lindsey, LaHaye and Jenkins insist that there is an evangelistic purpose behind their mass-market approach; but it could be argued that, by adopting the medium of the novel, they are unintentionally making it more difficult for their audience to take the Rapture doctrine seriously. The *Left Be-hind* sequence leaves intact the outline of dispensationalism, but neatly side-steps the question of its credibility. Instead, it presents it in a form—popular fiction—that is acceptable not only to secular society, but also to Bible-believing Christians who are not themselves "prophecy nuts." Arguably, the novels pro-vide evidence of an aspect of secularization. The authors claim that they are a way of reaching unbelievers; but might they reflect what the sociologist James Davison Hunter (1983, 1987) maintains is a shift in the cognitive style of evan-gelical Christians away from literal belief in difficult doctrines? We shall return to this question later in this study.

Obviously we cannot dismiss popular prophecy belief as pure entertain-ment; but there is not much evidence to suggest, as several commentators have done, that it supplies the hidden dynamic of evangelical Christianity. According to Barr, millenarianism probably has "much more influence within conserva-tive evangelicalism than would appear on the surface," and it is "likely that many conservative evangelicals personally entertain strongly millennial ideas, even when they know that it is not expedient to put them in the shop window"

(1977: 202–3). The more one studies the literature that serves as the major carrier of such ideas, however, the harder it is to take seriously as the expression of an ideology. Rather, it emerges all the more clearly as religious rhetoric, endlessly adaptable, sensitive to mood, whose propositions possess formidable explanatory power but rarely provoke significant social action.

Pentecostal Perspectives

Present-day Pentecostalism has a curious relationship with prophecy belief in both its official and unofficial variants. A minority of Pentecostalists are heavily "into the End Times" and buy uncritically into versions of the dispensationalist package of doctrines. This is not surprising, given that Pentecostalist Bible schools traditionally teach dispensationalism, and that many healing evangelists of the postwar years, such as Oral Roberts and Jimmy Swaggart, were dispensationalists (Prosser 1999: 258). What my fieldwork suggests, however, is that Pentecostalists who are preoccupied with the End Times are—to an even greater extent than in other evangelical churches—often marginalized within congregations: the whole subject is seen by some members of the community as somehow old-fashioned and un-Pentecostal.

The evangelical historian Peter Prosser (1999) argues that the sterile formulae of premillennialism are alien to the spontaneous spirit of Pentecostalism. He doubts that the movement ever really took dispensationalism to heart and questions whether, even in the early days, it was as millenarian as it appeared to outsiders. He lists the characteristics of Pentecostalism that were intensified by awareness of an approaching Last Judgment: diffidence toward worldly affairs, militaristic rhetoric, personal asceticism, and missionary zeal. But he adds that none of these is wholly explained by millenarianism; to some extent each was a product of other traditions inherited by the movement. "The point rather is that millenarianism seems to have sharpened the edges, stoked the fires, intensified the colours of their world," he concludes (1999: 26–27). Prosser's own view is that Pentecostalism should move away from Darbyite theology and concentrate instead on the more optimistic holiness tradition followed by many black and Hispanic Pentecostal churches, thus freeing the gifts of the Spirit to work socially and politically in the present (288–89).

Margaret Poloma, in a recent essay, also questions the importance of traditional End Times rhetoric to modern Pentecostals:

> While some Pentecostals joined their evangelical and fundamentalist cousins who focus on interpreting the prophetic elements in the Book of Revelation, many more downplay the details of premillennial eschatology. . . . These believers prefer a more practical, utilitarian and personal experience of the prophetic that is born through common experience of the prophetic and nurtured through prophetic myths. (2001: 169)

Prophecy is integral to the Pentecostal worldview, writes Poloma, but more as a prayerful religious experience of the individual than as a detailed blueprint for the Last Days. One question worth asking is whether this orientation reflects an attempt by the Pentecostal denominations—that is, church leaders rather than ordinary believers—to play down their millenarian inheritance. As we have seen, dispensationalism does exist as a respectable, quasi-scholarly discourse; but its overtones are fundamentalist rather than Pentecostal, and it is also associated with popular conspiracy beliefs that sit uneasily with the professional ethos of emerging denominations. There may be a parallel here with Seventh-day Adventism, a once overtly apocalyptic sect that has moved a long way toward accommodation with society. Ronald Lawson's survey of Adventists found that pastors gave a low priority to eschatology, and that their seminaries and religious departments generally avoided the subject (1997: 215–16). This suggests that, for Adventist leaders, the marginalization of apocalyptic doctrines was an effective way of lowering subcultural deviance. There is some evidence that Pentecostalism is moving in the same direction: witness, for example, Elim's 1994 decision to remove any reference to the Millennium from its list of "fundamental truths." As William Kay points out, this move in no way denies the return of Christ, allowing instead a variety of evangelical views to be held on the subject (2000a: 133); but, considered alongside Elim's increasingly vague statements about healing, it does point to some degree of accommodation with mainstream Christianity.

It is also true, however, that the routinization of Pentecostal healing and prophecy has been challenged by the high-tension claims of the "signs and wonders" movement. In much the same way, any downplaying of dispensational theory has been offset, in some churches, by a new eschatological fervor that also owes much to the Third Wave. The Wimberite excitements of the 1980s and 1990s did not just create an upsurge in reports of the miraculous: they also intensified some Pentecostalists' sense of living in the Last Days. The two key concepts here are Revival and Restoration. Pentecostalism has always been revivalist, but it became intensely so at the end of the twentieth century— and that, in itself, raised the eschatological temperature. Revivalism was described to me by one Kensington Temple pastor as "eschatology in disguise." According to an often quoted verse from Matthew's Gospel, the good news "will be preached throughout the whole world, as a testimony to the nations; and then the end will come" (Matt. 24:14). This prophecy and others lend an apocalyptic charge to the whole notion of revival: any sudden move of the Spirit resulting in many conversions becomes a candidate for the final outpouring of grace before Jesus comes back. It is only fair to point out that, as a result, many preachers are careful to qualify their use of the word "revival": they speak of the "coming" revival or a "possible" revival. But this hesitancy only underlines the potency of the concept: no sooner is the word used than the promise of the End is in the air.

Hand in hand with the prospect of revival, meanwhile, went an increasing Pentecostal fascination with the concept of Restoration. This word, too, is highly charged. The movement known as Restorationism, which surfaced in middle-class house churches in the 1960s, aims to return the worldwide Church to the New Testament pattern described in St. Paul's Epistle to the Ephesians: "And his gifts were that some should be apostles, some prophets, some evangelists, some pastors and teachers, to equip the saints for the work of the ministry, for building up the body of Christ" (Eph. 4:11–12). In the last decade of the twentieth century, several important Pentecostal and neo-Pentecostal churches, including Kensington Temple, declared their intention to restore the apostolic orders, just as the house churches had twenty years earlier. In doing so, however, they took on board ideas about the end of history that subtly contradicted the traditional doctrines of classic Pentecostalism. As Andrew Walker has pointed out, the very concept of Restoration is eschatological; but its vision of the future is not as catastrophic as that of premillennialism, which focuses on themes of tribulation and Antichrist. Restorationists believe that they are living in the End Times; however, instead of this era being characterized by chaos and wars, they expect it to be marked by "an outpouring of God's Spirit culminating in the establishment of the kingdom that is ready and fit for the return of the King" (1989: 30–31). Stephen Hunt argues that, by taking on board Restorationist themes of the return of a New Testament pattern, the Wimberite neo-Pentecostalists acquired some of the key tenets of postmillennialism, the idea that the rule of the saints will occur before Jesus returns (2001b: 58). Postmillennialism is traditionally foreign to classic Pentecostal churches; yet those closest to the Third Wave, such as Kensington Temple, have undoubtedly been touched by its apocalyptic optimism.

This development has created something of an ideological dilemma for classic Pentecostalists caught up in Restorationist revivalism. How can the notion of an emerging kingdom be reconciled with belief in the imminent rule of Antichrist and the Rapture of the Church? One way of squaring the circle for believers is to engage in complicated ideological work; another is not to let such theoretical considerations loom too large. Premillennialism and postmillennialism are sometimes treated by scholars as alternative beliefs separated by a vast theological gulf; the reality is that they are often mixed up with each other, and it is not uncommon for evangelical Christians to oscillate between a pessimistic premillennial scenario and an optimistic postmillennial one depending on their mood and circumstances. Susan Harding (1994) has shown how, during the 1980s, the premillennialist Religious Right in America was tempted by the success of its political project to flirt with postmillennialism. Something similar happened to many Pentecostals and Charismatics in the 1990s: confronted by the extraordinary growth of their congregations, they scented victory rather than preordained disaster. But, lacking the relish of their fundamentalist brethren for detailed eschatology, these Spirit-filled Christians did not let any ideological contradictions worry them too much. Instead, they reveled in visions of revivalism and Restoration, their relaxed attitude to their premillennial inheritance serving only to highlight the discursive, contingent, and utilitarian nature of apocalypticism in the Pentecostal tradition.[11]

Conclusion

This chapter has attempted to place Pentecostalism's relationship with apocalyptic theology in the wider context of routinization and boundary maintenance. Pentecostalism has always made claims about the empirical realm that require careful management. The vulnerability of such claims to disproof, and the difficulty of reconciling them with the exercise of traditional authority, has meant that Pentecostalism has undergone a degree of routinization; but it has also received regular infusions of charismatic authority in the shape of controversial revivalist ministries. The movement is therefore pulled simultaneously toward and away from accommodation with the reality of everyday life. This double movement is observable in the Pentecostalist relationship with the charismatic claims of millenarianism. The apocalyptic teachings that Pentecostalism has borrowed from American fundamentalism form an uncomfortable inheritance, and not just for Pentecostalists: as we have seen, many non-Pentecostal evangelicals are suspicious of the prophecy subculture. For Pentecostalists, dispensationalist prophecy belief poses special difficulties, since it sits uneasily with their understanding of prophecy as something spontaneous and personal. Yet some worshippers still subscribe to the traditional premillennial doctrine of the End Times, while others have been drawn by promises of revival into an unmistakably apocalyptic vision of the triumph of the Church.

Any attempt to consider the costs and benefits of millenarianism in a Pentecostal context must take into account a wide variety of competing ideas and practical dilemmas. There are bound to be conflicting ideas about the appropriate degree of subcultural deviance for a movement which combines strikingly countercultural beliefs and practices with a commitment to Christian orthodoxy. The sources of authority in global Pentecostalism are far too diffuse for any one leader or organization to hope to raise or lower the overall degree of tension that exists between the movement and the Western secular consensus. At the level of the local church, however, it is certainly possible to manipulate subcultural deviance through the management of Charismatic gifts and apocalyptic ideas; indeed, such management is essential if the believing community is to flourish and plausibility structures are to be maintained. To observe this dynamic at close quarters, we now turn to Kensington Temple.

4

Kensington Temple

This chapter sets the scene for our later discussion of the circulation of apocalyptic ideas at Kensington Temple. It describes the history and organizational structure of this large, multi-ethnic Pentecostal church and introduces its dynamic senior pastor, Colin Dye. We see how the life of the congregation reflects the religious trends discussed in chapters 2 and 3, such as the increasing role of consumer choice in the everyday spirituality of born-again Christians. Kensington Temple also reproduces on a small scale the conflicting demands of high- and low-tension religion, and in the second half of the chapter we see how Dye and his flock attempt to reconcile these demands by engaging in the rational management of charisma. On the one hand, they are open to the "signs and wonders" that swept through the Charismatic world in the 1990s; on the other, they take measures against cognitive dissonance and discourage excesses of enthusiasm and theology that might raise subcultural deviance to an unacceptable degree. Leaders and ordinary worshippers alike are wary of "difficult" or "superspiritual" people who attach disproportionate importance to miraculous phenomena or prophecy belief.

"KT": A Church with a Mission

The Church on the Corner

Every Saturday morning, hundreds of tourists pour out of Notting Hill Gate underground station and walk past a parade of coffee bars and antique shops on their way to Portobello Market. As they do so, they pass a grey stone Victorian church with imposing twin towers. Very few of them give it a second glance. There are dozens of these slightly forbidding neo-Gothic buildings in west London. Many of them have been taken over by Pentecostal Christians who speak in tongues and pray for miraculous healing—practices quite alien to the staid denominations that built the original churches. In London, Pentecostal congregations are largely made up of members of ethnic minorities: Africans, West Indians, Filipinos, and Latin Americans. Kensington Temple, known to almost everyone in the church as "KT," is one of these churches.

Every few minutes during the day, worshippers arrive on the local red buses and, after the services or meetings, form queues at the bus stops. Most of them belong to social groups traditionally associated with Pentecostalism. There are old black ladies in the straw hats beloved of the first generation of Caribbean immigrants. They are much in evidence on Sunday mornings, their cheerful banter in sharp contrast to the shy smiles of another KT "type," the middle-aged Filipina women who often work as checkout assistants in the local supermarkets. There are students from Brazil, Singapore, and Eastern Europe, clutching heavily annotated zip-up Bibles as they fish for change for the fare. On Saturday afternoons, while the tourists walk back from the market, the church hosts Nigerian or Ghanaian weddings; this produces the most colorful bus queues of the week, with departing and arriving guests dressed in the dazzling silk robes of tribal chieftains and their wives. On weekday evenings, in contrast, many worshippers are barely identifiable as churchgoers at all. They are young men and women, mostly black, dressed in businesslike suits; with their clipboards and mobile phones they could be delegates at a sales conference. Even so, most of the women arrive on the bus.

So far, there is nothing very surprising in all this: although some Pentecostal churches in London cater almost exclusively to one ethnic group, others create a rich demographic stew of races and nationalities. At Kensington Temple, however, there are unexpected ingredients in the mixture. A few worshippers are middle-aged white people who, judging by their well-tailored suits and skirts, belong to the professional classes who have colonized Notting Hill in the past decade. (This is an area in which, at the turn of the millennium, the average one-bedroom flat cost £250,000 and most houses well over a million pounds.) This in itself is unusual. In Britain, such people are rarely found in Pentecostal churches: if they are attracted to speaking in tongues or healing services they tend to go to churches that describe themselves as "Charismatic evangelical," in which the gifts of the Holy Spirit are experienced in a more restrained or sophisticated way than in the classic Pentecostal tradition. In addition, many visitors to KT look like typical student backpackers; a number of them speak with Australian or South African accents and sport the deep tan of the habitual traveler.

An observer might also notice that worshippers emerge from services clutching not a photocopied newsletter, as in other local churches, but an impressively glossy magazine called *Revival Times*. Produced once a month, its 28 full-color pages speak of ambitions and resources well beyond the reach of even the largest Anglican or Catholic parish. The issue of May 1999, for example, carried on its cover an image of thousands of worshippers filling the stalls and balconies of the Royal Albert Hall; many of them had an arm out-stretched in a gesture that indicated their openness to the Holy Spirit. Inside, a message from Colin Dye, KT's senior pastor, appeared underneath his photograph. He is white, slim, and pale-skinned, with neatly-cut dark hair dramatically streaked with grey. "What an amazing God we serve!" he wrote. "The Easter Monday services at the Royal Albert Hall were everything we hoped for. I will never forget the sense of the presence of God, the levels of high praise and passionate worship and the manifestation of God's power." The reader was left in no doubt that the rally, though attended by people from many churches, was a Kensington Temple event. There was, however, not one reference in the magazine to KT's mother denomination, the Elim Foursquare Gospel Church.

How can one small church afford to hire the Albert Hall, filling it twice in one day? The explanation is that "Kensington Temple" is shorthand for much more than one building. It is really a network of congregations which, during the 1990s, was sometimes described in the media as Britain's largest church; estimates of its size range from 3,000 to 15,000 worshippers, depending on whether affiliated congregations are counted as part of the whole. The pages of the May 1999 issue of *Revival Times* were sprinkled with references to zones and satellites, to ethnic fellowships, special conferences, and cell groups. There were advertisements for an evangelistic crusade in West Africa, to be led by Colin Dye (cost: £1,100) and a Christian school sponsored by the church (fees: £3,000 a year). All these were KT projects. Confusingly, though, the magazine also referred throughout to something called the London City Church (LCC), with offices in North Acton rather than Notting Hill Gate. In fact, the LCC is Kensington Temple writ large. In the mid-1990s, after years of spectacular growth, KT embarked on an ambitious plan to transform itself into a citywide network of Pentecostal churches, ministries, and cell groups. To this end it leased a former BBC warehouse building in Acton and divided it into offices, a Bible college and a 3,000-seater arena called the Tabernacle; KT would remain the spiritual home of this London City Church, but this would be its nerve center. At Easter 2000, however, these plans suffered a catastrophic setback. KT was unable to renew the lease on the building, and many staff and services had to be relocated at short notice to the cramped original building. As a result, scores of people who, until recently, traveled to Acton for the Sunday evening revival meeting have found themselves back in Notting Hill Gate; the bus queues have lengthened significantly.

The History of Kensington Temple

The foundation stone of Kensington Temple is dated August 20, 1848. It was laid by members of a prosperous Congregational church in Hornton Street, Kensington, who wanted to help "the poor and neglected people of Notting Hill Vale," then one of London's most insalubrious areas; at the meeting at which the project was commissioned, some of the Hornton Street worshippers were so moved that they wept. The new building was christened Horbury Chapel, after the Yorkshire birthplace of one of its founders. Wealthy Londoners began to worship there with their servants (Hywel-Davies 1998: 25–26). By the 1920s, however, attendance at the chapel had fallen so sharply that it was forced to close, and after a period standing empty it was bought by the Elim Pentecostalist Alliance. The Alliance was led by George Jeffreys, a young lay preacher who launched a campaign to evangelize Ireland at the beginning of the First World War. Jeffreys' initiative became the Elim movement, named after an Israelite encampment in the Book of Exodus (15:27). By 1920 it was holding revival meetings in borrowed halls and tents all around Britain. Jeffreys was a spellbinding preacher, capable of winning two or three thousand converts in each campaign. There were rallies in the Albert Hall and the Crystal Palace. The *Daily Express* reported incredulously on an Elim convention: "Swinging arms and resonantly clapping hands. Again and again—the same verse. . . . It was a species of trance creation. Hysteria seemed at hand. They were lashed and urged by massed melody into an unearthly joy" (quoted in Wilson 1961: 38). Under Jeffreys, Horbury chapel, renamed Kensington Temple, became the headquarters of a World Revival Crusade; it was dubbed by the newspapers "the Church of the Great Physician" because of the many miracles reported there.

This success did not last. The outbreak of war in 1939 and the subsequent evacuation emptied many London churches. More damaging for Kensington Temple, however, was the dispute about church government that broke out between Jeffreys and his colleagues. Jeffreys attempted to dismantle the administrative hierarchy of the movement; he lost the struggle and resigned from Elim. Bryan Wilson (1961: 49; 1990: 116) offers the controversy as an example of the tension that can arise between a charismatic leader and supporters of a routinized, denominationalized form of government.[1] From our point of view, it is interesting to note that the argument was also at least partly about Bible prophecy. Jeffreys was a supporter of British Israelism, a theory of divine history that identified the British with the lost ten tribes of Israel and predicted that the Battle of Armageddon would be fought between Britain and Russia.[2] British Israelism had been banned from Elim pulpits in the mid-1930s, but its influence persisted among the membership: in 1940 the Elim conference narrowly passed a resolution that "while all questions of prophetical interpretation should be decided by the governing body, liberty of expression on questions of prophetical interpretation should be permitted" (Wilson 1961: 51). British Israelism belonged to the cultic milieu of its day: despised by many educated Protestants, it threatened to increase the subcultural deviance of Elim Pentecostalism and was not surprisingly opposed by the forces of routinization. It was, however, supported by Jeffreys, who found himself in the position of a charismatic leader who, against the wishes of his lieutenants, espouses a deviant idea associated with his rank and file followers.[3] In the schism that followed, Jeffreys was able to keep Kensington Temple as the headquarters of his breakaway movement; but his following slowly dissipated, along with British Israelism, and the building reverted to Elim (Hywel-Davies 1998: 43).

Since the 1960s, Kensington Temple has had a succession of dynamic pastors, who, by concentrating on church growth and strengthening contacts with other evangelical Christians, have gradually moved it away from sectarianism. Wynne Lewis, a fiery Welshman who was senior pastor during the 1980s, turned the church into an international community. He visited West Africa, where religious leaders instructed their followers to attend Kensington Temple whenever they were in London. He set up fellowships for individual ethnic groups, effectively abandoning the philosophy of total integration previously adopted by the church. Chinese, Filipinos, and Ethiopians started holding services after which they served their own food—"culinary evangelism," as Lewis called it (Hywel-Davies 1998: 106). These ethnic fellowships accounted for most of Kensington Temple's spectacular growth during the 1980s and 1990s. Lewis's policy was to identify potential leaders and encourage them to recruit vigorously among members of their own community, many of them recent arrivals in London who felt detached from their roots. As a result, the KT congregation would sometimes swell by several hundred almost overnight. Admittedly, this strategy was not without risks. Some newly evangelized worshippers from the Third World brought with them controversial folk beliefs verging on the animist; during my fieldwork I occasionally heard rumors that voodoo practices survive on the fringes of the church's African, Caribbean, and Latin American communities. For the most part, however, Kensington Temple seems to have achieved on a small scale what Pentecostalism has achieved throughout the developing world: it absorbed indigenous traditions, such as belief in spirit possession, reinterpreting them in light of its own Charismatic worldview (Cox 1994; Martin 2001). Indeed, it used those traditions to enrich its own cosmology: in Hywel-Davies's book, the visions of demons and fire-breathing witches experienced by immigrant worshippers are offered as evidence of the assault of Satanic powers on KT, and therefore of its divine mission (1998: 119). A more serious risk was (and remains) that of large-scale defection by a particular ethnic group. On several occasions prominent members of fellowships left the network to join another church or start their own, taking their friends with them. When this happened, the ethnic balance within the church could change radically.

Colin Dye and the Central Organization

In 1991 Wynne Lewis was succeeded as senior pastor by his chosen successor, Colin Dye, an Elim pastor who had been instrumental in setting up KT's international Bible college. Dye possessed unusual qualifications. Born in Kenya in 1952, he moved with his family to Tanzania to escape the Mau-Mau rebellion, and then to Australia when he was 10 years old. He came to England at the age of 16 to train as a ballet dancer, joined the Royal Ballet and began to dance principal roles. It was during this time that he was converted to evangelical Christianity and started attending Kensington Temple, eventually abandoning dance to train for the ministry (Dye 1997a: 16–17). Today, Dye's much-admired platform performances draw on both his African childhood and his artistic training. He has a special rapport with the African men in the congregation, laughing with them and upbraiding them: "I want to speak to you African men before it's too late. Stop playing games with God! Do you think only African men are proud? All men are proud! The only difference between men and boys is the price and the consequence of their toys" (sermon, December 10, 1998). There is also a balletic gracefulness to the way he moves around while preaching, twisting and turning unexpectedly, sometimes leaping off the stage. His timing is impeccable, his jokes well crafted. Some of his younger colleagues copy his mannerisms.

First-time visitors to Kensington Temple are struck by Dye's nervous energy. His image is that of a man who pushes himself excessively hard: on the platform, in church meetings, in the gym, and above all in prayer. He has turned the Wednesday night prayer meeting into one of the central events of church life, attended by up to 800 people. He has been known to shut himself in his office for hours, praying for guidance. Sometimes his staff find the intensity of his commitment a little frightening. In early 2000, at around the time that KT lost the lease on the Tabernacle, Dye embarked on a 40-day fast, drinking only water. He emerged from it "looking like an inmate of Belsen," according to one colleague. Again and again during my research, conversations about aspects of church life or teaching drifted into discussion of his leadership style. "Colin is autocratic—all he does is surround himself with yes-men that are like bodyguards," said one former satellite leader. Yet the same person said he showed "wonderful" leadership qualities, for example, in championing the ministry of women pastors at a time when most pastors in the Elim denomination thought only men should be ordained. Dye himself told me that his leadership is "charismatic" in the Weberian sense. A minister in another Pentecostal church made a similar point: "Colin has grown into the role of charismatic leader, the sort of person who has a special kudos, almost an aura. He's a leader on a pedestal rather than one of the lads." A cult of personality has built up around "Colin" (as everyone calls him), which resembles that surrounding charismatic business leaders and can also be encountered in other big Charismatic congregations, such as the Faith movement's Word of Life Church in Uppsala, Sweden.[4] Moreover, the organizational structure of Kensington Temple has been refined in ways that increase the senior pastor's authority over it; the church has become increasingly responsive to his constantly evolving theological vision. But, as we shall see, this institutional reinforcement of Dye's personal charisma is in itself precarious: it depends heavily on his own responsiveness to the mood of the congregation and his ability to assess risk.

Dye is a classic example of a charismatic leader whose authority is dispersed throughout an organization. As Samuel Eisenstadt observes, the test of such a leader is "his ability to leave a continuous impact on an institutional structure—to transform any given institutional setting by infusing into it some of his charismatic vision, by investing the regular, orderly offices, or aspects of social organisation, with some of his charismatic qualities and aura" (1968: xxi). This is what Dye has set out to do at Kensington Temple: he has modified the chain of command within the church in ways that increase his freedom of maneuver. This approach is reminiscent of Jeffreys' attempts to remove bureaucratic constraints on his charismatic authority; the difference is that, although some leaders of Elim are critical of what they regard as Dye's dictatorial manner, he has mostly secured denominational approval for his initiatives.

Under Dye, Kensington Temple has been granted the status of an independent Elim region; this gives it the right to appoint and train its own pastors, award diplomas to students, set up new churches, and send missions abroad. Since these activities are supervised by the senior pastor, the effect of this change was to increase his personal authority. Dye has also assumed responsibility for appointing members of the board of elders that, in theory, was supposed to oversee his ministry. One former board member described the reconstituted body as "Colin's cabinet, appointed by patronage, over which he has almost total control." The choice of a political metaphor is significant. The church administration is divided into quasi-governmental "divisions" and departments. In the late 1990s, these consisted of pastoral ministry; satellites and planted churches; training (including the Bible college); evangelism and foreign missions; operations (including the bookshop and publications); and finance. Again, the point to note is that every department is answerable to the senior pastor. The structure of Kensington Temple can be usefully measured against the two templates of church organization described by Mark Chaves (1998: 189–90). Despite its affiliation to Elim, it is closer to the unitary structures associated with sects, in which liturgical and "worldly" activities fall under a single line of command, than to the dual structures of the mainstream churches, in which boards of education, finance, social justice, and so on operate relatively independently of the spiritual leadership. One could say that the church's administration has been streamlined in order to facilitate the operation of charisma.

But if the adoption of a unitary structure represents a rejection of the secularized agencies spawned by the mainstream churches, it does not imply a refusal to employ the tools and methods of the secular world. Like many fast-growing Pentecostal and Charismatic churches, Kensington Temple has some of the characteristics of an international corporation, carving out markets for its products both at home and abroad (Hexham and Poewe 1997: 45). In the late 1990s it employed graphic artists and marketing experts to create a corporate identity for the London City Church, complete with logo; the LCC offices in the Acton Tabernacle (now vacated) had more of the feel of a medium-sized company than of a church organization. It is worth remembering that the business world of the 1990s was strongly influenced by the operation of charismatic authority—by the personal charisma of corporate executives and their ability to achieve results that transcended the everyday reality of the stock markets. The central organization of KT during the same period was staffed by people who thought about Colin Dye in much the same way as employees of a software company might think about their dynamic CEO: as the originator of a "vision" to which the day-to-day business of administration must be subordinated.

Congregations and Worshippers

In purely administrative terms, the structure of Kensington Temple is relatively simple: all members of staff are answerable to the senior pastor. Viewed as a network of congregations, however, the church is more difficult to anatomize. Even the meaning of the words "Kensington Temple" is unclear. Estimates of the size of the congregation(s) vary enormously, reflecting confusion about where the boundaries of the KT/LCC network actually lie. During the late 1990s, it was quite common to encounter members of outlying LCC congregations who denied being part of Kensington Temple; yet they were invariably counted as part of the 10,000-plus total claimed for KT in media descriptions of it as "Britain's largest church." (The same people may also have been unaware that as members of the LCC they were part of the Elim Foursquare Gospel Church.)

During the period of my fieldwork, there were 120 satellite churches, most of them "planted" in the previous decade in an area bounded by the M25, the motorway encircling central London. These congregations did not own their own premises, meeting instead in rented church halls, community centers, and members' homes; the Covent Garden church, one of the most successful in the network with perhaps fifty regular attendees, met for a time in a branch of the Mongolian Barbecue restaurant chain. The names of the churches did not reflect their membership of the LCC: they had names such as New Way of Living Fellowship, Harrow Community Church, Jesus Reigns Gospel Centre, and Bible Life Foundation Ministries. Moreover, closeness to the center was not primarily a function of geography. It depended on a number of factors, including the age of the church (with those established first tending to be more independent); whether the pastor was a member of the Kensington Temple staff; how friendly he was with Colin Dye; and whether services were linked to the main church by satellite technology. Occasionally, churches left the network and placed themselves directly under the oversight of the Elim denomination; or the pastor might leave to found a fully independent congregation. When that happened, worshippers had to decide where their allegiance lay—with their local pastor, or with Dye and the network. I met several church members who faced this dilemma, and it reinforced an impression that Kensington Temple's reputation as a dynamic organization was achieved at the cost of structural fragility.

Some of this fragility can be attributed to the difficulties of holding together a community in which more than 100 nations are represented, and in which many worshippers are recent immigrants to the United Kingdom. When KT carried out its 1999 census of 2,973 worshippers at Notting Hill Gate and the Tabernacle, it found that 48 percent of respondents were African, 17 percent Caucasian, 10 percent Caribbean, 7 percent Asian (including South Asian), 3 percent Chinese, and 1 percent Hispanic.[5] These figures probably exaggerate the presence of Africans in the whole network, given that the satellite churches (many of which are predominately white) were not surveyed directly. Even so, Africans are overwhelmingly the largest group in KT and the wider LCC. This has been the case since the 1980s, when Wynne Lewis preached at a number of Pentecostal mega-churches in West Africa; afterwards, the pastors of these churches instructed their members to attend Kensington Temple when they were in England. The resulting influx of worshippers has had an impact on services at KT. The church regularly adopts an African style of prayer, in which members of the congregation stand up and shout out improvised messages, shaking their fists. "The Africans are very good at aggressive spiritual warfare," writes Colin Dye. "They bring their hand grenades to the meal table and blast the devil even when they are saying grace. We have learnt a lot from African believers in this way" (Hywel-Davies 1997: 159). There are, however, other big Pentecostal churches in London that compete for West African members, and there have been large-scale defections to them in recent years. Likewise, the number of Chinese worshippers fell dramatically in the 1990s after community leaders transferred allegiance to another church.

Ethnicity aside, the picture that emerged from the 1999 census was of a community whose members were predominantly female, young, and new to the church. Of the respondents, 45 percent were single women, 20 percent married women, 19 percent single men, and 15 percent married men.[6] As many as 61.7 percent of respondents were between 20 and 40 years old, with only 5.7 percent over 60; it is instructive to compare this to the 1999 statistics for English churchgoers in general, only 27 percent of whom were aged between 20 and 44, and a quarter of whom were over 65 (Brierley 1999: 4.9). Significantly, 70 percent of respondents had been members of KT/LCC for less than three years, a figure that the June 2000 issue of *Revival Times* attributed to "the mobility of the London population and the number of people coming to Christ." Not everyone put such a positive spin on this: one Bible college student told me it was evidence of a worrying lack of commitment among the core congregation. The census provided only incomplete data on attendance at services, but it did identify 469 respondents (15.7 percent of the total) who were "involved in KT ministry"; of these, 70 percent were women, a slightly higher proportion than for the church as a whole. This actually tells us little about what these 469 people do: "ministry" is a deliberately flexible term in the network, encompassing everyone from the senior pastor to bookshop assistants and tea-makers. It does, however, provide a rough method of comparing the most committed church members with worshippers in general. Inevitably, not everyone who regularly attends services is deeply immersed in the life of the church. Simon Coleman, in his study of the Charismatic Word of Life Church in Uppsala, Sweden, found that many people who went to its services and bought its products kept some distance from the congregation, adding that "such distanced participation is built into the structure of the group through its provision of relatively short-term educational opportunities, conferences, consumer goods and media communications" (2000: 109). Likewise, at Kensington Temple, the range of events, products, educational services, ethnic fellowships, and specialized ministries offers consumers a variety of modes of affiliation.

There is no single, approved way of being a member of KT: on the contrary, believers are faced with an array of spiritual choices that reflect new patterns of religious activity in modern society. As many scholars have noted, Western religious activity in general has become commodified, and no tradition makes more energetic use of commodities than Pentecostalism. The following observations about modern American fundamentalist churches, by the historian Joel Carpenter, could equally be applied to Pentecostalism:

> Denominations, which were once in effect the full-service department stores of American religious life, increasingly find that their members "shop around" to meet their religious needs. They order books and other educational materials from a variety of religious publishing houses. They support foreign missions and domestic missionaries organised independently by parachurch agencies, and they join nondenominational fellowships for prayer, Bible study, marriage enrichment and even recreation. (1997: 240)

Much the same could be said of Kensington Temple. When Dye steps forward to preach on Sundays, he is well aware that many in his audience hold a dual allegiance: an official one to the local church and an unofficial one to a preacher based in America or Africa whom they encounter through television, books, videotapes, and mailing lists. Significantly, KT's response has been to exploit this trend rather than to oppose it: recognizing the complexities of religious allegiance in modern evangelicalism, it has turned itself into a conduit for ministries and commodities that might otherwise be regarded as competition for its "own brand" products. In doing so, it is prepared to overlook quite substantial differences of emphasis and even basic theology between its own message and those of visiting preachers or authors stocked in the KT bookshop. Thus, the Mission to London rallies it held during the 1990s featured some of the most extreme of the black "prosperity Gospel" evangelists. One year, the American preacher Crefloe Dollar had the whole audience shouting "Money cometh to me!" to the embarrassment of church staff but to the delight of the Africans and West Indians in the audience. Another regular speaker was Grant Jeffrey, who used convoluted millennial arithmetic to demonstrate that the Rapture was imminent.

The diversification of religious taste is a feature of most Pentecostal congregations, and especially those, like Kensington Temple, which include a mixture of recent immigrants from other cultures. The everyday conversation of KT members yields plenty of evidence of what one might call the customization of cosmology. We have already encountered the idea that some church members are "into the End Times"; others will talk about being "into" spiritual warfare, prosperity teachings, or Bible study in much the same way as they might speak of being "into" a certain Christian rock musician. And the way they develop these specialist interests is through buying products—not just books, films, and recordings, but tickets to rallies, seminars, and training courses: worshippers are constantly writing checks or signing credit card slips to enable them to pursue a particular path of spiritual development. The content of all these products changes in response to changes in the Christian marketplace; interest in particular subjects waxes and wanes, often in response to media-driven spiritual fads, and that, coupled with the rapid turnover of worshippers, gives a kaleidoscopic quality to congregational beliefs. In this context it is worth bearing in mind an observation made by André Corten and Ruth Marshall-Fratani: that while getting born again represents a dramatic rupture in one's life, *being* born again is an ongoing existential project, not a state acquired once and for all (2001: 7). In a religious setting and a wider society that bombard the believer with information, the maintenance of faith may require complicated ideological work, and many small changes of spiritual direction. These changeable conditions do not make it impossible for a leader like Colin Dye to steer the faithful in a particular theological direction; but they do mean that, in order to do so, he has to calculate risk and anticipate the reactions of his audience.

Managing Charisma

Charisma, Rationality, and Risk

The rest of this chapter will attempt to demonstrate, among other things, that the operation of charisma at Kensington Temple reflects the "common sense rationality" (Garfinkel 1967) that governs religious choices in society generally. Colin Dye uses common sense when he frames his religious rhetoric: he asks himself how far he should go in advancing an argument and whether it is appropriate for a particular audience. Likewise, church members discriminate between the religious claims they encounter, their reactions ranging from unquestioning acceptance to outright rejection, with many subtle grades of response in between. These points might seem too obvious to be worth making were it not for the fact that it is often assumed—by hostile observers and the media—that charismatic religion involves the suspension of common sense on the part of self-deluded prophets and uncritical believers; the only rationality exercised according to this caricature is that of the charismatic leader who knowingly manipulates his audience or that of the ex-follower who "sees through" a preposterous claim.

In reality, the operation of charismatic authority in Pentecostal congregations is far from straightforward. In the first place, there is often considerable ambiguity regarding the source of the authority. As Bryan Wilson observes, no matter how vigorous the personalities and effective the ministries of Christian leaders, their claims are restrained by the pre-eminent charisma of Jesus Christ (1990: 111). Leaders such as Colin Dye are less restricted in this respect than ministers of the mainstream churches, since the Pentecostal tradition holds that the miraculous powers of Jesus can be exercised directly through the action of the Holy Spirit. But the attempt to demonstrate these powers carries with it the possibility of disconfirmation, and this means that the identification of the leader's actions with the will of God is inevitably precarious. If charisma is a "quality projected onto a leader by virtue of situation, opportunity and events" (Craib 1997: 134), then events can also lead to its retraction by the people who projected it—the charismatic audience. It is widely accepted in Pentecostal and Charismatic circles that supernatural gifts may be taken away by their divine giver at any time; as Csordas points out, this is "in effect a recognition that [the gifts] may vanish for a variety of reasons ranging from a failure of nerve to withdrawal of legitimating group consensus" (1997: 133). In Csordas's view, the perceptions of the audience are so crucial that charisma can be said to reside among participants in a religious movement rather than in the personality of the leader. Discourse and rhetoric play a crucial part in the creation of this charisma, which can be understood as "a product of the rhetorical apparatus in use of which leader and follower alike convince themselves that the world is constituted in a certain way" (139).

To understand the basis of Colin Dye's authority, we need to pay attention to the way he deploys rhetoric and, in particular, to his use of reason to persuade his audience of the validity of his claims. There is a paradox here that is characteristic of the whole Pentecostal belief system. On the one hand, his arguments insist on the inability of the scientific paradigm and human reasoning to explain the workings of the Holy Spirit. On the other, they are based on the rules of evidence and tailored to the rational expectations of his listeners. The underlying rationality of Dye's approach is detectable irrespective of whether his rhetoric moves toward or away from greater subcultural deviance—that is, whether he is engaged in a radicalization of charisma that increases anticipation of miraculous events or, alternatively, dampening down unrealistic expectations. In both situations, he works hard to make sure that neither he nor his audience is confronted by cognitive dissonance.

Dye's 1997 book *Healing Anointing* records a visit to Kenya during which he sought to exercise charisma in an immediate and dramatic way, as a channel for God's miraculous healing:

> A young man with a paralysed arm was the first person to be prayed for. I am not sure why, but I thumped his arm—and he was instantly healed. With that, everyone in the room went quiet and still. The disorderly woman [who had kept jostling people] was pushed forward for prayer, and I suddenly realised why she had been bumping into people: she was completely blind . . . I laid my hands on her eyes and prayed every type of healing prayer that I knew. When I took my hands away I asked her whether she could see. She blinked and gasped, "I can see!" . . . There was almost a spiritual riot in the hut. Of the 50 sick people, all bar one completely deaf boy was completely healed. (1997a: 14)

Dye comments that "the real Jesus has been at work" in the hut, thereby establishing the direct source of his power. During the same trip, however, that power appeared to fail. He and his party "prayed and prayed until we ran out of words" for a boy with a withered leg, but to no avail: the boy limped off unhealed. This experience left Dye feeling profoundly depressed:

The following morning I felt so low that I would not go out preaching with the team. . . . After they left I tried to be pious and pray. Finally, I stopped pretending and blurted out, "Why didn't you heal him?" Quick as a flash, God responded, "I have a purpose for that boy just as I have a purpose for you." The issue was closed. (12)

The effect of this divine message was to reduce cognitive dissonance. Significantly, something similar has happened when Dye's organizational initiatives have run into trouble. The following observations come from a Kensington Temple pastor who worked with Dye on church growth programs during the 1990s:

Colin takes enormous care over his initiatives from the moment he announces them to his inner circle, and the launch to the wider church is as important as it would be in, say, the publishing world. A few years ago we had something called "Group-Gather-Grow", which was Colin's new revelation from God about how individuals could attract other individuals and the church would grow. It was launched with immense aplomb by Colin, who announced that he was going to handpick lots of young men—it might have been as many as 100—to get this thing going. Anyway, basically it was a total failure, with only about 15 or 20 men coming forward, and only one or two of them had the necessary charisma. In private, we admitted that it had failed. In public, however, Colin said that the Lord had revealed to him that cell groups were the way forward, and Group-Gather-Grow was a *philosophy* rather than a specific programme. Well, we already had cell groups, so that was OK.

It is tempting to conclude that, in the cases of the boy with the withered arm and the Group-Gather-Grow initiative, God's messages have had the convenient effect of excusing failure. Before we question Dye's motives, however, it is worth noting Rodney Stark's observation that, throughout history, religious leaders have commonly interpreted mundane mental phenomena as supernatural revelation, and that these revelations have usually bolstered their own authority (1992: 21–23). For Stark, this is evidence not of mental illness or trickery, but of rationality: prayer is used to test the rightness of certain ideas, and those that pass the test are reinterpreted as divine communications. Seen in this light, Dye was merely applying a typically charismatic solution—a fresh revelation—to a typically charismatic problem—the apparent disconfirmation of God's promises. In talking about the Kenyan healing and the Group-Gather-Grow initiative, Dye implicitly conceded that it looked as if his powers had failed him; but he then presented new information that, once accepted by the audience, would reconcile faith and reason and preserve the community's sense that "the universe is constituted in a certain kind of way."

The whole Pentecostal system is predicated on the notion that God's activity in the modern world is visible and measurable, and that belief in it is therefore reasonable. Dye offers his listeners *evidence* of the operation of supernatural forces in the world, in the form of "true stories" of signs and wonders, or demonstrations of the miraculous in front of their eyes—and they, for the most part, accept their validity. Indeed, their rational assimilation of this evidence forms a crucial part of their encounter with the sacred. As Gerard Roelofs argues, the experiential character of Charismatic Christianity explains its self-confidence: experiencing God "brings forth the certitude that He exists" (1994: 225) and forms part of an exchange in which praise and gratitude are given in return for religious experience (219). This notion of an exchange fits neatly into the rational choice paradigm and helps us to understand the process of individual belief formation; but it also has implications for leaders such as Colin Dye, who in the Pentecostal tradition bear enormous responsibility to produce, through rhetoric and the staging of events, the experiences that sustain belief. For the exchange to take place, the religious product on offer must be of the right quality, and this requires sound judgment. Church leaders know that a demonstration of the working of the Holy Spirit must be sufficiently dramatic to hold the attention of the audience, but they are also aware that the more ambitious a charismatic claim is, the more likely things are to go wrong. A healing miracle may simply fail to occur, or it may be so carefully stage-managed that even a sympathetic audience questions its authenticity; alternatively, a Charismatic manifestation may be so effective that it encourages extremes of behavior and belief.

Throughout his stewardship of Kensington Temple, Colin Dye has frequently been faced with the dilemma of high versus low tension. He can encourage the radicalization of charisma, with its attendant opportunities and dangers; or he can move toward a safe but unproductive routinization of charisma. For the most part, he has chosen the former route: in the words of his predecessor, Wynne Lewis, he is a natural risk-taker (Dye 1997b: 10). Under his leadership, Kensington Temple has become associated with many of the strange phenomena about which Andrew Walker (1995b) warned the Charismatic world. Dye welcomed the thaumaturgical excitements that surfaced in the 1990s, including the Toronto Blessing and the mysterious appearance of gold teeth in the mouths of Christians. He has also invited controversial but crowd-pulling American evangelists to London, despite the reservations of some of his Elim colleagues about their "health and wealth" theology. In doing so, he has come under attack from the more cautious voices we encountered in chapter 3, including Britain's Evangelical Alliance;[7] the criticisms vary, but their common theme—echoed in private by some staff members—is that Kensington Temple has lent credibility to empirically dubious claims. Although Dye is aware of this criticism, he has been able to counter much of it by pointing to the spectacular results of his high-tension strategy: the much-criticized visits by the healing evangelist Morris Cerullo consolidated KT's following among black Londoners, and the miraculous happenings swelled attendance at Sunday services for several years. In other words, Dye has judged correctly that his constituency is comfortable with a relatively high degree of subcultural deviance.

On closer examination, however, it becomes clear that there are limits to the degree of tension that Dye is prepared to create. Certain risks are never taken, as the pastor quoted earlier points out:

> Colin would never get a person in a wheelchair up on stage and say: "If God exists, you will get up and walk." And the audience wouldn't expect him to. It's not spoken, but everybody tacitly agrees that this would going too far. People don't prostrate themselves before fate, because if they did their faith would be seriously damaged.

Furthermore, Dye has been careful not let subcultural deviance increase to a degree where thaumaturgical excitement becomes an end in itself. In September 2000 he preached a sermon in which he reviewed the miraculous happenings at KT since 1994:

> There was laughing experience [the Toronto Blessing]—we became a church of holy rollers, the church was filled with joy. The Holy Spirit came upon me, too, and I fell to the ground, rolling up and down. We took the aisles away, so that nobody could say we were rolling in the aisles. . . . [Some months later] at every service for 18 months, spots of oil came onto people's hands. In some instances it was clearly oil, really thick anointing oil. I remember a man whose whole thumb was dripping with oil. . . . A no-nonsense, retired policeman saw it. The whole of his head was covered. It wasn't so long after that that God sent holy gold, gold flakes: it's exactly the kind of thing God will do so people can say, "They're a bunch of flakes!"

The whole point of mentioning these events, however, was to stress how relatively unimportant they were:

> You can see how affirming I am of these phenomena, but none of that is revival. These were the trappings, the externals of revival. Whether we shake, rattle or roll, we need the heart of Jesus Christ. I'm not concerned whether people fall, or have oil on their forehead, or see angels bringing oil. God is in these things, but it's not what God is all about. We are so clever in Christian circles at taking things which are peripheral and making them central. We have got to have a revolution in our thinking and put first things first.

By talking in this way, Dye reveals an intuitive grasp of the need to reconcile the radicalization and routinization of charisma. While recognizing the potential of Wimberite signs and wonders for providing the experiences that dominate the Pentecostal "exchange" with God, he subtly reduces their significance; this is one of the dissonance-reducing strategies described by Festinger ([1956] 1964: 25–26).

In an interview in 1998, Will Napier, the young principal of Kensington Temple's Bible college, explained to me that there were "three levels of doctrinal importance" in the church. The first level consisted of "those doctrines that are necessary for salvation," such as belief in the divinity of Christ. The second level consisted of "fundamental and important truths," such the inerrant authority of Scripture and the future bodily return of Jesus. The third level was reserved for "lesser doctrines" such as belief in a pre-, mid- or post-Tribulation Rapture, or belief in the validity of certain Charismatic gifts. We shall come back to the status of eschatology in the next chapter; the point to note here is the relegation of *charismata* to a low level in the hierarchy of Christian truth. Such phenomena are central to Kensington Temple's popular appeal, yet they also carry the risk of involving the church in controversies. Their "third level" status limits the damage done by disconfirmation, public criticism, or—always a possibility in the Pentecostal world—a sudden change of fashion: put on the spot, church spokesmen can argue that these high-tension phenomena were peripheral to the life of the community. Napier himself now takes the view that the hierarchy of doctrines he had outlined was essentially an insurance policy. In 1999, after a spectacular falling-out with Dye, he left the staff and ceased to identify himself as a Christian. Afterwards, he commented:

> Kensington Temple wants to have its cake and eat it—to take advantage of certain phenomena, but also to have a way of dodging the consequences when they are discredited. It's paradoxical, when you think about it. KT is quietly ambivalent about the very things that make it culturally distinctive.

To an outsider, or to an ex-believer such as Napier, the leadership's fine-tuning of charismatic claims might appear manipulative. It does not strike most worshippers that way, however, because they themselves are engaged in an often unconscious process of charisma management. Like the Charismatic Catholics studied by Neitz (1987: 80), they test hypotheses. If an evangelist tells them that their finances will miraculously improve if they donate money to a certain cause, they may do so—but they will only carry on doing so if the experiment succeeds. Likewise, they may say specific prayers that are intended to bring about physical healing and wait for results. Or they may listen to a sermon expounding a particular doctrine and ask themselves whether it makes sense in the context of their own lives. Often a claim will fail a test of experience or rationality; but that does not mean that it brings the whole edifice of Christian faith collapsing around it. Just as Colin Dye performed ideological work that explained the apparent failure of his healing powers in Kenya, so many of his flock find methods of reducing cognitive dissonance. One young woman offered the following example: "Someone might find the house of their dreams, put in an offer, and it's accepted. So immediately it becomes 'the house that God wants me to have'. Then the deal falls through, and they say, 'well, that's not what God had in mind after all—he has something else in store for me.' " There are, in fact, many ways of reducing and forestalling disappointment— thanks, in part, to those features of contemporary Charismatic religion that are sometimes described as postmodern: its juxtaposition of global and local sources of authority and its appeal to consumer taste. In such conditions, it becomes much easier to edit and customize one's personal cosmology. Worshippers who are uncomfortable with a charismatic claim promoted by Kensington Temple need not expose themselves to it. A part-time pastor told me: "Because I'm not on the staff, I have the freedom to say, if you're having Benny Hinn [a controversial healing evangelist] to preach, then I'm not coming." By the same token, church members who dislike "health and wealth" theology may avoid guest appearances by Faith preachers—and those who are skeptical about the End Times subculture can avoid apocalyptic talks and literature.

Yet the circulation of contentious, and some would say disprovable, religious claims remains an important feature of life at Kensington Temple. How can this be reconciled with the operation of common sense rationality? Two points are worth making. First, the process of hypothesis testing is far from scientific. People tend to search for evidence that reinforces their existing beliefs; as J. L. Simmons notes, "confirming evidence . . . is sought and found because most situations are ambiguous enough to allow them to be interpreted as confirming evidence" (1964: 256). Neitz adds that "disconfirming evidence may go unacknowledged because the explanations provided by the non-conventional [i.e., empirically disprovable] beliefs are 'more satisfying' on some level than are conventional explanations" (1987: 81).[8] The second point has to do with the nature of worshippers' engagement with controversial religious claims. Most members of Kensington Temple—including those who delight in "signs and wonders" and read popular prophecy literature—implicitly accept Dye's argument that such areas are peripheral to the main life of the church. They approach them in the spirit of consumers searching for spiritual entertainment, whether in the form of satellite broadcasts by "health and wealth" preachers or the Left Behind thrillers. This almost light-hearted attitude to spiritual claims helps explain how high-tension theology can be popular and peripheral at the same time. Although Kensington Temple is open to spiritual risk-taking, there is a consensus among pastors, part-time ministers, and many ordinary worshippers that things must not be allowed to get out of hand—and an unspoken agreement that individuals who manifest excessive enthusiasm should be discouraged from doing so.

Policing the Boundaries

Even religious organizations that are judged deviant by society have their own deviants: individuals who, while belonging to the group, are distinguished from the rest of the membership by virtue of their unusual opinions or behavior. These are the people described by their fellow members as "troublemakers," "eccentrics," "fanatics," and so on—labels whose vague, subjective nature reflects the complex nature of deviance itself. Whether someone is labeled a troublemaker or a harmless eccentric depends partly on his or her personality and social skills. A dissident with persuasive powers represents a threat to authority and may be regarded as dangerous; someone who holds the same views but lacks personal magnetism may be written off as a harmless eccentric. Some people fall between these stools: while they have no significant personal following, they are mistrusted by the religious authorities because they waste time and sow low-level dissension among fellow worshippers. These potential troublemakers are familiar to religious leaders in many traditions: rabbis and imams as well as Christian ministers are forced to deal with "difficult" types in the congregation.

Charismatic Christianity, whose very name conjures up the exercise of disruptive powers, positively invites behavior that disturbs the peace of the congregation. Certain worshippers become known for showing off or nurturing obsessions, and in doing so they create a degree of tension between themselves and the church environment that reproduces on a small scale the subcultural deviance of whole groups. Csordas (1997: 185) lists some "pastoral slang" terms in use among American Catholic Charismatics, several of which identify mild forms of deviance. "Charismania" refers to the "over-extensive cultivation, use, or attention to Charismatic gifts"; "hothouse spirituality" is the "over-intensive cultivation of Charismatic gifts, with the danger of being carried to potentially destructive excess"; "superspirituality" is a surrender to the divine will so total that the believer is reduced to inactivity. This last term is used at Kensington Temple, though its resonances are different. Will Napier, while still principal of the Bible college, put it as follows:

> Americans would use the word "flaky" and we would use the word "superspiritual"—people who tell you that God told them to do this or that, and the way you know that they are a bit flaky rather than wonderfully prophetic is that they don't usually have the personal credibility to back up their claims. It's very common for these people—in fact, it's one of the signs of being one of these people—that they will latch on to some particular doctrine. Often it's Israel, often it's also End-time stuff. A lot of people in the world, and they are reflected in this church, are strange in that they are competent and intelligent enough to hold down responsible jobs, but you get them onto this one subject and they don't seem to have a grasp of reality.

Note that, according to Napier, the people who claim to receive divine messages are also likely to be theologically unbalanced: this implies the existence of a sort of multi-dimensional deviance, in which unsuccessful claims to charismatic authority go hand in hand with distorted opinions on other matters. In an interview in 2003, Napier spoke more frankly about the management of the theological margins at Kensington Temple. I asked him whether staff members tended to identify deviant ideas with deviant people. He replied:

> Definitely, yes. I used to call them "fruit bats," and they weren't hard to spot. People who issued weird and wild prophecies were always suspect. In a Pentecostal church, the issuing of spiritual messages happens all the time, of course—but ordinary church members would do so very cautiously. They might say: "This is going to sound strange, but last night I had a dream in which . . ." Whatever significance they attached to the dream, it would be surrounded by these

apologetic phrases, to show that they weren't fruit bats. If, on the other hand, someone related a dream which directly usurped the authority of the leaders, that might be a sign that they were a bit batty. And there were other, rather obvious clues: they might smell, or look unkempt, and have poor social skills. As a Pentecostal pastor, I was always rather uncomfortably aware that hearing messages from God is one of the diagnostic signs of schizophrenia.

In practice, however troublesome the "fruit bats" or superspiritual worshippers might be, they can at least be easily identified. The usual sanction is for a member of the KT ministry team to have a quiet word with a disruptive worshipper; in rare cases, people have been banned from services or the church premises. Policing the boundaries in these cases is relatively straightforward. Milder forms of deviance, on the other hand, pose more of a diplomatic challenge for the leadership. Dye's radical approach tends to be copied by his protégés in the congregation, some of whom lack his innate sense of just how far to push a charismatic claim. Sometimes, they are encouraged to take risks— to indulge in attention-seeking street evangelism, for example, or use violent images in their rhetoric of spiritual warfare. At other times, they are reprimanded for overstepping the mark. One interesting case from the mid-1990s involved a young evangelist called Ravi Holy, an Old Etonian of Indian extraction who had been a teenage "punk anarchist" and drug-taker. Before his conversion, Holy dabbled in the occult and espoused an elaborate conspiracy theory in which both the American government and Hitler were representatives of the Satanic secret society known as the Illuminati; we shall look at his ideas more closely in the next chapter. The problem from Kensington Temple's point of view was that Holy carried on spreading these conspiracy beliefs as a Pentecostal. In an interview after he left KT, Holy talked about the church's attempts to moderate his opinions:

> I was told by three of Colin Dye's lieutenants on separate occasions that all this stuff about the Illuminati and a New World Order was inappropriate—they said it was giving Satan too much power in the physical realm. I felt it was a bit hypocritical of them, because from time to time Colin himself would hint that there was a conspiracy in public life. He would drop some remark in the middle of a sermon about how prostitution and organized crime were controlled by Satanists, and it sounded as if he basically believed the same things as I did.

But there was a big difference, of course, between a senior leader hinting at a conspiracy from the platform and a junior evangelist "banging on to anyone who would listen"—his own phrase—about 33rd degree Freemasons traveling in the astral plane. Holy's cosmology owed more to the cultic milieu than it did to evangelical tradition; it was the wrong sort of subcultural deviance, created by someone without any particular spiritual authority. Yet, at the same time, Holy's adventurous spirit appealed to Dye. As Napier recalls:

Ravi was in danger of tipping over into being a fruit bat, and some-times he was chastised. But on the whole KT encouraged him, be-cause it was friendly to people who lived close to the edge. That was how we liked to think of ourselves. It gave us a buzz to think of our-selves as counter-cultural, and to realize that the rest of the world thought of us as a bit strange.

In the final analysis, though, you have to ask whether we were really as radical as we thought we were. Our view of what constituted ex-treme behavior or ideas was heavily influenced by societal norms—we could recognize mental problems or crazy conspiracy theories as readily as anyone else. You might say that we employed a secular criterion of battiness.

In fact, my impression was that all sorts of societal norms were internal-ized by members of Kensington Temple. Worshippers did not just draw on their common sense in assessing religious claims: they were also influenced, sometimes unconsciously, by the boundaries of acceptable thought and behav-ior associated with secular liberal democracies. Younger church members were strongly anti-racist and committed to the equality of the sexes, and they had some difficulty reconciling this with the evangelical doctrine of male headship. At one satellite service, to my surprise, I heard two young black women com-plaining about the anti-gay rhetoric of a visiting American preacher. One of them told the other that she was worried that visitors "might think we were all like that" (i.e., vehemently anti-homosexual). Generally speaking, I found sup-port for James Davison Hunter's thesis (1987: 40), based on his fieldwork among American Bible students, that in modern society even members of conservative religions are keen to play down aspects of their cosmology that might be considered socially offensive, such as the doctrine of eternal dam-nation for all unbelievers. One of the questions Hunter asked his subjects was about Mahatma Gandhi: was he, too, burning in hell? I tried this litmus test on my interviewees and received the same response as Hunter: people were extremely reluctant to state that he was not in heaven, even though he was not a Christian. It was as if church members kept looking over their shoulders at secular society, supposedly the province of Satan but also the source of many of their social attitudes. This apparent contradiction goes to the heart of the debate about religion and secularization; we shall return to it in the final chap-ter of this study.

Conclusion

Although this chapter has hardly touched on the subject of the End Times, its description of the organizational structure and Charismatic theology of Ken-sington Temple provides an essential background to the next two chapters of this study, which discuss the place of apocalyptic belief within the congregation.

Ideas about the end of the world are always rooted in a social context, and the context here is one in which the experience of high-tension religion is moderated by the operation of an underlying rationality. Members of Kensington Temple test hypotheses along lines dictated by their common sense. Leaders and most worshippers share a sense that certain boundaries should not be crossed, though these boundaries are not necessarily marked by specific doctrines: rather, the danger is that believers will concentrate too much on elements in the Pentecostal tradition that are regarded as peripheral to salvation. Eccentric or disruptive people are identified and dealt with in much the same way as they are in the outside world. Seen from a rational choice perspective, the situation is one in which worshippers seek to maximize the benefits and reduce the costs of belonging to a Charismatic community: they want to experience empirical proof of their status as God's chosen people while retaining the freedom to reject or modify spiritual claims that strain credulity or are considered socially offensive.

5

Living with the End

This chapter asks how members of Kensington Temple relate to, and live with, the full range of End Times tradition they might encounter in their church, including biblical images of Rapture and Armageddon, theological arguments about divine dispensations and the shape of history, and conspiracy theories involving Antichrist and the New World Order. The first half of the chapter studies this question from the perspective of the church leadership. It examines the "official" treatment of apocalyptic doctrines in sermons and Bible classes and the "unofficial" material sold in the church bookshop; at both levels, there is evidence that the transmission of millenarian ideas is affected by the personal dispositions of pastors and church employees, many of whom find this a difficult area to manage. The second half is based on interviews with ordinary church members and survey data. It explores the different strategies employed by worshippers in dealing with potentially troublesome apocalyptic ideas: these include a policy of ignoring them, a focus on explanatory rather than predictive motifs, and the use of language that reduces millenarianism to the unthreatening proportions of a professional discourse.

Managing Apocalyptic Belief: The Perspective of Leaders

Official Millenarianism: Teaching about the End Times

Kensington Temple publishes a 30-page booklet[1] for visitors, which, in addition to introducing Colin Dye and describing the church's activities, sets out a "statement of our beliefs"—in fact, the official credal formulation of the Elim denomination. The statement begins with the Bible: "We believe the Bible, as originally given, to be without error; it is the fully inspired and infallible Word of God and the supreme and final authority in all matters of faith and conduct." It declares belief in the Holy Trinity, the bodily resurrection of Jesus, justification by faith alone, and the eternal, conscious punishment of the wicked. It affirms the fivefold ministry of Ephesians, the baptism of believers in water, and "baptism in the Holy Spirit with signs following." On the subject of the Second Coming, it says only this: "We believe in the personal, physical and visible return of the Lord Jesus Christ to reign in power and glory."

Such a minimalist statement of eschatological belief might seem surprising for a denomination founded amid intense and detailed expectation of the Second Coming. Bryan Wilson, writing about Elim congregations in 1961, summarized their apocalyptic beliefs as follows:

> Elimites expect the physical return of Jesus Christ to earth at any time. In their more cautious discussion it is conceded that the exact time is unknown, but ever since the earliest days of the movement it has been believed that all the usual signs portended the imminence of this event. Christ will appear in the upper air, the saints be caught up to him, and a period of woe and martyrdom will occur on earth. The righteous dead will be resurrected and caught up unto Christ, and this episode is literally awaited. "Watch the coffin lids fly open", is the exhortatory vision of one writer. At that time the earth, without the leavening influence of Christians, will know a period of orgy and license, crime and war. The complex pattern of events which Elimites believe will then occur—the emergence of the Anti-Christ; the battle of Armageddon, to be fought between Britain and Russia; the ascent of the saints; the casting of the Beast and Anti-Christ into the lake of fire; the Millennium itself—are all depicted in terms familiar to those acquainted with fundamentalism. A brief revolt at the end of the Millennium will lead to the new heaven and new earth. (1961: 25–26)

It is instructive to compare these ideas to Kensington Temple's current position on the End Times. On the one hand, the church does offer its members some teaching on the subject, and this outlines a sequence of future events similar to that described by Wilson, though it reverses the sequence of the Rapture and the Tribulation. On the other, such teaching is no longer central to the life of the congregation. Church members who are interested in the End Times have to seek it out—and, when they do, they are likely to be told that they are free to disagree with their teachers on major points of interpretation.

During the period of my fieldwork, the major source of apocalyptic teaching at Kensington Temple was a series of six lectures by Pastor Bruce Atkinson entitled "End Times Truths," originally delivered before the main Sunday evening services in 1997 and subsequently sold as tapes in the bookshop (Atkinson 1997). Atkinson, a fiery young preacher from Yorkshire, is Colin Dye's second in command and widely believed to be his anointed successor. He is well known for taking a specialist interest in the End Times: "It's the Second Coming that drives me, that motivates me, that gives me hope," he announces in the first lecture. It is also one of the reasons he is a classic Pentecostal rather than a Charismatic. In the same lecture, he criticizes middle-class Charismatics who have become so preoccupied by their own spiritual journey that they have lost sight of the Second Coming. He also reveals himself to be a millenarian, in the sense that he expects the end of history to occur in his lifetime:

> I believe that we are in the beginning of the End Times revival that will herald the coming of Christ. We need to shake ourselves and wake ourselves. We are not just moving into another time of bless-ing or revival. I believe with every part of my being that we are in the beginnings of the revival to end all revivals. . . . Jesus is sending his Spirit stronger and stronger. I fully expect to be here when Jesus returns. I expect it, I feel it so close! I can't doctrinally state that, of course I can't—no man knows the hour. But I feel it in my bones. I feel it so near, I don't expect to die, I expect to see him come in the clouds of glory. The End is coming.

We noted in chapter 2 that many apocalyptic preachers and authors seem rel-atively uninterested in the millennial reward awaiting believers, concentrating instead on the world's slide into chaos. This is not true of Atkinson. He tells his audience:

> The Second Coming will deal once and for all with every injustice that has happened on this earth. It will deal with every trouble, every-persecution, every enemy of Christ and his Church—and of you. . . . The bad guys don't always win! . . . At the Second Coming, sickness and death will finally be dealt with. . . . There's coming a day when every saint in God who has ever lived and been sick will be raised up with a perfect whole body. There will neither be tears, nor fears, nor sickness. And Jesus' Second Coming is great for those that have lost loved ones, who are Christians, for those struggling with sick-ness, to know that one day every believer will be raised from the dead with a new body, an immortal body.

The message could hardly be clearer: *you* will have a new body; *you* will see your enemies confounded. There is one promise, however, that Atkinson is not prepared to make. Unlike most premillennialists, he does not believe that the Church will be secretly raptured to safety when the Antichrist appears and the Tribulation begins (the premise of the *Left Behind* books). Both he and Dye believe in a post-Tribulation Rapture, a minority evangelical position some-times known as historic premillennialism (Grenz 1992: 127–47). One of the purposes of Atkinson's lectures is to explain this "post-Trib" view to the con-gregation as simply as possible—but without demanding adherence to it, since the Elim church takes no official view on the matter. The lectures therefore tell us as much about the difficulties of locating the boundaries of KT's official End Times theology as they do about its precise content.

Atkinson refers several times to the "confusing" nature of his topic. He wants to clear away that confusion, he says, by using the Book of Revelation to provide the skeleton of a single coherent narrative of the End Times, supplemented by references to the Book of Daniel, the Gospels, and Paul's letters. His second lecture, entitled "Last Days Overview," offers a condensed account of sacred history from the Day of Pentecost to the final defeat of Satan after the Millennium. Atkinson argues that Pentecost marked the beginning of the Church Age, which is now drawing to a close as the signs of the Church's growth—and of the diabolical wickedness of the enemy—accelerate and multiply. He suggests that the visions that follow the breaking of the first five of the seven seals in Revelation depict events that have already occurred, though he is careful to add that there are "many possible interpretations." The white horseman of the apocalypse may represent the spread of the Gospel throughout the earth, while the other three horses indicate the wars, famines, and pestilence that reached a climax during the twentieth century; the breaking of the fifth seal, which reveals martyrs slain for the faith, points to the persecution of the Church up to and including the modern era.

In Atkinson's view, it is only with the breaking of the sixth seal, with its vision of the sun growing black and the moon turning to blood, that the Revelation narrative reaches events that have still not occurred (though dispensationalists would disagree, arguing that none of the prophecies has yet been fulfilled). The key verses describe the servants of God, who receive a seal on their foreheads: "And I heard the number of the sealed, a hundred and forty-four thousand sealed, out of every tribe of the sons of Israel" (Rev. 7:4–5). Dispensationalists usually identify the 144,000 as the saved Jews who are about to go through the Tribulation, reasoning that the Church has already been raptured (Grenz 1992: 106). Atkinson insists that this is not the case:

> This verse isn't talking about the Jewish people. It's a number that talks about fullness, about the Christian population, who have been sealed so that during the Tribulation they can be protected and not punished in the judgment of God. We will have to go through the Tribulation persecution of the Antichrist, but none of the wrath of God will affect us because we will be sealed. . . . Others will be touched by the demonic plague [and other punishments], but people will look at the Church and say, "Why isn't this happening at Kensington Temple? Why isn't it happening at Holy Trinity Brompton?"[2]

Some serious ideological work has gone into this argument. In order to make the 144,000 sealed believers represent the Church, Atkinson has to move away from his usual literal interpretation of Scripture, explaining that neither the number nor the reference to Jewish tribes is to be taken at face value. He also has to explain that Christians, although they will not be touched by any of the punishments God visits on the earth, will be terribly persecuted during the Tribulation. Anyone who expects to be whisked up to heaven at the first sight of the Antichrist is in for a nasty surprise:

When the Antichrist is revealed, there'll be a lot of Christians
bouncing up on trampolines saying, "Take me, Lord! Take me!", or
skydiving out of planes hoping to meet the Lord in the air. But he's
not coming then. He's not coming before the Tribulation. You'll just
have to bounce on your trampolines for seven years. [Pause.] And if
you disagree with me, just bless me.

This last comment rather undermines what has gone before. It shows that,
although Atkinson believes passionately in a post-Tribulation Rapture, he has
no authority to insist on this interpretation. The question of whether Jesus will
pluck his Church to safety before or after the reign of the Beast has been
relegated to one of the lower "levels of doctrinal importance" that Will Napier
described in chapter 4—which is just as well, perhaps, because the majority
of the world's born-again Christians, including many of the international evangelists who preach at Kensington Temple, believe that the Church will be raptured before the Tribulation.

If the pre- versus post-Trib argument is largely a matter for evangelical
scholars, the same cannot be said of the speculation surrounding the Antichrist, the seductive world leader depicted in the Book of Revelation who, after
the nations bow down before him, reveals himself as a demonic "Beast." As
we saw in chapter 2, Christians have spent 2,000 years attempting to identify
the historical or contemporary figure who fits this description (see Boyer 1992;
McGinn 1994; Fuller 1995). In the process, they have created a culture of
conspiracy belief that, in the eyes of modern society, is both more deviant and
closer to popular culture than any scholarly theological discourse. The verses
most often quoted by conspiracy theorists are as follows:

Also it [the Beast] causes all, both small and great, both rich and
poor, both free and slave, to be marked on the right hand or the
forehead, so that no one can buy or sell unless he has the mark, that
is, the name of the beast or the number of its name. This calls for
wisdom: let him who has understanding reckon the number of the
beast, for it is a human number, its number is six hundred and sixty-
six. (Rev. 13:16–18)

Interpretations of this passage bring us close to the border between official
and unofficial millenarianism, where orthodox theology shades into the cultic
milieu. Atkinson is aware of this and treads carefully, warning his audience
that some Christian speculation about the Antichrist has got out of hand:

We know that the Mark of the Beast will be an economic measure
that affects buying and selling—but we don't actually know what it
will be. It's interesting to speculate, and many people do, but the
problems start when they present their speculation too strongly,
causing confusion. It's like those people who presented Henry Kissinger as the Antichrist; when it turned out that he wasn't, other
people said, "This End Times stuff is a load of rubbish."

There will be some sort of mark. Will it be a tattoo, or one of those electronic gadgets that you put in your wrist or forehead so you don't have to use a credit card? I don't know. But the Christians of that time [the Tribulation] will know what it is. What about this number, 666? Is it like those price tags on your loaf of bread, with three strips coming down that read 666? We don't know.

Atkinson has singled out two ideas from the prophecy subculture ridiculed by the evangelical author B. J. Oropeza in *99 Reasons Why No One Knows When Christ Will Return* (1994): Reason 75 is "There is no evidence that Henry Kissinger is the Antichrist," while Reason 88 is "The current Universal Product Code is not the Mark of the Beast." Atkinson and Oropeza are equally dismissive of the Kissinger allegation, which first surfaced in the 1970s and survived long into the former U.S. Secretary of State's retirement.[3] But, while Oropeza rejects the barcode theory, explaining that "the paired longer bars in the front, middle and end of the code are not secret configurations meaning the number 6 and adding up to 666" (1994: 164), Atkinson seems to regard it as legitimate speculation. He appears well disposed toward the prophecy subculture.

Perhaps the most revealing moment in Atkinson's talks comes when he expounds on the meaning of the Whore of Babylon in chapter 17 of Revelation: a "great harlot . . . with whom the kings of the earth have committed fornication," bedecked in gold, jewels and pearls, drunk with the blood of the saints (Rev. 17:1–6). He explains that the harlot is the false church of the End Times, spreading the diabolical message of the Antichrist under the guise of a beneficent world religion. Then he adds:

It wouldn't surprise me if Rome brought forth this End Times false whore. That's my opinion, it's not the opinion of many pastors in this church, so don't go away saying that Kensington Temple says it— you can say that Bruce Atkinson says it. It wouldn't surprise me if some later demonic Pope gets hold of this [idea of a new world religion], though it might be something different; it might be the World Council of Churches. . . . I know there are many wonderful, beautiful, saved Roman Catholics. I know God is teaching his gospel through that church and blessing pockets of it. I'm not talking about individuals and specific priests, I'm talking about an institution that could possibly become that. I'm not bashing Catholics.

Atkinson is here restating one of the traditional beliefs of Elim and many Pentecostal denominations: the idea, central to the Reformation, that the whore of Babylon refers to the Pope. But the virulently anti-Catholic ethos of the early days of Kensington Temple has long since been routinized: the Elim denomination does not wish to be associated with the sort of subcultural deviance associated with extreme Northern Irish Protestants. Atkinson is probably the most anti-Catholic of the KT pastors—but note that he presents the idea of a diabolical Pope in a carefully modified form. He acknowledges that many Roman Catholics are saved (a concession that would have horrified the early Elimites) and goes so far as to suggest that God is working through "pockets" of the Catholic Church. Significantly, he is at pains to distance Kensington Temple from his theory: he backs it with his personal charismatic authority, qualifying his argument in much the same way as he did his prediction that Christ will return in his lifetime. Moreover, Atkinson seems anxious not to cause too much offence to any Roman Catholics who might be listening. It might be worth noting here that, according to James Davison Hunter, modern evangelicalism contains "both sectarian and accommodationist tendencies" (1987: 196); in other words, as we have already noted, it is pulled toward and away from the societal consensus. Atkinson's lectures illustrate what a complicated process this can be: even when reviving a sectarian teaching about the apocalyptic role of the Roman Church, he seeks to establish common ground, in typical late twentieth-century fashion, between Pentecostals and "saved" Roman Catholics.

To what extent do Atkinson's "End Times Truths" represent the theological position of Kensington Temple? On the one hand, the lectures were delivered during official teaching services and sold as audiotapes bearing the KT logo. On the other, Atkinson is at pains to emphasize that his more controversial digressions express his *personal* views, not those of the church. But this raises another question. Why does Kensington Temple allow a leading pastor to express speculative, dissonance-inviting ideas from the platform that it does not itself teach? One possible answer is that it regards Atkinson's fondness for prophecy speculation as the price it has to pay for his unusually fervent ministry. The historical record suggests that Pentecostal ministers can be just as susceptible to ideas emanating from the cultic milieu as rank and file believers: the British Israelism controversy in Elim (Wilson 1961: 46–47) is an illustration of this. A pastor's attraction to deviant ideas may form part of a broader commitment to the faith that benefits his colleagues. Atkinson's flirtation with popular prophecy belief cannot easily be disentangled from his intense devotion to classic, high-tension Pentecostalism; therefore Dye is prepared to indulge him, allowing him to present mild conspiracy theories to a KT audience provided that they do not invoke the authority of the church itself. A second explanation, not incompatible with the first, is that apocalyptic belief simply does not matter enough to the authorities to make it the litmus test of orthodoxy. We have seen that Napier consigned belief in the bodily return of Jesus to a secondary level of doctrinal importance, describing it as a "fundamental and important truth" rather than a "doctrine necessary for salvation," while belief in a pre- or post-Tribulation Rapture belonged to a third level of "lesser doctrines." Atkinson's lectures imply that some ideas hold an even lower rank in the hierarchy of truth: they are not doctrines at all, but "speculation" which may or may not be valid. Unlike many pastors, Atkinson takes some of these ideas seriously; but he does not invest heavily in them, being prepared to concede that they could be wrong.

My fieldwork suggests that the imminent return of Christ plays a less important part in the official teaching of Kensington Temple than it did in the first half of the twentieth century. During the late 1990s—in some respects, a period of raised eschatological expectation—the End Times were barely mentioned in the main services: one worshipper told me that he had been attending KT for three years and had never heard Dye preach about them.[4] Most of the satellite church leaders I interviewed displayed no enthusiasm for apocalyptic teaching: Larry Grant, who ran the Porchester Hall service in Bayswater, had spent twenty years in the Jehovah's Witnesses and said that the experience had taught him the folly of speculating about the End; Ron Tomlinson, former pastor of a satellite church in South London, told me he had never thought seriously about the apocalypse, let alone preached about it. A member of KT who was determined to receive instruction in this area would therefore either have to wait for a teaching service on the End Times or enroll at the Bible college. But, even at the college, the topic did not loom large. During the academic year 1997–98, there were 160 students, most of them first years studying for a diploma of Christian ministry. The first-year course consisted of 120 lectures over two terms. Of these, only three or four were devoted to eschatology, and these reflected the noncommittal position of the Elim denomination, which in 1994 removed premillennialism from its list of fundamental truths (Kay 2000a: 133). In the Bible classes, not only was the timing of the Rapture left open, but so was the larger question of whether Jesus would come back before or after the Millennium. Napier said this was because the college wanted to attract students from evangelical churches whose theology was post-millennial. From an outsider's point of view, this looks suspiciously like the loosening of doctrinal constraints to increase market share. (Not everyone appreciated the college's *laissez-faire* eschatology. Metin Tilki, pastor of KT's Covent Garden congregation, told me that, as a student, he was so confused by the presentation of contradictory theories about the Second Coming that he walked out of the lecture.)

In sociological terms, the marginalization of apocalyptic teaching at the Bible college appears to be a textbook case of the routinization of troublesome charismatic claims. Many sects have lowered the degree of tension between themselves and society by gradually distancing themselves from their millenarian beliefs, and it is often their educational institutions that lead the way: in the Seventh-day Adventist Church, for example, Bible colleges deliberately ignore their apocalyptic heritage (Lawson 1997). Moreover, there is evidence of similar routinization in the End Times teaching offered to the KT congregation, which rarely ventures beyond the sketchy statement of belief set down by Elim and has effectively designated once important doctrines—relating to the Tribulation, for example—as matters of opinion. We must, however, be careful not to oversimplify the picture. Several qualifications need to be made. First, it should be stressed that there is nothing historically inevitable about the playing down of millenarian themes at Kensington Temple; if Bruce Atkinson were to take over from Colin Dye as senior pastor, he might choose to emphasize them. As it is, the content of teaching is dependent partly on the accident of who is available to teach: there was one year when Bible college students received detailed instruction in eschatology, thanks to the presence on the staff of a premillennialist who kept bringing the End Times into his lectures on the Old Testament. Second, it is important to recognize that the routinization of apocalyptic doctrines does not indicate an across-the-board lowering of tension between Kensington Temple and its environment. Although Dye places little emphasis on the End Times, he is prepared to take considerable risks with "signs and wonders." Napier, likewise, assigned a low priority to eschatology in the Bible college, but happily embraced the controversial miraculous claims emanating from various American preachers. Third, the scarcity of explicitly apocalyptic claims should not blind us to the *implicit* millenarianism of Dye's discourse: we shall consider evidence of this in chapter 7. Finally, we should note that Kensington Temple not only permits its members to read the sort of flamboyant prophecy material that it refuses to endorse from the platform, but it also sells it to them in its bookshop. This unofficial millenarianism provides an interesting counterpoint to the official teaching of the pastors; we shall now look briefly at the range of material on offer and the extent to which its content is monitored by the authorities.

Unofficial Millenarianism: The KT Bookshop

During the 1990s, members of Kensington Temple who were "into the End Times" were offered a choice of dozens of prophecy books and videotapes in the bookshop, situated in the basement of the old church building. The shop can be entered directly from the street; there is a constant trickle of customers even when there are no services upstairs. At any one time there are around 1,000 titles in stock; when I was conducting my fieldwork, around fifty of these were non-fiction books about Bible prophecy; this total has since shrunk, though the number of fictional treatments of the End Times, in the shape of the *Left Behind* sequence and its imitators, has greatly increased. Jim Saunders, the bookshop manager, said that apocalyptic material had never been as popular as books on prayer and spirituality; however, a number of prophecy authors sold steadily. Three in particular were well represented on the shelves in the late 1990s: the Korean evangelist Paul Yonggi Cho; Grant Jeffrey, a Canadian fundamentalist author specializing in Israel and the End Times; and Barry Smith, a New Zealand-based Christian conspiracy theorist. All of them had spoken at Kensington Temple services or events; their work is interesting because they represent different degrees of immersion in the cultic milieu.

Cho is one of the most successful pastors in the Pentecostal world; his church in Seoul, which claims 750,000 members, is listed in the *Guinness Book of Records*. Colin Dye admires him, and in 1995 arranged for him to preach at a large rally at the Wembley Arena in London, at which large numbers of Cho's book *Revelation: Visions of Our Ultimate Victory in Christ* (1991) were on sale. Most of this book consists of straightforward exegesis of Revelation; but some passages are heavily influenced by the work of Hal Lindsey. Cho predicts that the Antichrist will assume power after the EEC (as it then was) is unified; there will be a peace treaty between Europe and Israel, but then Russia and the Arabs will attack Israel after the Jews try to rebuild the Temple (78–82). He believes that the Rapture of the Church will take place seven years before

Jesus comes back to earth: "Unsaved husbands will awake in the morning to find their wives missing, or wives will find their husbands missing. Some pilots will suddenly disappear from their aircraft. In schools, some of the teachers and pupils will be missing" (1991: 9–10). Given Dye's vigorous promotion of Cho as one of the world's great religious leaders, it would hardly be surprising if a KT member reading this passage were to treat it as authoritative. In fact, of course, this is precisely the "pre-Trib" view that Dye rejects, and that Atkinson mocks in his lectures.

The first edition of Grant Jeffrey's *Armageddon: Appointment with Destiny* (1988) was available in the church bookshop for several years. The book is, essentially, an exercise in date-setting. Jeffrey argues that Christ's apparent warning against calculating the time of the End, "But of that day and that hour knoweth no man" (Mark 13:32), does not forbid "careful, prudent consideration as we see the signs of the approach of the last days" (164). He believes that it is his task to offer clues as to the date of the Second Coming. He does so by juggling scriptural numbers to demonstrate that the Second Coming may occur in the year 2000. Several calculations are built around the Jewish and early Christian notion that human history will consist of six "days" of 1,000 years each, running from Creation to the dawn of the millennial sabbath (see Campion 1994: 323). Jeffrey shows that, because the Jewish year had 360 rather than 365 days, a biblical 1,000-year "day" consists of 985.626 modern years. Taking Hosea's prophecy that the Messiah will revive the people "after two days" (Hos. 6:1) as a reference to Jesus, he adds two periods of 985.626 years to the start of Jesus' public ministry in "AD 28.8," and arrives at 2000 (177–78). (As we shall see in chapter 7, Jeffrey radically scaled down his predictions when he came to revise the book in the 1990s.) Quite what the leadership of Kensington Temple makes of Jeffrey is not easy to establish. He has spoken at KT's Mission to London rallies, and Bruce Atkinson quotes him as a recognized authority on prophecy. Other members of staff find his theories preposterous. One pastor told me that Jeffrey was a "complete parasite," feeding off the latest fads in the secular world, such as the so-called "Bible Code" or the Y2K scare, and repackaging their dubious claims for a Christian audience. "With Benny Hinn or Grant Jeffrey I get the same feeling I would if I was on a plane being flown by someone with vague amateur experience," he said. "Sooner or later they are going to crash. They don't have theological subtlety in proportion to their grand claims."

The third author is Barry Smith (1933–2002), a preacher from New Zealand who believed that Satanic Freemasons were plotting to take over the world. As this suggests, he was more deeply immersed in the cultic milieu than either Cho or Jeffrey. Yet, of the three, he had the strongest personal following at KT, thanks to his weekly broadcasts on a Christian radio station; the bookshop was selling three or four of his books every week during the late 1990s, and the KT survey results showed that 23 percent of worshippers had read or listened to him. In *Better Than Nostradamus, or The Secret World Takeover* (1996), Smith argues that some of the sixteenth-century seer's prophecies were correct—but only because his master, Lucifer, allowed him a glimpse of the future. He goes on to show how the Freemasons are working to establish a New World Order presided over by an Antichrist who will probably turn out to be Henry Kissinger. Smith is not certain of this, but offers supporting information: if A is 6, B is 12, C is 18 and so on, KISSINGER adds up to 666; tradition holds that Antichrist will probably be a Jew; and the former Secretary of State has an "owl-like stare" that resembles the sinister gaze of Antichrist (1996: 158–73). Most KT pastors I spoke to regarded Smith as an eccentric and tended to smile when his name was mentioned. Jim Saunders, assistant manager of the bookshop in 1999, said Smith's identification of Kissinger as Antichrist was "crazy" and suggested that most of his theories could be put down to his lack of education.

Why sell his books, in that case? The obvious answer is that there was a demand for them. Moreover, it appears that no one from the shop took the time to read Smith's many titles before agreeing to stock them. When I asked Saunders what the bookshop was prepared to sell, he replied:

> It's a committee decision. I don't think we've discussed it for four or five years, and obviously not every person would agree with every single choice. There are really only three things we don't stock. Anything that sets the date for Christ's return is number one. Number two, we don't stock anything by Rebecca Brown, which is very heavy spiritual warfare stuff.[5] And, third, we don't stock books that give detailed descriptions of what heaven and hell are like.

This is interesting because it draws a parallel between date-setting millenarianism and other theological extremes. Yet these boundaries are not policed with particular vigilance. Jeffrey's *Armageddon* provisionally names the year of Christ's return; the fact that it slipped through the net implies that the prohibition against date-setting was not taken very seriously, or that Jeffrey's assurances that he was only *suggesting* a date were enough to satisfy the authorities, or that no one bothered to read the book before buying it in. I asked Saunders whether he ever found himself selling people End Times material that, in his opinion, would be unhelpful to them. He said: "Many times. It would be a different situation if I was in sole charge of the bookshop." In the event, Saunders did take over the shop, and in 2001 he removed Barry Smith's books and other colorful prophecy titles from the shelves. But, when questioned about this, he said I should not read too much into it. He had stopped stocking the End Times material, but only because he personally disliked it: it was not a policy decision by the church, and he had not discussed it with the leadership. (By 2002, prophecy titles had begun to reappear in the shop, though there was still nothing by Smith.) One is struck by the haphazard nature of the process: just as the doctrinal content of teaching depends on who happens to be giving the lecture, so the range of ideas expressed in the bookshop literature is affected by the vagaries of the ordering system and the tastes of the manager.

To what extent does the material in the Kensington Temple bookshop determine the boundaries of what it is permissible for church members to believe? This is a difficult question to answer. On the one hand, it is hard to see how the church's pastors could discipline worshippers for discussing the possibility that Dr Kissinger is the Antichrist, given that it was happy to sell them a book floating this idea. On the other, we can be sure that anyone who used the KT organization to publicize this conspiracy theory would soon find himself reprimanded. From the perspective of the leadership, what matters is not the content of unofficial apocalyptic ideas, but *how* they are held, and by whom. No great harm is done if church members read Barry Smith's books for their entertainment value, treating his wilder claims with skepticism. But, if his theories become the basis of people's personal faith, then there is a risk that they will become a source of tension between KT and other Christians, or between KT and society. Furthermore, while an out-and-out "prophecy nut" may do little damage on the fringes of the congregation, a pastor or evangelist holding the same views could create confusion among the faithful. Hence the warning to Ravi Holy to drop his conspiracy theories: they were seen as inappropriate coming from someone who was being groomed as a youth leader.

In the final analysis, apocalyptic belief does not require or receive much in the way of special attention by the Kensington Temple leadership: rather, its management is integrated into the broader policing of boundaries. There are one or two apocalyptic ideas that serve as warning signs that a particular worshipper is "superspiritual" or a troublemaker; John Starr, a senior member of Dye's ministry team, told me: "As soon as people start talking about conspiracy or producing an exact date for the return of Christ, then I don't want to know. That's it, mate, you've lost your audience." But he also said that someone with eccentric views on the End Times might be a formidable evangelist. Indeed, ministers generally emphasized that "over-the-top" views in any area—spiritual warfare and prosperity teachings as much as eschatology—were forgivable so long as they did not deny Christian orthodoxy, damage the unity or reputation of the congregation, and, most important, were rooted in a commitment to evangelism.

Managing Apocalyptic Belief: Individual Strategies

As we have seen, apocalyptic doctrines tend to be played down in the official teaching of Kensington Temple. Yet anticipation of the Second Coming remains an important strand in Pentecostal tradition. For the believer, certain questions are hard to avoid. Is Jesus' return really within sight—and, if so, what difference should that make to believers' lives? When they watch the television news or read the newspapers, should they do so with one eye on the prophecies of Daniel and Revelation?

The rest of this chapter is based chiefly on interviews with a relatively small number of members of Kensington Temple. My sample of around forty interviewees included people from different levels of the organization and ranged across the many demographic groups represented in the church. It was not, however, a representative or random sample. Fortunately, I was able to compare the complex opinions gathered during the interviews with the data from the "census" of nearly 3,000 worshippers that KT conducted in October 1999. The census consisted of a four-page questionnaire designed to provide the church with a detailed picture of its core membership; Colin Dye kindly allowed me to add several questions about the End Times and related subjects to the last page. As the following pages suggest, there was a significant degree of correspondence between interview and survey data.

Deciding how to group the interview responses proved difficult. Only four or five of the forty interviewees could be described as millenarians, in the sense that they firmly believed or thought it was likely that Jesus would return in their lifetimes; their ideas will be considered in some detail in the next chapter. Everyone else acknowledged that Jesus would return one day, though for some it seemed a distant prospect; the relevance of the Second Coming to daily lives varied, but rarely seemed very great. One way of organizing the data is to say that most interviewees seemed to have a *strategy* for coming to terms with the potentially difficult eschatological teachings of Pentecostalism, even if that strategy was to ignore them. Some people adopted broadly the same strategy, performing similar ideological work on doctrines, or cordoning off those doctrines from their lives in roughly the same way. The following list of strategies is not exhaustive, however, and it should be stressed that the categories overlap: a person might adopt more than one strategy, or abandon one in favor of another.

1. *Ignoring or Marginalizing Apocalyptic Doctrines*

The strongest evidence for the general lack of interest in apocalyptic doctrines at Kensington Temple came from the survey data. The questionnaire presented 2,973 worshippers with a list of spiritual activities or interests and asked them to number them in descending order of importance to their personal faith. Table 5.1 shows how the respondents distributed their first preferences. The picture could hardly be clearer: the End Times are at the bottom of the list. But even this does not fully convey the unpopularity of the option: a full 45

TABLE 5.1. Spiritual priorities, showing percentage of respondents who chose each activity as their first priority

Spiritual priority	First preference (%)
Evangelism	9
Spiritual warfare	4
End Times	2
Bible Study	9
Gifts of the Holy Spirit	11
Prayer	51
No response	14
Total	100
	N = 2,973

Note: Figures shown are to the nearest percentage point.

TABLE 5.2. Responses to the question "When do you think it likely that Jesus Christ will return? (a) within 10 years; (b) within 50 years; (c) not our place to speculate"

Options	Responses (%)
10-year return	8
50-year return	9
Not our place to speculate	73
No response	10
Total	100
	N = 2,973

Note: Figures shown are to the nearest percentage point.

percent of respondents made it their last preference. Respondents were also asked a direct question about the Second Coming: "When do you think it likely that Jesus Christ will return?" The options were (a) within ten years, (b) fifty years, and (c) not our place to speculate. Only 8 percent of respondents chose the ten-year option, 9 percent chose the fifty-year option, while 73 percent declined to speculate and 10 percent did not answer the question (see table 5.2).

These statistics, which became available toward the end of my fieldwork, could be interpreted narrowly as signifying no more than disapproval of date-setting. In fact, it was obvious from my first encounters with church members that many of them were genuinely uninterested in Bible prophecy. "I haven't even read the Book of Revelation all the way through," a middle-aged Nigerian man told me after a satellite service in Bayswater. "I know Jesus is coming back in my lifetime is a possibility, but it's just not something I think about." Most interviewees, when asked for a description of the end of the world as they imagined it, produced conventional statements along the lines of "the Bible says Jesus will come again, to judge the living and the dead" or "I believe there will be a Rapture, but I can't say what form it will take." Emmanuel Johnson, a Ghanaian in his twenties working as an estate agent in West London, offered a fairly typical response:

> Well, it's all a bit bizarre. I imagine what the Bible says about it: Jesus coming in clouds of glory. Every activity will be completely normal, and then he will just come, in the twinkling of an eye. There will be an angel of light coming dressed in royal clothes, majestically. . . . [Did he mean Jesus?] Yes, Jesus in the form of an angel. Armageddon? That will definitely take place, and the Rapture, too. We will be lifted physically up, as the Bible says.

Note the clichés—"clouds of glory," "twinkling of an eye"—and the slightly defensive invocation of the Bible as an authority for these "bizarre" concepts.

The reference to an angel was an unusual embellishment, but I suspected that Johnson made it up on the spot, and only added the clarifying detail that it was Jesus at my suggestion. No doubt I could have stimulated some worshippers into producing imaginative apocalyptic scenarios, rather as Charles Strozier did in his fascinating psychological study of fundamentalists (1994). But I was interested to discover what people would say about the Second Coming without prodding; the answer, in most cases, was relatively little.

Several interviewees told me that they had better things to do with their time than pore over the prophetic Scriptures. This was the line taken by Rajiv Gupta, a young South Londoner who converted to Pentecostalism from Hinduism:

> Soul winning is the priority, you're talking about winning a soul. Getting saved—that's the whole purpose why we're here. End Times is good, but it has its place. We've got the prophetic Scriptures, but in the meantime what do you do when those prophecies are being fulfilled? What's the point of spending your life finding out who the Antichrist is?

Adam Knight, 27, who was brought up in an evangelical family, made a similar point:

> I believe that it's every Christian's duty to know the Bible well, and that includes the End Times, but an unhealthy focus on the End Times can make us neglect more important issues that God wants us to face: obedience, issues of character, prayer, daily battles for the Christian to fight.

Ron Tomlinson, who had pastored a satellite church with his wife, Sarah, said that apocalyptic teachings had never appealed to him:

> I never had a strong sense of the End approaching. I'm one of those people who believes that it may be quite a long way off, even though it's a logical necessity that every day it must be a day nearer than it was. I was leading the church and I never recall thinking about the End being nigh—it didn't present itself.

Will Napier, while principal of the Bible college, told me in an apologetic tone of voice that he found it difficult to focus on the Second Coming:

> Speaking very personally, I do find it a challenge to live in the light of the imminent coming of Jesus, and if you spoke to most Christians they would say the same: that they have to keep pinching themselves to remember that they are in the Last Days, and that time is precious, time is short. . . . If somebody said, "do you believe in the imminent return of Christ?" we would tick that box. But the extent to which that is an every day, every second, reality in our lives is a matter for personal discipline.

In an interview following the loss of his faith, he took a rather different line: he told me that, even at the height of his infatuation with Pentecostal signs and wonders, he had been uncomfortable with the End Times tradition and tried not to think about it. (He felt the same way about Creationism, he added.) But, finding himself on the staff, he could hardly avoid the subject altogether: "It's a bit like joining a political party: there are going to be some commonly recognized beliefs of the party that are a bit of an embarrassment, but you are prepared to take them on because of the notion of cabinet responsibility." There is no reason to think, however, that Napier or other worshippers found it difficult to sideline these "embarrassing" beliefs. If church members had to keep pinching themselves to remember they were living in the Last Days, that was at least partly because they were rarely reminded of this fact from the platform. Even though it sold prophecy literature, Kensington Temple did not supply a strong plausibility structure for millenarian doctrines; nor—judging by the interview and survey data—was there any great demand for one. Some worshippers positively welcomed the lack of emphasis on the End Times. For Larry Grant, who had left the Jehovah's Witness only four years earlier, it was one of the advantages of belonging to Kensington Temple:

> I've spent too many years in the Witnesses listening to people talking about apocalyptic prophecy for me to feel comfortable with that stuff today. It's put me off the whole area—Barry Smith, Grant Jeffrey, they're not my cup of tea. There's been an utter change of my central focus. My Christian faith is about my relationship with Jesus. I know He's coming back and that we should live accordingly, but now I have a more balanced view.

2. The Stigmatization of "Prophecy Nuts"

Many interviewees who distanced themselves from apocalyptic teachings had a ready excuse for doing so: they felt that the whole area had been taken over by extremists whose eccentric ideas might discredit evangelical Christianity. For the most part, this stigmatization of popular prophecy belief went hand in hand with the playing down of eschatology we have just described; but some worshippers with quite a strong sense of the Second Coming were keen to balance it with criticism of "prophecy nuts," so I have considered it separately.

One young woman expressed her doubts as follows:

> It's important to study and understand Revelation, but there's a fringe, not really in the church but in Christian society, who get an obsession with figuring out all the metaphors and figurative language. . . . I tend to write it off when people start predicting when Jesus will come back. It's very clear that man cannot know these things—the Bible says that even the Son doesn't know but only the Father.[6]

The reference to date-setting is reminiscent of John Starr's reaction to attempts to date the return of Christ—"that's it, mate, you've lost your audience"; almost no one I spoke to had a good word to say for predictive millenarianism. There was condemnation, too, of the excesses of explanatory millenarianism. Napier, while still part of the church leadership, spoke disparagingly of a small number of "Israel-watchers" in the congregation who were perfectly sane on most subjects; but, as soon as the subject of the Middle East came up, their eyes would "swivel upwards" and they would start talking about the fulfillment of prophecy in the Holy Land. (He added that an attempt to found a pro-Israel fellowship at Kensington Temple had foundered through lack of interest.)

There was some confusion, as there is in evangelical circles generally, about where to draw the line between well-meaning Christians who got the End Times "out of proportion" and apocalyptic fanatics. Adam Knight implied that the main problem lay within the Church:

> Some people can cover up their responsibilities by having too much
> of a focus on the End Times, or equally the beginnings, Creation,
> the start. I have a gut instinct that these things can be used as an
> excuse for Christians that can't deal with the issues God is raising,
> so [they say] let's find something in the Bible that I can be fasci-
> nated with. People in my childhood and the past were so stuck in
> their opinions on the End Times.

Tom Rayner, a Bible college student, saw apocalyptic extremism as both a Christian and a non-Christian phenomenon:

> Well, sadly, there are a lot of books on eschatology both inside and
> outside the Church. Although I find it very strange, the Book of Rev-
> elation was Aleister Crowley's favorite book[7]—it's often used by oc-
> cultists and the media, the idea of the Beast and the Antichrist are
> figures in the popular imagination. On top of that there are people
> on the fringe of the Church who point out that this person is likely
> to be the Antichrist, and depending on who the author is, the actual
> identity of the Antichrist changes as well. I've heard everything from
> the Pope to particular grand rabbis to theories that the person would
> have to be Jewish or a leader of the European Union, and a lot of
> the backgrounds are very spurious.

Emmanuel Johnson suggested that the worst excesses occurred outside the Christian mainstream:

> Some sects, all they believe in is the End Times—they have End-
> Time ministries, End-Time churches, which can be quite dangerous.
> Some people even look at specific dates, like that one in Korea or
> Japan where a sect said Jesus is coming on a certain date and every-
> one should get ready. . . . I've seen people praying in the street, fa-

natics who say Jesus is coming back, repent! It's not the way I
would approach the issue. I used to work with the homeless, giving
them teas and coffees and sandwiches, and we didn't even preach
the Gospel to them until they opened up. That's my kind of approach, not preaching to thousands in the street.

Surprisingly, though, the only apocalyptic believer who Emmanuel had met
recently was from the secular world, a young woman client of his, who during
a business meeting had suddenly brought up the subject of the End:

She said, "I believe the world is coming to an end, you can see it all
around you, with an accident here, a plane crash there." She asked if
I was religious, but I didn't push. I do think there's a question mark
on the top of each human being about this subject. This girl came
out with it straight out of the blue, and she wasn't even a Christian.
A fanatic would have wanted to preach to her, but I have to be professional in my job; that's very important.

There was a sense that, for many worshippers, intense apocalyptic belief
was a particularly unenticing form of subcultural deviance, demanding a price
that was not worth paying. The people who used words such as "fringe" and
"nuts" to describe the excesses of the prophecy subculture were not necessarily
afraid of deviance per se. Some of them were happy to support Pentecostal
preachers such as Cerullo, who had been denounced as snake-oil salesmen by
the secular media, and accepted reports of the miraculous appearance of holy
oil or gold teeth without subjecting them to serious scrutiny. Apocalyptic theology inspired more skepticism, and even downright hostility, than other charismatic claims. One reason for this was an awareness that Christian apocalyptic
believers had been proved wrong in the past: not necessarily in a dramatic
fashion, by the passing of specific deadlines, but by the slow dying out of
generations that were convinced that they had been chosen to witness the
parousia. "I can't see the world going on for another hundred years, but I'm
sure they thought that a hundred years ago," said Adam Knight. Tom Rayner
told me that he found it "sobering" to discover that Christians throughout
history had used the Book of Revelation to justify their belief that the End
would come in their lifetimes. Jim Saunders made a link between millennial
disappointment and conspiracy theories involving the European Union:

The way that prophets always tie up the End Times with Europe is
surprising because the Bible doesn't talk about Europe, not in that
context. It doesn't talk about ten states of Europe. They are only saying that because that is what is happening in their particular lifetime. They haven't got enough historical imagination to realize that
in almost every age people thought they were living in the Last
Days.

Saunders was, however, unrepresentative of my interviewees. He holds a doc-
torate in church history, and his critique of prophecy belief was more sophis-

ticated, and went further in the direction of mainstream theology, than any other I encountered. Other members of Kensington Temple, although not predictive millenarians, happily embraced End Times conspiracy theories.

3. Explanatory Millenarianism

The KT survey results suggested that a substantial minority of church members were receptive to conspiracy theories. On the last page of the census, underneath the question about Christ's return, I had added two familiar statements of conspiracy belief: "The move towards a single European Currency is a sign of the Antichrist"; and "Supermarket barcodes may contain hidden Satanic information." Of the respondents, 38 percent agreed with the first statement and 27 percent with the second—far higher totals than the 8 and 9 percent who thought it likely that Jesus would return within ten years and fifty years, respectively. This finding seemed to support an observation I had made during the interviews: that, while there was a widespread reluctance to engage with the concept of the Second Coming in anything more than general terms ("the Bible says . . ."), there was a greater willingness to toy conversationally with conspiracy belief. The 73 percent of respondents who said it was "not our place to speculate" about Christ's return were almost as likely to espouse conspiracy ideas as those who did speculate: a third of them agreed with the European currency statement.

In short, it appears that explanatory millenarianism was far more popular at Kensington Temple than the predictive variety. The 1,121 respondents who agreed with the statement about the euro cannot be dismissed as a small fringe of "prophecy nuts." It is true that they had consumed more apocalyptic material than other people—36 percent had read or listened to Barry Smith, as opposed to 23 percent of the whole church—but in terms of sex, ethnicity, and education they were close to the norm. All sorts of people made use of explanatory millenarianism in their analysis of the world around them. They ranged from mild-mannered KT office staff who would talk hesitantly about dark forces at work, but deny that they had a special interest in the subject, to colorful characters such as Ravi Holy who "banged on" about the Illuminati. Interestingly, some conspiracy theorists were also strongly opposed to predictive millenarianism and poured scorn on date-setters.

Anna Lomax, a single woman in her forties who had converted from Roman Catholicism, was distinctly reserved about her conspiracy beliefs, which had to be coaxed out of her. She said she had known nothing about the End Times until after she joined the church and was initially skeptical: "I heard Barry Smith preach six months after becoming a Christian at KT, and I thought: Is this what I'm supposed to believe in? I've joined this?" Instead of dismissing Smith's ideas, however, she carried on reading conspiracy material and eventually decided that there was something in it:

> He did open my eyes and help me to make sense of what is going
> on with Europe and the monetary system. He said there was going

to be a single currency, and ten years ago that wasn't so obvious. It was the first time I had heard that, and also the things concerning Revelation. I didn't know anything about that at all. . . . I do think we are approaching the End, the way things are going—the issues of gay rights and the homosexual issue, just the way society is going. . . . There's only so far you can go down that road before you get to the Mark of the Beast.

For Keith Dickinson, a 35-year-old warehouseman who was studying part-time at the Bible college, conspiracy theory represented a path back to faith after he drifted away from the Pentecostalism of his West Indian parents. He had always known about the End Times, but had never encountered Christian conspiracy writings until one of his sisters left a book by Barry Smith lying around:

> The book talked about certain economic policies related to the Bible, so I started looking on TV for certain things that might correspond with what Barry was talking about. And I did find them. And me being a curious cat, I started asking more questions. I was led by the Holy Spirit. I walked into a Christian bookshop and asked the guy at the counter if he had any books on the New World Order and he pointed me to the cults and religion section. And I went over and found a book that talked about Communism, Marxism, socialism. It talked about the beginnings, from Babylon as it were, and it came up the twentieth century, what's going on now. And so I applied it to today, and I saw what's going down with certain governments right now.

Unlike Smith, however, Keith was dismissive of predictive millenarianism— partly because his parents had told him as a child that Jesus was coming back soon:

> I was always taught in the 1970s that Jesus would come back in the 1980s along with the silver car and the silver dress that we saw in the adverts. My mum and dad were always saying, when we talked about the 1980s, that Jesus would be coming by then . . .
> It's risky to talk about dates. There are people who measure the years from Adam and get into the seven-day week. I think it's interesting, but I won't go there. When Christ comes back it's going to be a surprise; why should we speculate? If he did tell us [Christians], I'm coming back on the 12th of August, we wouldn't be able to keep our mouths shut. We'd blurt it out. People would go around murdering each other, then decide to get holy at the last minute, five to twelve.

Comparing the testimonies of Anna and Keith, it is difficult to say who was the more intense apocalyptic believer. Judged by his fondness for prophecy material, Keith was heavily "into the End Times." But there was something light-hearted about his encounter with it. He was entertained by details of the New World Order; one might describe it as his hobby. Anna would not list the End Times as one of her interests and viewed the subject with foreboding. Yet she employed an apocalyptic narrative to explain things that really troubled her, such as homosexuality. What united Anna and Keith was the way they used the apocalyptic analysis of current events to impose order on a disordered world and to neutralize the operation of evil, whether manifested in the machinations of foreign governments or the gay rights lobby. Conspiracy theory was here performing the historic function of explanatory millenarianism, reducing the dissonance between religious teaching and the world, rather than increasing it as date-specific prophecies tend to. Its logic might be flawed; but even the most unsympathetic critic would be unlikely to accuse Anna and Keith of ex-hibiting delusional behavior. Even so, they were, in a sense, playing with fire: the currents of conspiracy theory run directly into the furthest reaches of the cultic milieu, where they are associated with fanaticism and paranoia. The fact that explanatory millenarianism deploys its arguments rationally is no guar-antee against extreme subcultural deviance: on the contrary, its internal logic can drive Christians further along the spectrum of stigmatized knowledge— not toward doomsday millenarianism, necessarily, but into a worldview similar to that of conspiracy theorists on the political fringes. This danger was ac-knowledged at Kensington Temple, where the more extravagant conspiracy believers ran the risk of being reprimanded by the leadership, as Ravi Holy had been, or marginalized within the congregation. At the time, Holy felt that he had been unfairly treated because Dye himself entertained conspiracy the-ories; but even a cursory glance at the book-length memoir he posted on the Internet helps explain why some members of Kensington Temple found his views disturbing.[8]

As a teenage dropout, Holy had flirted with anarchism, punk rock, witch-craft, and Satanism, and it was during this period that he was introduced to the "Illuminatus" trilogy of science fiction novels by Robert Anton Wilson (1975). These books, which have acquired cult status, draw on a vast range of subcultures to produce one dazzlingly complex conspiracy theory; many fans regard them as truth lightly clothed as fiction.[9] Holy certainly took this view and offers his own summary of Wilson's ideas in his memoir. At the center of the conspiracy are the Illuminati, a secret society ostensibly founded by the Bavarian mystic Adam Weishaupt in 1776 but actually dating back thousands of years. Holy describes the Illuminati as "totally evil, pan-dimensional beings" who were once known as the Knights Templar and worshipped the dark God Baphomet. They also built the pyramids of Egypt, and there are still pyramids at the bottom of the Atlantic Ocean, the last traces of the Illuminati-controlled civilization of Atlantis. The society controls the U.S. government through a vast pentagram centered on the Pentagon; its ultimate aim is to "feed" its evil gods by bringing about the eschaton, the end of the world, in the shape of a thermonuclear catastrophe. In a classic demonstration of the adaptability of the motifs of the cultic milieu, Holy carried out only minor adjustments to this narrative after he became a born-again Christian; indeed, it served as a bridge into his new religious culture. He recalls:

> Becoming a Christian helped me tidy up my mishmash of conspiracy ideas—it gave me the full picture, instead of just glimpses of what was going on. I had to let some of the occult stuff go, such as reincarnation and astral travel, but even then I'm not sure I really did let it go. Kensington Temple told me that astral travel didn't exist, but I just concluded that you weren't supposed to talk about it. At the time I arrived at KT, Barry Smith was in favor, and some of his ideas were totally crazy, so you could say that the church's worldview wasn't very different from mine.

As his spiritual odyssey suggests, Holy's experience of the late 1980s and early 1990s was one of extreme disorientation; the usefulness of conspiracy theory in providing a moral and cultural compass for him is revealed by the way he clung on to it through several dramatic changes of religious allegiance. In the late 1990s, he left Kensington Temple and reinvented himself yet again, this time as a liberal Anglican; but, even then, he was still toying with the notion that world events were controlled by an international secret society.

Conspiracy theory also seems to have operated as a spiritual lifeline for Linda Symondson, a widow in her sixties who worked as a part-time tourist information officer. She told me that she had been struggling with her faith until she came across Christian literature that revealed that astonishing archaeological discoveries were being kept secret:

> I was in a specially bad time in my faith . . . when the Lord put me right next door to a Christian couple who had a Christian lending library with videos and tapes, and they had videos by these people. The Lord put it on my heart to borrow this tape. They found the undersea crossing where Moses took the children of Israel across. They found the road under the sea, and to their amazement the chariot wheels, wood wrapped in gold . . . They also found Sodom and Gomorrah, and it still exists: the buildings are solidified ash. They found the Ark of the Covenant; that is a bit of a bombshell. The government is keeping it low key because they don't want a holy war with the Muslims.

I asked her which government was keeping this secret. She replied: "Let me think. It's the government that's ruling now where there is all the trouble. The Ark of the Covenant is so valuable and so powerful that if the Muslims knew the Jews had it they would fight to get it off the Jews." Linda went on to talk about an End Times conspiracy in which Satanic forces would arrange for fire to come down from heaven; it would look real but it would have been arranged by sending light rays through the ionosphere to come back as fire. Who was behind it? "It's a conglomeration. The Pope is at the centre of it," she said, though, tantalizingly, that was all the information she had.

As a conspiracy theory, this was not necessarily stranger than that espoused by Ravi Holy; the difference was that Linda possessed few of Holy's persuasive skills. This became clear during my interview with her, which took place outside a service, in the Kensington Temple forecourt. We were overheard by Barbara, a Kenyan convert to Pentecostalism, who began to interject skeptical questions. "What is the evidence for this?" she asked. "If the government is keeping these discoveries secret, how do you know about them?" Barbara's tone was incredulous, almost mocking; and I discovered later that Linda was regarded as a marginal presence in the KT community, a wandering eccentric rather than a permanent member of the church. She told me she had been a member of several evangelical congregations, but left them after deciding that they were "cult churches." She did seem a troubled individual, and one could understand why other worshippers thought of her as only a step or two removed from those mental patients who think that the CIA is sending death rays through their television screens. Her explanatory millenarianism served only to explain things to herself; for her fellow worshippers, it confirmed an instinctive association of deviant ideas with deviant people.

4. Apocalypticism as an Option

Many Kensington Temple worshippers seemed to occupy a middle ground: they neither ignored apocalyptic ideas nor made heavy use of them. Instead, they distinguished between helpful and unhelpful concepts, sometimes working on the End Times narrative until it made sense to them, and they dipped in and out of the apocalyptic paradigm as it suited them. We have already cited Neitz's argument that converts do not suspend their rationality when confronted by the claims of the new belief system: doctrines are evaluated and tested against experience (1987: 78–90). My fieldwork suggested that many members of Kensington Temple—not just recent converts—used this sort of informal hypothesis testing to evaluate apocalyptic claims. They asked themselves, in effect, "Does this proposition make sense to me? Does it go too far?" The answers were heavily influenced by their personal outlook. Claire Henderson, a Scots-born businesswoman in her twenties, was particularly wary of conspiracy theories involving modern technology:

> The End Times is very interesting, but I wouldn't go much further than that. I know that one of the prophecies is of a One World Order, and you can see some of that coming together—the way Europe is being formed, and NATO. But I stand back and watch with interest; you can't be fanatical about it. When people say we are all going to get barcodes stamped on our hand, I tend to be very cautious; I should know more about it and think it through more. I don't think the conclusion is that we are all going to get *this* [points to her hand]. Something will happen, but how it works itself out . . . I almost don't *need* to know. There's a hundred and one theories, but people are missing the point. Yes, there's going to be persecution,

and we should start thinking about it. But you hear of people who shun all uses of technology and say the Internet is the root of all evil and I personally think that's fanatical.

A similar ambivalence was expressed by Sophie Kempff, a German woman in her thirties living in London:

> I know from the Bible that Jesus is coming back, and I am con-scious of living in the End Times. Everything is getting more global, with the Internet; we are receiving a lot of news from other coun-tries and we see how dictators and leaders are misusing their coun-tries. Jesus said, look at the signs in Matthew 24. I'm very aware of wars, that people hate each other, there are other catastrophes . . . [Did she feel that moves toward greater European union might be a sign of the End?] No, it's not my opinion. I personally feel that it's not good to put countries with different histories under one roof and currency—but I wouldn't say that this is the Antichrist. I'm very careful about that. [Did she expect Jesus to return in her life-time?] It could happen, but Martin Luther said we should still plant apple trees even when we expect the world will finish.[10]

For Claire and Sophie, apocalyptic conspiracy theory had some ability to explain the shape of the modern world, but not as much as its most enthusiastic proponents imagined. They could see political events "coming together," but worried that some Christians were misreading the signs and becoming fanat-ical. Each had her own sticking point: for Claire, the notion that people would be forced to carry computer chips implanted in the hand; for Sophie, the iden-tification of moves toward a united Europe with the Antichrist. These were the points at which the strength of conspiracy theory—its rootedness in the real world—became a weakness; the moment at which it overreached itself and proposed an unacceptable hypothesis. The two women responded by perform-ing the ideological work of drawing a line between its believable and unbeliev-able claims.

The survey data suggests that this sort of discrimination was common at Kensington Temple. For example, only 50 percent of the people who thought that the single currency heralded the Antichrist also agreed that supermarket barcodes might contain Satanic information. We can sense the influence of secular society here. The euro was constantly in the news at the time of the survey and was presented by its political opponents in a sinister light. This gave European conspiracy theories a surface plausibility that was missing from the rather dated apocalyptic warnings about the Universal Product Code. As a result, some worshippers thought it appropriate to apply a prophetic paradigm to Europe, but regarded the barcodes conspiracy theory as a silly American notion aimed at the unsophisticated. (Interestingly, 70 percent of people who assented to the barcodes statement assented to the euro statement; there were also slightly fewer graduates among them than in the church as a whole.)

The process of discrimination took people in and out of an apocalyptic framework for analyzing the world. Sophie Kempff was reminded of Bible prophecy when she read about dictators and the Internet, but not when Europe was being discussed. When I asked Adam Knight if he thought about the End Times when he watched the television news, he replied: "Only when I hear stuff about the Middle East, stuff on Jerusalem. Yesterday they talked about the Temple and I thought, this is classic prophecy stuff, they're talking about peace but all sides are building up their armed forces to go to war." But, where the European Union was concerned, Adam felt he did not know enough to make a religious judgment, so his understanding of it was based on whatever secular analysis he picked up from the media.

Sometimes, church members disagreed about whether it was appropriate to analyze current events in the light of eschatology. I attended a service at KT's Royal Oak satellite in October 2000, just after Israeli troops had fired on rioting Palestinians, killing teenagers and children. The crisis dominated the headlines that Sunday; worshippers were not surprised to be asked about it, but hardly spoke with one voice. A young Nigerian told me he was certain that the End Times drama was being played out in Jerusalem: there was "nothing that human beings could do to bring about peace." An English housewife thought it was only a "possibility" that prophecies were being fulfilled. "I need to do some more reading, to have a greater depth of knowledge about Revelation," she said. "But I don't feel that the world is coming to an end right now—it's too soon." Larry Grant, who was leading the prayers, said pointedly: "We pray for Israel, that it might show wisdom and restraint. There are those in the Church who say that whatever Israel does, praise it and bless it. But should that be the case now? Is that nation perhaps being punished for its excesses?" After the service, the apocalyptic and secular options came face to face in an animated debate between two middle-aged men: Joseph, a lifelong evangelical from Ghana, and Henry, an English convert. Joseph felt that the search for peace in the Middle East would fail because it ran counter to Israel's prophetic destiny:

> The Jews are God's chosen people, no matter what happens. We may pray for peace, but we have got to believe that the End is going to be ushered in through wars and rumors of wars. This may be a prophetic sign, in as much as the whole world is trying to get peace in the Middle East, yet every time they get close to it something is triggered off and the peace is broken. That doesn't happen for nothing—there's something powerful going on.

Henry took a different line:

> Do you think we should not interfere and just let them start a big war? This could just be another spat. Israelis and Palestinians are killing each other and I think we *should* interfere. The Israelis have very hard hearts towards the Palestinians when they should be showing some compassion. You [Joseph] see this as more prophetic than I do. If this is God's way of starting the End Time, then there's

nothing we can do about it—but if it isn't, then we are missing an opportunity to be compassionate. We mustn't say, this is God's will so we'll just let them get on with it.

Joseph and Henry both believed that civilization would enter its final crisis in the lands of the Bible, in accordance with the visions of Daniel and Revelation. But they disagreed on a crucial point: was it happening now? Much the same question was asked by church members after the terrorist attacks of September 11, 2001. In America, some fundamentalist prophecy writers hailed the destruction of the World Trade Center as the beginning of the End Times (Barkun 2003: 158–59). The response from members of Kensington Temple was far more muted. There was a brief flurry of interest in Bible prophecy, but by the late autumn of 2001, when various apocalyptic books based on September 11 appeared in the bookshop, it had died down. "We had an awful job getting rid of those books—no on wanted them because it was old news," commented one staff member. According to Emmanuel Johnson, "September 11 didn't make people think about the End Times—they saw it more as a wake-up call to the Church." Jason Robinson, a young accountancy student from Jamaica, offered an unusual interpretation of the event that toyed with calendrical millenarianism while rejecting the prospect of an imminent apocalypse:

> After September 11, I thought about the year 2000. They had kept
> telling us that something significant would happen, and when noth-
> ing did I just thought that it was another wrong prediction. Then
> something did happen, even if there was a year in between. And I
> thought: this is God's way of letting himself be known—every
> 2,000 years something really significant happens. But I didn't think
> it was the end of the world. God works slowly. It's human nature to
> want to make everything happen in our lifetime, it's a way we have
> of exalting ourselves. But not even the angels know when the End is
> coming, so why should we?

This sort of relaxed speculation emphasizes the freedom of maneuver enjoyed by members of Kensington Temple, as opposed to the tighter control of prophecy belief in the present-day Jehovah's Witnesses or the Pentecostal denominations early in the twentieth century. KT worshippers were encouraged to reach their own conclusions about the usefulness of explanatory millenarianism; no one protested if they molded aspects of apocalyptic tradition until they fitted more comfortably into their own worldview.

As we saw earlier, Bennett Berger (1981: 114) uses the term "remedial ideological work" to describe changes to received ideas that are made in order to resolve the intellectual or practical difficulties they cause. In a religion that makes as many empirical claims and interprets Scripture as literally as Pentecostalism, these adjustments are frequently necessary. Apocalyptic concepts are no exception to this. One motif that was subjected to frequent remedial work by KT members was the Mark of the Beast. The Book of Revelation says that everyone carrying the mark will "be tormented with fire and sulphur"

(Rev. 14:10). According to popular prophecy literature, Satanic agents are planning to insert computer chips (or some other device—the details are constantly being updated) under the skins of unwary people. But if the latter genuinely have no idea what the mark means, how can God's punishment be fair? Several worshippers were mildly troubled by this contradiction. One pastor told me that the mark could not be something forced on people, but must correspond to some "inner corruption" that would merit divine punishment. A similar thought had occurred to Debbie Mowbray, a student from New Zealand:

> The Mark of the Beast has to be something in our hearts. If somebody forced me to have it, it's not going to mean I denied Jesus Christ in my heart . . . I was talking to someone who reckons that it could be something like we discover aliens on another planet, and we start genetically modifying ourselves with aliens or plant species. The human race could become so deformed that God could only destroy it. I've been thinking about that ever since he said it.

This statement gives us an insight into how apocalyptic ideas are constructed in practice. Debbie had modified her concept of the Mark of the Beast as a result of a casual conversation with a friend that drew on current events and science fiction (she was speaking at the height of the controversy over genetically modified foods); in effect, she customized it so that it made better sense to her. But, although she had been "thinking about it ever since he said it," it was not central to her faith. She told me she was vaguely aware of living in the End Times, but rarely gave the subject her full attention:

> It's there in the back of my mind, but I don't think about it. When I read the newspaper I look around, for example at natural disasters, and think "This is really getting quite serious, it could be any time now." But as far as my everyday Christian life goes, I just try to make every day as fulfilled as possible, so it's not a huge focus of mine. I've got tapes at home on the End Times [by Barry Smith], and I really should listen to them at some point.

What one notices here is the sheer ordinariness of the mental processes applied to the prospect of the end of the world. Even in its explanatory mode, millenarianism is constructed around intrinsically frightening notions; yet Debbie and many other church members worked on them in much the same way as they worked on other doctrines. It was as if the threat of cognitive dissonance, of ideas not making sense, bothered them more than the threats conjured up by the apocalyptic narrative, which in the version approved by Dye involved the shocking persecution of Christians during the Tribulation. On the occasions when Debbie applied a prophetic paradigm to the world around her, she reflected that "it [the emergence of the Antichrist] could be any time now"; but the series of eight audiotapes by Barry Smith that she had borrowed from a friend, which purported to reveal much secret information regarding the approaching crisis, remained unopened in their box.

5. *Apocalypticism as Rhetoric*

During our interview, Debbie said something that pointed toward another aspect of apocalyptic tradition: the way that the words in which it is expressed can take on a life of their own. She told me: "Me and my girlfriends often say 'Jesus is coming soon, it's the End Times,' but none of us are into studying it or have a particular interest in it." What this statement implies is that the concept of the End Times, which is an exotic one by the standards of secular society, is so familiar in the Pentecostal world that people throw it about in conversation almost without thinking about it—and, perhaps, without believing in it very strongly. As we saw in the Introduction, O'Leary (1994) argues that apocalypticism is best understood as rhetoric, an attempt to persuade an audience that history is structured in a certain way. But the analysis of apocalypticism as rhetoric need not be confined to the formal propositions of preachers and authors. As the social psychologist Michael Billig points out, rhetoric and argumentation are spread throughout social life. It is too readily assumed that in striking an attitude people are giving an outward expression to an inner mental state; in reality, they do not possess a single "attitude," but use complex and frequently contradictory patterns of thought to accomplish different functions (1991: 15–17). For example, they might engage in a particular discourse without investing much in it, out of custom as much as conviction. A non-evangelical who overheard Debbie saying to a friend "It's the End Times" would probably conclude that this young woman was living in the shadow of the apocalypse. But that was not really the case: her mention of the Second Coming entailed no serious practical consequences. Far from corresponding to some inner excitement or turmoil, this fragment of apocalyptic rhetoric formed part of what Billig calls "the chatter and argument of ordinary life" (11).

Most worshippers do not find themselves referring to the End Times very often: I came across only one reference to the subject that was completely unprompted by me, and that was when a pastor was asked to clarify a complex question of eschatology. In doing so, he employed a specialist discourse quite unlike that of Debbie and her friends—yet there was a similar mismatch between the content of the rhetoric and what the person speaking it privately believed. I was sitting one morning in the office of Andrew Kenworthy, a Cambridge engineering graduate in his early thirties who was acting head of the KT Bible college. While we were talking, a member of staff came in and asked for the answer to an exam question that had been set for the students. Kenworthy turned to the Book of Daniel and started talking about the seventy "weeks" that Daniel is told by the angel Gabriel will elapse until the dawn of everlasting righteousness (Dan. 9:24), a passage understood by many born-again Christians to reveal the amount of time left before the Second Coming. The colleague left, and I asked what his question had been. This is a transcript of Kenworthy's reply:

> The question was, at the end of the 69th of Daniel's weeks, what
> happens? Is it (a) Rapture, (b) the Crucifixion, (c) something else—

and the answer's the Crucifixion because the argument would be
that you've got a literal time-span that you can peg from the calendar to the week. You can even take into account that they are different years, 360 days or 365: whichever one of those you take it still
fits, and the better one is to go from the decree of Cyrus that Israel
can be a nation again, which is found in Jeremiah or somewhere,
and from that date until the Crucifixion is a literal 483 years using
the year they would have had, without having to juggle things.[11] So
you've got a literal time there; if the next seven-year period is a literal one as well, it's quite difficult to find a historical event that
would match up with that. And because the prophecy is given from
Gabriel to Daniel, saying "this is a plan for your people," the seventy
weeks reflect God's dealings with the Jews. So at the point of the
Crucifixion, when the veil was torn in the Temple, that ushered in
the Church Age, because people whether Jews or Gentiles were now
able to have clear access to God, and the premillennial or pre-
Tribulation would be . . . actually, no, it wouldn't depend on your belief about when the Rapture happens, it would simply be . . . no, it
would be a pre-Tribulation Rapture because you could either say that
the remaining week is a seven-year period, the seven-year Tribulation, so the end of the Church Age is when the Church is raptured,
so the Church goes from the Crucifixion to the Rapture, and the
Church is out of the way, so the Jewish time clock starts ticking
again for the last seven years, even though there's been a disconti-
nuity. Or you could say that the Aramaic word for week, or seven, is
more accurately translated as a number divisible by seven, so you
could have a 483, 69 times 7, literal years at the beginning, and the
last seven years could be more figurative: it could be 7, 14, 21, and
so on. So you're not quite sure how long that goes on for.

All this was spoken almost without a pause for breath; even when he hesitated,
Kenworthy sounded like a mathematician solving a problem rather than someone genuinely confused. I confessed that I was unable to follow his argument
after the first sentence or two, and I asked how much of it he had worked out
for himself. He replied:

If you said to me, "what does that passage [in Daniel] mean?" I
would give you that explanation. If you asked me when I believe the
Rapture will happen, I would give you another answer. But that is
the clearest explanation of that passage, which I have probably
gleaned from reading books since I've been here at this church.

Kenworthy was raised in the Church of England; I asked if this sort of millennial speculation would have meant anything to him before he was a Pentecostal.

No, I couldn't have cared less. And I still couldn't care less in one
sense. The reason I started caring was not because of a need to pin

down my own eschatological belief to one party or the other, that's
not what's driving me. But I wanted to be aware of the different arguments and approaches out there, and in order to do that you've
got to familiarize yourself with them all, and in doing so you are
likely to come down on one side or the other.

But which side *had* he come down on? Let us look again at his odd statement
that if he were asked to explain the passage in Daniel he would give one answer
and if he were asked when the Rapture would occur he would give another.
His explanation of Daniel's "weeks" points to a pre-Tribulation Rapture, since
the Church would be "out of the way" before the start of the 70th week, the
Great Tribulation. Yet he did not actually believe that this was when the Rapture
would happen. As he said later:

> The reason I would come down on the side of a post-Tribulation
> Rapture is that the only way the Church will be purified is if it goes
> through hard times. Plus, in the Bible, God is always saving people
> *out* of things, he's not saving people *from* things.

In other words, Kenworthy's personal convictions led him to a conclusion
different from that of the complex explanation of Daniel that he had "gleaned
from reading books." So why did he not reject that explanation? Partly, one
suspects, because he wanted to be fluent in the eschatological discourse of
born-again Christianity. He was not driven by his own need to know exactly
how the End Times would unfold; rather, having become a Pentecostal minister, he wanted to understand the "different approaches that are out there."
Eschatology was an area of knowledge rather than the key to salvation. "I still
couldn't care less in one sense," he said—which may explain why he felt able
to perform an exegetical exercise that he suspected was flawed.

That exercise was also a demonstration of how the intimidating raw material of Jesus' prophecies has become routinized. Like one of the medieval
clerks described by McGinn ([1979] 1998: 35), Kenworthy adapted apocalypticism to the requirements of a specialist discourse, demonstrating in the process that he was what Max Weber called a religious virtuoso. The blood-
drenched images of the Book of Revelation lose much of their disruptive power
once they are subsumed into a debate about the order in which they will occur.
Not only is attention diverted from their more disturbing aspects toward her-
meneutical technicalities, but the professional ethos of the debate discourages
extreme reactions to them. Furthermore, the knowledge that there are recognized experts in eschatology relieves ordinary worshippers of some of the burden of thinking about the terrible things to come: the smooth flow of rhetoric
renders the subject of the End Times manageable in everyday life.

6. Apocalypticism as Entertainment

Some members of Kensington Temple encounter the End Times chiefly as
entertainment, in the form of taped sermons by celebrity preachers, prophecy

books, or novels. This mediation does not necessarily rob the apocalyptic narrative of its force; but, like the eschatological rhetoric discussed above, it can make the subject easier to manage. Admittedly, "entertainment" is a rather loose concept. Purely theological material can function as entertainment if it is packaged in the right way and that is how the consumer experiences it. Alternatively, fiction may convey a powerful theological message. For some people, novels and feature films based on the prophecies of Revelation are a way of sustaining a belief in millenarian doctrines, albeit at a comfortable distance; others may derive apocalyptic beliefs from secular entertainment.

When I first visited the KT bookshop in the mid-1990s, it stocked a small range of apocalyptic videotapes, including the made-for-television film *A Distant Thunder* (1986), which told the story of a young woman trying to escape being given the Mark of the Beast by the Satanic forces known as UNITE. There was no sign of any great appetite for this sort of material, which appeared to be aimed only at worshippers with a special interest in the End Times. By 2002, however, a bookcase in the center of the shop was given over to the *Left Behind* novels and their spin-off comic books, DVDs, and videos, supported by slick promotional material. The irony was that Jim Saunders had only just removed most non-fiction prophecy literature from the shelves; it was tempting to interpret this as evidence that, even in the conservative evangelical world, apocalyptic motifs were increasingly the stuff of fiction rather than literal belief. In fact, *Left Behind* did not enjoy a huge following at KT: the sales figures for 2003 showed that, in the previous few months, the novels had sold only about 20 copies each. Most of the worshippers I asked about the subject had seen the feature film based on *Left Behind* but had not read the books. Their responses to the film were mixed. David, a rock musician in his twenties, said he was perfectly comfortable with the presentation of the End Times in a fictional form; he felt that the film had grappled with its difficult subject as realistically as possible. "I had been a Christian for a long time when I saw it, so I already had my own views about the End Times," he said. Like Dye, he personally expected a post-Tribulation Rapture, a doctrine directly at variance with the central concept of *Left Behind*. This did not worry him: "It's an area where people honestly disagree. It doesn't matter, so long as people know that the End Times are coming and prepare for them." In effect, David had agreed to differ with the film's producers about the sequence of the apocalyptic events. Katherine, another young church member, had seen the film but had not even noticed that its depiction of a Secret Rapture contradicted Dye's teaching; nor was she very interested when I told her. "I knew that the film wasn't completely accurate, but I do believe that these things will really happen one day," she said. She had heard someone criticize the theology of the *Left Behind* books, but could not remember what the criticism was.

These and other discussions implied that apocalyptic fiction had failed to intensify millenarian beliefs at KT: although it reminded worshippers that the End was coming, it acted as an agent of routinization, allowing them to encounter it from a safe distance. Paradoxically, however, some interviewees derived an apocalyptic message from secular products that were intended purely as entertainment. I was occasionally told that blockbusters such as *The Matrix* and *Independence Day* contained subliminal clues to the development of a New World Order: Hollywood was hinting at things in its screenplays that could not be revealed directly—which was also what Ravi Holy believed about Wilson's "Illuminatus" trilogy. As Michael Barkun observes, this way of approaching fictional material is very common on the cultural fringes of society. "The common sense distinctions between 'fact' and 'fiction' melt away in the conspiracist world," he writes. "More than that, they exchange places, so that in striking ways conspiracists often claim that what the world at large regards as fact is actually fiction, and what seems to be fiction is really fact" (2003: 29). In the 1970s and 1980s, the evangelist John Todd visited Pentecostal churches spreading the message that the *Star Wars* films represented a battle between Satanism and the false Christianity of the Illuminati (30); the apocalyptic believers of Waco and Heaven's Gate also interpreted films and television in this way (see Thompson 1999a). Yet the encounter between the entertainment industry and the cultic milieu was a two-way process: Hollywood during the 1990s was fascinated by conspiracy theories, many with millenarian overtones. Whether these ideas were taken seriously is another question. In Barkun's view, conspiracy-orientated motion pictures, television series, and books have increased the reach of "stigmatised knowledge"—but they may also have devalued the common currency of conspiracy theorists by placing it in everybody's hands (2003: 35). The same could be said of the appropriation of the Christian End Times narrative by popular culture. As I shall argue in the final chapter, the presentation of apocalyptic ideas in such an accessible form represents a lessening of subcultural deviance: it is consistent with theories of secularization and routinization.

Conclusion

When they were asked about the End Times, the vast majority of members of Kensington Temple—pastors as well as ordinary worshippers—failed to strike the confident, unambiguous note of the fundamentalist Christians interviewed by Nancy Tatom Ammerman (1987) and Charles Strozier (1994), for whom a sense of an imminent End appeared to supply the hidden dynamic of their Christian life. One could not say of Kensington Temple, as Ammerman did of the fundamentalist church in New England that she studied, that "the doctrine of the Rapture . . . produces a sense of impending doom that invades the sinner's consciousness" (157). Nor did most KT members "feel the dangers of the signs of the end acutely, and [alter] their lives accordingly" (Strozier 1994: 145). The most noticeable quality of eschatology at Kensington Temple was its ambivalence. Everyone appeared to believe (with differing degrees of intensity) that Jesus would return one day, and many people made the rhetorical concession that it might happen soon. But even those church members who employed the tools of popular prophecy to analyze the contours of the modern world did not say much about the imminence of the Second Coming. The survey results reinforce the message of the interviews: this was a church that, its traditions notwithstanding, assigned a relatively low priority to the End Times. Crucially, it did not provide a strong plausibility structure for millenarian ideas; and this lack of a social base was both a cause and a consequence of individual worshippers' unenthusiastic response to the subject. In any religious community, the cost of expressing belief in an apocalyptic event is increased if other members of the worshipping community are reluctant to do so. In the absence of formal rhetoric and informal conversations that confer plausibility on counter-intuitive millenarian ideas, the ordinary member's opinions will drift toward the secular consensus.

Why was there such a contrast with Ammerman's and Strozier's findings? One possible explanation is that this study concerns Pentecostalists, not fundamentalists (though some of Strozier's interviewees were Pentecostalists). The Pentecostal movement has an uneasy relationship with a prophecy subculture that it has borrowed from the conservative evangelical mainstream (Prosser 1999; Poloma 2001). Another factor is that Kensington Temple, despite its multi-ethnic congregation and American-influenced worship, is a British church, and prophecy belief has never played as prominent a role in evangelical churches in the British Isles as it has in the United States. It is worth examining the results of the KT questionnaire in the light of a survey of the pastors of Charismatic "new paradigm" congregations in America carried out in the early 1990s by the sociologist Donald Miller. More than a third of the pastors from the Vineyard movement (the least fundamentalist of the churches surveyed) thought that Jesus would return in their lifetimes (1997: 231). Meanwhile, only 12 percent of KT ministers expected the Second Coming within fifty years. Although the figures are not directly comparable, the contrast is striking. Given that the middle-class Charismatic Vineyard is traditionally *less* orientated toward the End Times than classic Pentecostalism, the difference could possibly be accounted for in terms of America's apocalyptic heritage.

Even so, I suspect that a through ethnographic study of the circulation of millenarian ideas in an American fundamentalist church would identify some of the patterns revealed by this chapter, such as a concentration on explanatory rather than predictive imagery and the use of a routinized rhetoric to take the sting out of the prospect of the end of the world. Above all, it might find that, in America as much as in Britain, the tension-inducing propositions of prophecy belief—irrespective of whether they carry the stamp of official theology—need some sort of management at the levels of both the group and the individual. The nature of this management is dictated partly by the special characteristics of millenarianism and the peculiarly intense cognitive dissonance created by the failure of prophecy. But, in the final analysis, many of the strategies for dealing with apocalyptic claims can be applied, *mutatis mutandis*, to other high-tension claims.

6

Millenarians

A small number—maybe four or five—of the forty people I interviewed at Kensington Temple communicated such an intense expectation of the Second Coming in their lifetimes that I felt it was possible to label them millenarians. I was not entirely comfortable ring-fencing them in this fashion, since the way they thought and behaved did not present that much of a contrast with their fellow worshippers; but it did seem worth asking how they came to possess an unusually heightened awareness of the coming apocalypse, and whether, in conjunction with the survey results, their testimonies threw light on the debate about the causes of millenarianism.

This chapter divides into three main sections. The first consists of a single case history: the story of Maureen, a woman in her early sixties who not only gave me a full account of how she was introduced to the concept of the End Times but also claimed to have received an apocalyptic message from Jesus. The second section uses the interview data to explore the social and psychological factors that might dispose a member of Kensington Temple to move beyond explanatory millenarianism to belief in an imminent *parousia*. The third section brings in the questionnaire data, treating responses to the question about the return of Christ as a dependent variable and examining the effect on them of sex, age, ethnicity, and participation in the life of the church.

The Making of a Millenarian: Maureen's Story

Maureen Archer was doing the washing up at home when she realized that Jesus was coming back soon:

> Two years ago I was at the sink, not in prayer, and the Lord said to
> me: "I'm coming soon, I'm coming soon." It was like a thought, not
> audible. It was like a butterfly alighting on my thoughts. I told one
> of my friends, Angela, and she said to me that the Lord had told her
> "This is the Last Hour." Now we know that with the Lord a thou-
> sand years is but a day, so if you work it out there's probably about
> 30 years left, if you divide 1,000 by 24.

It is a strange little story, from the perspective of the secular world, and also a
complicated one. The more we scrutinize Maureen's words, the more questions we need to ask. Did the revelation really come out of the blue, or was
Maureen—a part-time legal secretary living on her own in a distant suburb—
somehow prepared for it by previous religious experiences? If her friend Angela had not told her about the Last Hour, would she still have attempted to
work out when Jesus was coming back? How did she produce such a characteristic piece of millennial arithmetic, similar in many ways to the apocalyptic
calculations of the early Church? And what should we read into the fact that
she got her sums wrong? (1,000 divided by 24 is 41.7, not 30.)

Maureen's revelation may have taken her by surprise, but it was hardly
unprecedented: the history of apocalyptic thought is full of messages delivered
to ordinary people at a time when they least expected it. It was not even the
first time that an End Times revelation had been granted to a woman while
standing at a sink:

> Missionary Ms Young Shin Kim in New York area was not quite
> sure about His [Jesus'] return in 1991 and she prayed about it for
> any possible certain answer. . . . Later one morning when she was
> going to wash her face she saw the vivid number 10/28/92 in the
> water sink (Mission for the Coming Days c. 1990: 36).

This quotation is taken from a typewritten anthology of visions and testimonies
circulated by the Mission for the Coming Days, a South Korean church that
attracted international ridicule after prophesying that the Rapture would take
place in October 1992 (Thompson 1996: 239). The narratives of its members
are similar to Maureen's. They are not distinctively Korean, any more than
hers is distinctively English; nor is their form determined by the precise content of the theology. They belong in a long tradition, encompassing many religions and cultures, in which narratives of sudden enlightenment—not
necessarily apocalyptic in character—are given rhetorical power by the ordinariness of the setting: other Koreans were playing golf, walking in the street,
or driving their cars when they heard the message. But, however unexpected
these experiences, they did not strike members of the public at random. Most
of the visionaries were active evangelical Christians: missionaries, pastors, pastors' wives, or deacons. They were already connected to a plausibility structure
in which millenarian ideas were taken seriously.

Maureen is an unusually committed member of Kensington Temple.
When I met her, she was half way through a course at the Bible college; she

was more than twice the age of most of her fellow students, but as eager to learn as any of them. She witnessed to passers–by in the street and to people in shops:

> The Lord gave me the gift of evangelism—and I had been an intro-
> vert! The Lord has never stopped talking through me. Sometimes
> He will give me six or seven souls in a day. He gives me opportuni-
> ties wherever I go: I set foot outside my front door, and there it is.

Maureen was as close to the popular stereotype of the convert as anyone I met at Kensington Temple. The sudden awakening of her faith in middle age colored her whole life. As a young woman, she had been a practicing member of the Church of England, but she was more interested in parish social life than religious teachings. Then, when she was 48 years old and no longer a regular churchgoer, she had a dramatic experience:

> I was asleep in bed, the children were away at university, and I was
> awoken by this thunderous voice and a scripture from Isaiah which
> was very detrimental to me. When God's got his hand on a person
> he never lets you go, and I realized I was in a total mess. Then the
> Lord led me to a [Pentecostal] hall on the corner of the road where
> they were all dancing and singing. I've never seen such joy—I was
> used to a vicar and a pew. I realized I could have a relationship with
> Jesus and that I had to be baptized according to what the Bible says.
> Baptism in the Holy Spirit seals you into the Kingdom of God. He
> gives you the gifts like the fire on the disciples in the upper room.
> It's such a privilege to be on fire for God. I'll say it from the roof-
> tops: I'm willing to die for Jesus.

She discovered the teachings about the end of the world some months after becoming a born-again Christian, and then almost by accident:

> I first heard about the End Times when I went to a Jews for Jesus
> meeting at Westminster Central Hall. I wanted to learn about the
> Jews, and they gave me a little glimpse about the End Times and
> what would happen to the Jews, but it wasn't a big thing.

Messianic or Christian Jews form a small but valued part of the culture of conservative evangelicalism (see Cohn-Sherbok 2000). It is not surprising that Maureen should want to find out more about them, or that their meeting should deal with the subject of the End Times, a central preoccupation of many born-again Jews.[1] What is mildly surprising is that until then Maureen—a new believer very enthusiastic about her faith—had managed to attend a Pentecostal church without learning anything about apocalyptic doctrine. But that situation was rectified when she moved to Kensington Temple:

> When I came to this church they taught me about the End Times
> and the Book of Revelation. It was all Bible-based, sermons and

teaching. Revelation is a bit of a difficult book to comprehend without teaching: you have to find out from the Hebrew scriptures the
deep meaning of Revelation—beasts and horns that are nations, the
correct interpretation.

This teaching was delivered during study sessions in the church and at the
Bible college, where Maureen enrolled; she might not have encountered it if
she had merely attended Sunday services. The reference to *correct* interpretation implies that the lectures were attempting to discourage over-the-top speculation; but, as we have noted, Kensington Temple has an ambivalent relationship with the End Times subculture and acts as a channel for unofficial
prophecy material. Maureen is one of the people to whom such material was
channeled. In the early 1990s, she was in the audience when one of the evangelical world's most controversial prophecy authors spoke at KT's Mission to
London rallies:

> I've heard—what's his name?—Grant Jeffrey at Mission to London.
> He's a professor or something, a very, very clever man. He's studied
> scriptures and Revelation for years and written a lot of books. He
> gave us interpretations of Revelation for about seven years [i.e.,
> seven years running] and I received an interpretation of Revelation.
> He's very much a learned man, a doctor, I believe he's got a Ph.D.

As we have seen, Jeffrey's work comes very close to explicit date-setting: he
takes the view that, in these Last Days, the confusion surrounding the year of
the Lord's return will finally disappear; and, at one stage, he believed that 2000
was the most likely candidate (see Jeffrey 1988). Maureen learned the rudi-
ments of millennial arithmetic from him, and it is unlikely that it would have
occurred to her to work out the rough date of the apocalypse if she had not
been to his lectures.[2]

Maureen told me that she hoped and expected to live long enough to
witness Christ's return. But what difference did this make to her daily life? It
seemed to have had little effect on her actions, apart from possibly increasing
the urgency of her witness. She used a familiar rhetorical strategy to distance
herself from her prediction: "It's my own interpretation, and I don't live by
that," she told me, echoing Atkinson's insistence that his expectation of the
End during his lifetime was only an opinion. But apocalypticism did mold her
understanding of the world:

> I do believe I'm living in the time when Jesus will come again. I can
> see wickedness and degradation all around, a decline in respectabil-
> ity and the respectfulness of people, the rebelliousness of young-
> sters, the hopelessness of people. The general flaunting of sex on
> the trains last thing at night, I see it on the British Rail trains, peo-
> ple doing what they shouldn't. Even in broad daylight on a tram in
> Croydon. A couple of teenagers, the girl hovering over him, his
> hand up her privates, it almost made me sick.

By this stage in the interview, Maureen had retreated to the safer territory of explanatory millenarianism; it is interesting to note the similarity between her diagnosis and Anna Lomax's conviction that homosexuality was a sign of the End. Indeed, when I raised the subject of the survey questions, she talked more readily about conspiracy than she had about the Second Coming:

> It's not our place to speculate, so I just ticked that box—but if you asked me what I think, I would say [Jesus will come back] in fifty years. [And the single European currency?] I do think that! It gives that in the Bible; it says in Revelation there will be one world rule, no money exchanged at all. This is where the thing in the wrist will go if you go to the supermarket—and that's when we flee to the hills. I don't have a credit card. I like to pay cash or nothing; I never liked credit.

> Did you know about Procter & Gamble? The director was inter- viewed on American television late at night, but one Christian saw it. He said he gave all his profits to Satan's church. The interviewer said, don't you think you will lose trade? He said, there's not enough Christians to make an impact. On the actual packets of soap powder there was a goat's head. I think I saw it once, then they de- cided to take it off.

The Procter & Gamble story is one of the most persistent of recent urban myths;[3] Maureen did not question its veracity—but, significantly, it had no effect on her shopping habits. Far from scrupulously avoiding Procter & Gam- ble products in the supermarket, which one might expect her to do if she believed that the money would go to Satan, she was unable to name a single item the company manufactured and must have bought many of them un- awares. Once again, a professed belief failed to translate into social action. But this is very much of a piece with her attitude to apocalyptic calculation: having apparently discovered the key to the date of the Second Coming, which involved dividing 1,000 years by 24 to produce the length of the Last Hour, she did not even perform the calculation properly.

We might conclude from this that Maureen's millenarianism was essen- tially rhetorical: the act of expressing certain ideas was the culmination, not the beginning, of her engagement with apocalypticism. Even so, the sequence of events that led her to the point of articulating those ideas is representative of important social processes, such as the mastering of an unfamiliar culture, negotiation with fellow believers, and ideological work. There may have been no single cause of Maureen's belief that Jesus would return to earth in about thirty years; but that does not mean that the search for factors that predisposed her to reach this conclusion is pointless. On the contrary: Maureen's case history is instructive because it displays evidence of three factors that appeared to incline other members of the congregation toward millenarianism: conver- sion, subcultural immersion, and individual psychology.

Factors Influencing Millenarian Belief

1. Conversion

Maureen's expressions of belief in the Second Coming were informed by, and difficult to distinguish from, "the zeal of the convert." This figure of speech is rooted in a real sociological phenomenon: many scholars have observed that converts tend to hold to a group's doctrines more firmly than those who have grown up with them.[4] For some new believers, the fact that certain teachings are considered extreme or odd by the outside world adds to their appeal. Converts are often drawn to the controversial teachings of the movements they join; indeed, a high proportion of converts in a group helps to maintain a state of tension with the surrounding environment. By the same token, the birth of a second generation of believers often has the effect of lowering tension within a group, of knocking the rough edges off difficult teachings (Stark and Bainbridge 1985: 152; Bainbridge 1997: 81). Rodney Stark and William Sims Bainbridge, in their book *The Future of Religion* (1985), argued that the difference between converts and later generations can be explained by the statistical phenomenon of regression to the mean: the unusual personality traits or social circumstances that lead converts to join a group—and perhaps to respond to its more distinctive teachings, such as millenarianism—are unlikely to be passed on in the same degree to their children (154). Bryan Wilson has made a similar point, arguing that "there is certainly a difference between those who are converted to a revolutionist sect, and those who accept adventist teachings at their mother's knee" (1966: 207).

If millenarianism is the sort of high-tension concept that appeals to converts, then one might expect to find that, in groups with apocalyptic teachings, converts are more likely to be millenarians than non-converts. The evidence for this hypothesis is sketchy, but one ethnographic study can be cited in support of it. Adam Jacob Szubin (2000), who conducted fieldwork among the Lubavitch sect of Hasidic Jews, found that converts to the movement from non-orthodox or secular Jewish backgrounds were more likely than those born in the movement to be millenarians—that is, to believe that the sect's leader, Rabbi Menachem Schneerson, who died in 1994, was in fact the Messiah, who would soon return from the dead (or, alternatively, never really died and was just about to show himself again). Szubin puts forward three complementary explanations for this. The first is that millenarianism prolongs the excitement of conversion. He quotes one convert or *ba'al teshuveh* (literally, "penitent") as saying: "Coming into religion is an eye-opening experience which contradicts everything that you previously knew to be possible. So you are more open to a belief which also contradicts everything you know to be possible." A non-convert told Szubin: "It's like giving a child a candy. If you give a child one candy, he will want a second candy"—the first candy representing the transformative experience of becoming newly religious and the second the belief that God will imminently put an end to all worldly travails. Szubin adds:

Ba'alei teshuvah, particularly recent immigrants, are more prone to
see the world in extremes of right and wrong, especially in the spiritual sphere. They tend to be drawn towards activist ideologies which
promise revolutionary upheavals rather than gradual evolutions.
Thus, the doctrine of millenarianism, which predicts a sudden if not
violent usurpation of human chaos by divine order, would particularly appeal to *ba'alei teshuvah*. (2000: 223)

Szubin's second explanation has to do with time. The converts, most of whom
grew up as secular Jews, had not acquired their religion through historical
transmission; their faith was orientated toward their own generation and the
short-term future. Millenarianism "complements this perception, depicting the
present generation as the most spiritually significant generation in time"
(2000: 225). The third explanation presents millenarianism as a way of overcoming marginalization. Converts were eagerly sought by Lubavitch, but, once
they become members of the sect, found themselves second-class citizens. The
promise of millennial transformation rendered this irrelevant: "What could be
more welcome news to the *ba'al teshuvah* . . . who has barely lived among Has-
idim, than to hear that the central requirement of his faith is to publicise his
belief in the Messiah's imminent coming?" (2000: 234).

Needless to say, it is not possible to draw an exact parallel between Lubav-
itchers and members of Kensington Temple—not least because, in a tradition
such as Pentecostalism, in which everyone is supposed to go through a conversion experience, the distinction between those born inside and outside the
faith is not especially important. But my interviews did suggest that a millenarian worldview could be a natural accompaniment to the cosmology of the
recent convert. Maureen was an example of this. The impact of apocalyptic
teachings on her was magnified by the fact that she was encountering them
for the first time; that made them fresh and exciting. The same could be said
of another interviewee who can be classified as a millenarian: Tim Bradshaw,
a 26-year-old white South African studying at the Bible college.

Tim's ideas about the end of the world were closely tied to a life-changing
conversion experience; indeed, they formed part of his testimony. He first became a Christian in South Africa at the age of 20:

I only got saved because I was scared of dying. Some new Christians had said to me: 'Where are you going when you die?' I stopped
smoking, swearing, became part of a closed community in an Assemblies of God church.

Then one of his Christian friends showed him a video about the End Times,
a subject that was entirely new to him:

I was a new Christian and the video made me really scared. It said
we'll be taken up and forced to have a mark on our arm, and all the
early signs of that are here already. That was when I first began to

think, my gosh, the Lord is coming back! . . . My friends said my
mother [who was not a Christian] would die and I was scared of the
persecution that was coming and hoped that we would be raptured
before it. Then I backslid. I pushed those thoughts away. I was very
scared. I didn't want to think about the End Times, or about the
Church and God. I got back into cocaine, ecstasy, smoking grass,
and some of my best mates are still into that.

In other words, the prospect of the end of the world contributed to Tim's
decision to abandon his new faith: it was simply too painful to think about.
But the subject also played a part in bringing him back to Christ after he moved
to London:

After backsliding for three years, I was out drinking with my mates,
my girlfriend was staying at our house, and I passed a guy preaching in Leicester Square. He looked at me and said "God is talking to
you." I walked past him, and I think that was when he said, "Christ
is coming back, the Lord is returning soon." And that hit me, and I
thought, oh my gosh, it's that Jesus Christ word again. I said to my
mates, I don't want to go drinking, I just want to go home. The guy
said, Christ is coming back: that's what got my attention, I couldn't
get it out of my mind. That night I went back home, broke off with
my girlfriend and said, what we're doing is wrong and I don't love
you. And I recommitted my life a week later.

He now looks forward to the apocalypse and thinks the Church should make
teaching about it a higher priority:

Very recently I've begun to realize that the awareness of the End
Time truth in the Church is not that great. We hear about prosperity
and holiness and personal sanctification, and people know there is
an End coming—but the message that we need to be prepared and
ready is not getting across. I think there needs to be a great teaching
on the fact that Christ is coming, and that it's imminent although
we don't know when, and we need to be ready for that time. Christians generally shy away from persecution, and it's a teaching which
is not embraced fully in the Western Church.

The fact that Maureen and Tim were classic converts *and* millenarians
does not prove anything in itself, of course; but the interviews also yielded
evidence to suggest that "cradle" Pentecostalists or evangelicals who had been
introduced to the subject of the End Times as children found it difficult to
sustain an interest in the subject in later life. Keith Dickinson, whose parents
told him that Jesus would return in the 1980s, was left with a strong distrust
of predictive millenarianism (though he subscribed to conspiracy theories).
Several African church members told me they remembered learning about the
prophecies of Daniel and Revelation in the schoolroom and not taking them

very seriously. For them, descriptions of horned beasts and apocalyptic battles were no more immediate than any other images in the Bible; they were passed on routinely as part of a conventional Pentecostal education, much as images of the Sacred Heart might be in a Catholic school.

Only one "cradle" Pentecostal said that she had lived in expectation of the Second Coming ever since her childhood. This was Silvia, a Brazilian Bible college student in her early twenties:

> I was born in a Christian family, Assemblies of God, and since I
> was little I heard about eschatology, and it was a subject that inter-
> ested me but it was more like fear or a scare. When I started to read
> the Bible and got to the Apocalypse, I was frightened. I remember
> being nine years old and wanting to say to everybody "Jesus is com-
> ing" through my fear of the End. But then later I realized that we
> cannot have fear of what is happening, because we can have confi-
> dence that we will not be confused or lost, because God is not a God
> of confusion and he will step by step reveal what is going on. We
> are almost there.

Two points are worth noting here. First, Silvia's parents were first-generation converts in a Catholic society where Pentecostals often live in relatively closed communities (D. Martin 1990: 285). The apocalyptic faith to which she was introduced was far less routinized than that of Keith's parents, and this may help explain its lasting impact on her.[5] Second, although Silvia's expectation of the Second Coming may have been sustained, it changed its quality over time. Her fear dissipated as she learned to put a more positive and cheerful construction on the teaching; in effect, she adjusted it in a way that lowered its subcultural deviance, though without diminishing her expectation that she would live to see the return of the Lord.

Clearly, familiarity with apocalyptic doctrines can play a part in reducing their impact; one of the reasons that recent converts find it relatively easy to embrace millenarianism is that, unlike some non-converts, they have not had time to grow bored of the rhetoric of prophecy belief, nor experienced the endless awkward adjustments of apocalyptic predictions in response to the flow of disconfirming events. Converts of long standing, in contrast, can find themselves subject to the same routinizing pressures as non-converts. Larry Grant discovered just how difficult it was to sustain millenarian beliefs during his two decades as a Jehovah's Witness. He joined the Watch Tower movement at the age of 19 in 1975, a year that many Witnesses believed would usher in the Millennium (Schmalz 2000; Singelenberg 2000):

> I was baptized in '75. I remember, having only been associated with
> the Witnesses for about six months, telling a friend in the park—I
> look back on this with horror—that we were not going to be around
> in two years' time and she had better become a Jehovah's Witness.
> How does one imbibe that certainty after such a short period?

Although Grant rose rapidly in the organization, he was increasingly troubled by the inflexibility of its prophetic eschatology:

> The Witnesses went completely over the top in prophetic interpreta-
> tion. It's as if you compared the Christian to a ship in a storm,
> needing an anchor. I can understand that, but when you start ex-
> plaining the precise significance of every stitch on the sails, then the
> mind can't handle all the detail and you lose it. The Witnesses went
> to that sort of extreme—crazy, crazy speculation in which they didn't
> just go for the big picture, but every single detail of a verse has to
> mean something.

The more Grant thought about the Witnesses' intricate eschatology, the more he was struck by its inconsistencies.

Similarly, several Kensington Temple members said they had gradually turned away from the less intense prophecy teachings of evangelical Christianity: they had gone through a period of expecting Christ's return at any time, but had then "matured" or "grown up." Adam Knight told me: "As a young Christian [a teenager] I thought about the Second Coming, I thought: wow, this is new to me. But as I have grown in character it doesn't come into my mind at all. That's not to say I'm not interested, but I don't base my life around trying to find out about the End Times."

Pedr Beckley, now an Anglican priest in his forties, went through a similar experience with conspiracy belief. He joined Kensington Temple as a student in the 1970s after developing an interest in popular eschatology: "I first went to KT because it was acceptable to talk about that sort of stuff. But after about three months common sense clicked in and I said to myself, some of this is absurd: Hal Lindsey is bizarre and just false."

These testimonies imply that the novelty of apocalyptic teachings is sometimes crucial to their acceptance by converts; adapting Szubin's ideas, we can hypothesize that the challenge of mastering a new religious culture often leads the convert to express belief in an imminent Second Coming, perhaps as a way of compensating for previous unfamiliarity with apocalyptic ideas. But, once the novelty wears off, the convert may find that a mixture of common sense rationality and the weakness of local plausibility structures pulls him or her in the direction of routinization.

2. Subcultural Immersion

As a member of Kensington Temple, Grant found it easy to push apocalyptic theology to the back of his mind; all he had to do was stay out of the way of certain preachers, books, and broadcasts. Worshippers who were "into the End Times" did the opposite: they sought them out. Will Napier told me that the millenarian beliefs of people in the KT congregation could usually be sourced to various ministries or authors:

If you speak to someone who has a particularly strong belief in the imminent return of Christ, you will find that in order to support that interest they have read a lot of the popular prophecy literature or watch videotapes on the subject. Or they might have picked it up from one of the ministries—Morris Cerullo, for example. You get a lot of Africans who come to KT on Sundays, but on Tuesday or Fridays they might be going to some other ministry which is much more based on the idea of Jesus coming back soon.

Napier was keen to stress that the material used to support the apocalyptic worldview originated outside Kensington Temple. But, as we have seen, the church often acted as a conduit for such material, and most of the millenarians and conspiracy believers I interviewed derived at least some of their ideas from books or tapes purchased through KT. To cite an example: one morning when I was in the bookshop, a Nigerian prophecy enthusiast called Francis dropped by to see whether any new titles by Barry Smith had arrived. He told me that he had been introduced to Smith's work by his brother, who worked for Morris Cerullo. Whenever Francis bought a new videotape by Smith he would show it to his KT prayer group in South London, thus helping to extend the circulation of apocalyptic ideas in the church network. A bookshop assistant commented: "People who buy Barry Smith will often buy nothing else in a particular transaction. I suppose they might buy other End Times stuff as well."

The crucial question is whether, in addition to sustaining millenarian belief, the church environment was responsible for creating it. Let us look again at Maureen's story, and the social processes that surrounded her personal revelation. The words of Jesus might have appeared to come out of nowhere; but she was prepared for them, in the sense that she was already thoroughly immersed in the subculture of Pentecostalism and had a passing knowledge of prophecy belief. We cannot say that this immersion directly *caused* her revelation, since that would involve pronouncing on its authenticity.[6] What we can say is that by the time it happened she had acquired specialist knowledge that enabled her to make sense of, and to interpret further, the words "I am coming soon." This is what the anthropologist T. M. Luhrmann calls interpretative drift—"the slow, often unacknowledged shift in someone's manner of interpreting events as they become involved with a particular activity" (1989: 312). First came Maureen's visit to Jews for Jesus that introduced her to the End Times; then the KT sermons and lectures that fleshed out this concept with biblical references; then the talks by Jeffrey that legitimized a do-it-yourself approach to dating the Second Coming. Moreover, Maureen's personal ties to Pentecostalism continued to shape her understanding of the revelation after it happened. She consulted her friend Angela, a fellow member of a KT satellite church, and it was only after Angela told her about the Last Hour that it occurred to her to work out how much time was left before the apocalypse.

This tells us something important about immersion in a subculture: that it is a process whose outcome is determined partly by accidental social encounters. As the symbolic interactionist school of sociology points out, ideas are often hard to divorce from the people who express them or act on them; "communications are at the very centre of action, and must form the basis of a true perspective on social events" (Skidmore 1979: 192). If Maureen had not talked to Angela, her understanding of the message from Jesus would have been different. As it was, the meaning of the words "I'm coming soon" was, in effect, *negotiated* by these two ladies over coffee. It is easy to forget that, although millenarianism envisages the end of the world as we know it, its prophecies are issued in and through everyday life. (The historian Garry Wills made this point in his book about religion and American politics, *Under God*, by describing how the Republican candidate and End Times author Pat Robertson drank steaming cups of tea and coffee while formulating his theories; the chapter is entitled "Coffee-cup Apocalypse" [1990: 172–73].) By following the story of Maureen's gradual accumulation of social ties to Pentecostalism, we can join the dots, as it were, between the housewife who knew very little about the Bible, let alone the apocalypse, and the millennial believer who suspected that Jesus would return in her lifetime. The more we know about her engagement with the subculture, the less surprising her eventual position becomes. We can see that she moved in a succession of small steps, none of them particularly remarkable. As the sociologist Howard Becker puts it:

> The pathway that leads to any event can be seen as a succession of events that are contingent on each other. . . . You might envision it as a tree diagram in which, instead of the probability of getting to a particular end point getting smaller the farther you get from the starting point, the probability of reaching point X increases the nearer you get to it (1998: 33).

Becker offers an example from the work of James Driscoll (1971) that is roughly comparable with Maureen's odyssey, though she would no doubt find the analogy distasteful: the decision by a young man to have a sex-change operation. Driscoll demonstrated that the final result was "the end of a long line of prior decisions, each of which . . . did not seem so bizarre in itself." These decisions involve moving in new company (that of cross-dressing homosexuals) and learning new behavior (dressing in women's clothes). In Becker's words, "each step is intellectually and emotionally understandable to people who themselves are nothing like this young man, once the circumstances are made intelligible to them" (1998: 27).

But, just as there was nothing inevitable about this outcome, so the experience of immersion in a Pentecostal environment need not (and usually does not) lead to millenarianism. Interaction with fellow worshippers may move the believer in another direction right from the beginning; alternatively, he or she may develop a temporary belief in the imminent Second Coming but then gradually move away from this conviction in response to disconfirming events and discouraging conversations. In short, it is dangerous to generalize about the effect of subcultural immersion on the individual. The Pentecostal environment in particular is not nearly "closed" enough for high-tension beliefs to flourish unquestioned. The testing of hypotheses can lead individuals toward a reduction of subcultural deviance that reproduces, on a small scale, the routinization that takes place in organizations over decades. Or, like Maureen, they can move in the other direction. Either way, decisions are not made in a vacuum: millenarianism is created and sustained by social interaction.

3. Individual Psychology

Having recognized the role of historical accident and subjective rationality in the development of Maureen's beliefs, we need to add an important qualification. It is obviously not the case that everyone passing through the same force field of encounters and influences would develop roughly the same opinions as Maureen. Although her millenarian rhetoric was heavily influenced by socially acquired religious ideas, it was also an expression of her own unusual personality. The consensus among those of my informants who knew her was that she was essentially a loveable eccentric. This verdict did not surprise me: the first time I met her she expressed her enthusiasm for Jesus by jumping up and down like a little girl in a playground, which did indeed look strange coming from a woman of retirement age in a dark skirt and sensible shoes. One pastor described Maureen as "the sort of person who gets things out of proportion." It was widely assumed—as it was in the case of Linda Symondson's conspiracy theories—that her unorthodox ideas reflected a gullible and unsophisticated outlook on life. Indeed, several people assured me that a preoccupation with the End Times was one of the marks of such a personality. Paul Wallis, an Assemblies of God minister with ties to Kensington Temple, said he associated millenarianism with two sorts of people: "new Christians," who might well lose their fascination with the subject as they grew spiritually; and "time wasters"—"people who always have some urgent thing to occupy the time of their minister. Often it's End Times stuff. They say, 'This is something you should be aware of, pastor, you should watch this video and show it in church.' "

The notion that millenarians are psychologically distinctive is well established in the scholarly literature, though there is less of a consensus as to whether this can be ascribed to nature or nurture. Norman Cohn's *Pursuit of the Millennium* ([1957] 1993) paints a picture of mass psychological disturbance caused by extraordinary circumstances, of ordinary people radicalized beyond recognition by social dislocation and the arguments of demagogues. It is an explanation that works well for the revolutionary millenarians he describes; but, as we noted in the Introduction, it was never intended to account for the routinized rhetoric of stable religious movements with an apocalyptic tradition. A much closer parallel with Kensington Temple's millenarians is provided by Strozier's interviews with Christian apocalyptic believers in New York. He found that all of them "described their narratives as broken in some basic way. . . . Their stories were discontinuous and full of trauma; faith healed them." He also suggested that the mythical transformation of the future offered by millennialism played a part in that healing (1994: 43–46). These observations are similar to those made in the scholarly literature about religious converts, who since the pioneering work of William James ([1902] 1985) have often been portrayed as people responding to intense mental stress (see Lofland and Stark 1965; Rambo 1993); and also about fundamentalist Christians, who have been accused of manifesting a range of undesirable psychological traits (Savage 2002). The problem with these ideas, as we have already noted, is that they are difficult to demonstrate empirically: not only is stress virtually universal, but it is hard to record people's mental states *before* they assume the beliefs in question. The psychologist Sara Savage argues that there is "little or no hard evidence of significant mental disturbance for individuals before conversion relative to the general population" (2000: 11). She has also drawn attention to the lack of evidence demonstrating that Christian fundamentalists are psychologically unusual, despite many attempts to produce it (2002). Any systematic attempt to discover psychological factors that predispose people to millenarian belief is likely to run into the same methodological difficulties.

It is, in any case, impossible to generalize from my own tiny sample of millenarians; but I was still left with a subjective impression that, in at least three cases, the subject's apocalyptic hopes and fears resonated with other distinctive personality traits. Thus, Maureen's message from Jesus seemed to reflect a more general receptivity to unorthodox ideas, and perhaps an unwillingness to scrutinize them. Tim's impatience with other Christians for not looking forward to the Second Coming fitted comfortably into his all-or-nothing approach to faith: it was as if millenarian theology, which had earlier encapsulated his own fears about the future, now stood for the sort of total commitment to Christ that more faint-hearted believers could not achieve. The third case is that of Sarah Kim, a young Korean woman whom I met at a Sunday afternoon service at the Tabernacle. She was the only interviewee whose experience seemed to bear out Strozier's argument that the promise of millennial transformation can help to heal individual suffering (1994: 43–46). Sarah's conversion to Christianity was opposed by her family. Her spiritual crisis began in childhood and lasted for years:

> I had trouble with spirits since I was 12 and it was getting worse. A lot of people thought I was a witch doctor; I used to see ghosts and hear them, I couldn't go to bed without a light. I saw millions of ghosts and demons.

Then Jesus appeared to her: "I saw this vision; something white, I can't explain, it was so splendid, so bright, like a garment; I couldn't see his face. He opened his arms. It was so powerful, I fell over—but it was like falling into clouds." She was certain that Jesus would come back soon, though she was less sure about the mechanics of it: "He will come back, as the Bible says. One day people will wake up and lots of people will have gone. I believe that I will go up to the sky with Jesus—or maybe we will disappear and be transported to heaven." What is striking about Sarah's testimony is the consonance between her conversion story and her vision of the apocalypse. Being taken up into the sky with Jesus would complete the salvific experience that began when the radiant stranger opened his arms to her; where once she fell metaphorically into the clouds, she would now soar physically into the heavens. There is strong sense here of the easing of tension.

But if Maureen, Tim, and Sarah were psychologically unusual in some respects, their thought processes were usually unremarkable. Maureen may have had the rare experience of receiving a message from Jesus about his Second Coming; but Pentecostal Christians frequently claim that Jesus talks to them about other subjects, and these messages usually take the low-key form that Maureen's did, of words intruding on everyday thoughts rather than the hearing of voices. Furthermore, Maureen did not feel that the message required her to do anything beyond telling a few fellow worshippers about it, any more than she changed her purchasing habits after deciding that Procter & Gamble was Satanic. She did not take practical steps, such as stockpiling goods in preparation for the Tribulation or boycotting certain goods, that would have significantly increased the degree of tension between herself and society. Her millenarian and conspiracy beliefs remained confined to the level of rhetoric— unlike her commitment to evangelization, which did lead her to tension-inducing actions, such as witnessing to strangers in shops. As for Tim, it was interesting to discover that, like Will Napier, he sometimes found it difficult to sustain his sense of living in the Last Days. In a second interview, he told me that "I don't spend much time thinking about the end of the age, although Jesus talks about it. . . . Even with my mates, it's not too much in our thinking, although it should be: we should be living our lives for Christ's return." Sarah, meanwhile, spoke confidently about her belief that she would be raptured, but also criticized the Korean evangelist Paul Yonggi Cho for flirting with date-setting, which she thought was "dangerous." She described "attempts to put barcodes into human beings" as one of the signs of the End, but when I showed her the barcode on my notebook and asked her if that was Satanic, she laughed and said, "No, actually."

In short, however intense their beliefs, the Kensington Temple millenarians managed apocalyptic ideas in much the same way as other church members did. They drew a line between rhetoric and the actions that might spring from it; they distinguished between acceptable and unacceptable ideas emanating from the prophecy subculture; and at least one of them struggled to keep the "end of the age" uppermost in his mind.

Survey Data

Until now, we have avoided speculating about the effect of the standard demographic variables—sex, age, ethnicity, education, and so on—on millenarianism. My interview sample was far too small and not sufficiently random to permit such generalizations; it was not until the questionnaire data became available in 2000 that it was possible to look for demographic patterns that might throw light on the formation of millenarian belief. The interview and survey data, different in so many respects, had one thing in common: they were measuring *expressions* of millenarian belief. The questionnaire asked respondents whether they expected the return of Jesus within ten years, fifty years, or whether it was not their place to speculate. As we have seen, 8 percent chose the first option, 9 percent the second, and 73 percent the third. (For the sake of convenience, I am going to call these respondents *ten-year millenarians, fifty-year millenarians,* and *non-speculators.*) Willingness to assent to the first or second of these options is not a very profound measure of millenarianism, and it does not correlate neatly with the expressions of belief recorded in the interview data: Maureen, for example, was a non-speculator. On the other hand, the responses do constitute a form of apocalyptic rhetoric; questionnaires covering this area are extremely rare—the only other example known to me is Miller's survey of American evangelical pastors (1997)—and there has never previously been an opportunity to subject one to extensive multivariate analysis. And, as I hope to demonstrate, there is a limited but significant degree of overlap between the interview and survey data. The following analysis is broken down into sections based on independent variables: sex, age, ethnicity, education, religious upbringing, and participation in ministry; it also examines the correlation between responses to the statement about the Second Coming and those dealing with conspiracy and Creation.

Sex

In his interviews with American fundamentalists and Pentecostalists, Charles Strozier found that the women were "generally more gentle in understanding the apocalyptic" and they "deflected end time violence onto more immediate human concerns like personal salvation and morality" (1994: 124–29). My own interviews did not pick up this difference: men and women were equally keen to emphasize the primacy of personal salvation, irrespective of whether they also attached importance to the apocalyptic narrative. The survey questions could not address subtle points of interpretation, but they did ask people to list their spiritual priorities: the results show almost no difference between the sexes, with a mere 2 percent of both men and women making the End Times their top spiritual priority, and a similar distribution of preferences overall. Nine percent of men and 8 percent of women were ten-year millenarians, though the gap was wider for fifty-year millenarians: 11 percent of men and 8 percent of women. This suggests that men at Kensington Temple might have slightly stronger millenarian impulses than women, though it would be foolish to build a theory around such small variations in the data.

Age

Early in my research, John Starr, a senior staff member, had told me that the greatest enthusiasm for the Second Coming was among young members of the church. Another pastor suggested that church members might look for the return of Christ at roughly the time they might expect to die. One of the reasons for offering respondents a choice between ten- and fifty-year deadlines for the return of Christ was to see if the old would gravitate naturally to the first and the young to the second. Table 6.1 shows how different age groups responded to the question about the return of Jesus. The findings bear out Starr's observation—up to a point. Young people were no readier than anyone else to predict the return of Jesus within the decade, but they *were* more likely to opt for fifty-year millenarianism: 11 percent of people aged 20–35 chose this option, as opposed to 5 percent of people over 65. But the oldest respondents were no keener than any other age group on the idea that Jesus would return within ten years. So, despite the relative popularity of fifty-year millenarianism among young adults, the figures offer no real support for the notion that millenarians in general imagine Christ coming back at around the time they might expect to die.

Ethnicity

Table 6.2 shows a breakdown of responses according to the ethnic background of KT members. The most striking detail here is the contrast between Africans, the largest group in the church, and Caucasians, who dominate its leadership. Only 5 percent of Africans expected Jesus to appear within ten years, compared to 13 percent of Caucasians; 6 percent of Africans expected him within fifty years, compared to 16 percent of Caucasians. This was an unexpected result: Colin Dye told me before the questionnaire was administered that he thought African worshippers would be more apocalyptic than others because "they have been exposed to more of that sort of material" back home in Africa. How can we explain it? Further analysis of the figures does not reveal a significant intervening variable; the answer may lie in the special qualities of African Pentecostalism.

Pentecostalism spread to Africa within a year of the Azusa Street revival in Los Angeles in 1907. Large independent churches sprang up which, as in

TABLE 6.1. Responses of age groups to the question: "When do you think it likely that Jesus Christ will return? (a) within 10 years; (b) within 50 years; (c) not our place to speculate"

	Born after 1979 (%)	Born 1965–79 (%)	Born 1950–64 (%)	Born 1935–49 (%)	Born pre 1935 (%)	Whole church (%)
10-year return	8	9	7	9	7	8
50-year return	9	11	7	8	5	9
Not our place to speculate	72	72	75	73	77	73
No response	10	8	11	10	11	10
Total	100	100	100	100	100	100
	(n = 149)	(n = 1377)	(n = 909)	(n = 299)	(n = 82)	(n = 2973)

Note: Chi square test: $p = 0.954$; reject null hypothesis ($p < 0.05$): no.

Figures for people who did not give their date of birth are not shown. "No response" indicates no box ticked.

TABLE 6.2. Responses of ethnic groups to the question about the return of Jesus

	Caribbean (%)	Chinese (%)	African (%)	Caucasian (%)	Asian (%)	Whole church (%)
10-year return	11	9	5	13	10	8
50-year return	7	8	6	16	16	9
Not our place to speculate	74	82	79	62	61	73
No response	9	2	10	8	13	10
Total	100	100	100	100	100	100
	(n = 307)	(n = 104)	(n = 1,415)	(n = 519)	(n = 180)	(n = 2,973)

Note: Chi square test: $p = 0.000$; reject null hypothesis ($p < 0.05$): yes.

Some smaller ethnic groups and people who did not state their ethnicity are not shown but included in the Chi-square calculation.

Latin America and the Far East, reinterpreted animist traditions of territorial spirits, magical healing, and ancestor worship in light of Christian teaching about the action of the Holy Spirit (Cox 1994: 243–62). Sometimes their spiritual message was anti-colonial; occasionally it was messianic, as in the case of the Congolese preacher Simon Kimbangu, whose followers cast him in the role of black messiah during his long imprisonment by the Belgian authorities (Wilson [1973] 1975: 367–73). But African Pentecostalism has rarely been millenarian. According to Paul Gifford, Africa has been exposed to dispensationalism; its chief tenets are widely known, and when Barry Smith undertook a tour of Uganda "his assumptions and methods came as no surprise to his listeners." But the message was, and is, largely ignored:

> The popular Christianity [Smith] encountered was personalised, not
> cosmic. It was not concerned with a renewed order or any "new Je-
> rusalem," but with a job, a husband, a child, a car, an education, a
> visa to the West. It was about succeeding in this realm, through
> faith or (increasingly, at least in West Africa) through faith and deliv-
> erance from Satanic blockages. . . . On the face of it, it might be
> thought that there are millennial images that could resonate power-
> fully with African's truly apocalyptic plight (Rev. 6:1–8), or (at least
> in the optimistic interlude of 1989–93) the imminent dethroning of
> evil powers and the dawning of a new order. But these images have
> not been widely developed. (1998: 339–40)

If anything, millenarianism is losing ground in Africa. Rather than employing prophecy belief to help them cope with the turmoil of the last decade, African Pentecostalists have turned to two other American spiritual imports: the Faith movement, with its promises of victory over poverty and sickness, and the church growth movement, with its emphasis on the dynamic potential of megachurches (Gifford 1998: 41–42). Both movements emphasize this-worldly success over the promise of the millennial kingdom. The fastest-growing Pentecostal churches in Africa today are no longer the older independent denominations that celebrated traditional culture; they are new churches linked to large congregations in the West—such as Kensington Temple—whose patronage helps their members to acquire Western-style prosperity. In Nigeria and Ghana, the focus of these churches is relentlessly international. Part of their appeal is that they offer a route out of poverty through overseas mission contacts: going abroad to study or work is seen as a special mark of God's favor (Gifford 1998: 92).

The typical West African Pentecostalist living in Britain is far removed from the stereotype of the illiterate peasant compensated for material deprivation by promises of apocalyptic transformation. Stephen Hunt, in his study of Jesus House, a West London congregation of the (overwhelmingly Nigerian) Redeemed Christian Church of God, found that membership of the church was "solidly middle class." Nearly 60 percent had degrees or professional qualifications. The church's teaching reflected the emphasis on personal purity and hard work that characterizes the new wave of Pentecostal churches in Nigeria. The promise of financial prosperity was held out, but not in a crude way; instead, members were given help with controlling expenditure and managing debt (2000: 11). Much the same could be said of the West African fellowships of Kensington Temple. Many members are engineers, doctors, lawyers, and academics, and there is a similar stress on professional success and financial probity. For example, 46 percent of African survey respondents had read or listened to tapes by the "health and wealth" evangelist Kenneth Hagin. This is a higher percentage than for any other ethnic group and seems to confirm the observations of KT bookshop staff that African customers are particularly interested in financial and practical subjects. Seen in this light, it is hardly surprising that Africans were less likely than anyone else to speculate about the return of Christ: there were more pressing things to worry about.

Education

Moving on to education, we are confronted for the first time by what looks like a coherent pattern, one suggesting that less qualified people were more likely to expect Jesus to come back soon. Fourteen percent of respondents with no formal qualifications were ten-year millenarians, compared to 9 percent of those with only school qualifications, 8 percent of current students, and 7 percent of graduates. This brings to mind an observation of Strozier's: that, while the working-class people he interviewed imagined an apocalypse in the near future, middle-class believers tended to postpone the End well beyond their anticipated lifetimes (1994: 116). The KT survey did not provide a measure of social class (which is an elusive concept, anyway, in a congregation made up of worshippers from such widely differing societies). But, if we assume that social class increases with educational level, then these findings are broadly consistent with Strozier's theory.

The picture becomes more complicated, however, when we look at how different groups felt about the return of Jesus within fifty years. Eight percent of those with no qualifications were 50-year millenarians, compared to 8 per-

TABLE 6.3. Educational levels of respondents to question about the return of Jesus

	No qualification	School	Student	Degree	Other	Total
10-year return	9	39	12	36	4	100
(%)						(n = 247)
50-year return	5	31	16	45	4	100
(%)						(n = 264)
Not our place to speculate	5	34	14	43	4	100
(%)						(n = 2,169)
No response	8	38	10	34	10	100
(%)						(n = 293)
Whole church	5	35	14	42	5	100
(%)						(n = 2,973)

Note: Chi square test: p = 0.219; reject null hypothesis (p < 0.05): no.

"Other" includes people who did not state an educational level or wrote in an alternative description (e.g., professional qualification).

cent of those with only school qualifications, 8 percent of current students, and 10 percent of graduates. In other words, the neat inverse correlation between expectation of the Lord's return and educational level has disappeared: although still overwhelmingly reluctant to speculate, graduates were more likely than any other group to plump for the return of Jesus within fifty years. The impression that the latter is in some respects an "educated" option is confirmed when we turn the figures round and look at the educational levels of ten-year millenarians, fifty-year millenarians, and non-speculators: 45 percent of fifty-year millenarians had degrees, as opposed to 36 percent of ten-year millenarians and 43 percent of non-speculators.

Religious Upbringing

The theory derived from the interview data that millenarianism can be the product of a conversion experience receives partial support from the survey. Although the whole notion of converts is a difficult one in a conversionist religion such as Pentecostalism, in which it is possible, even commonplace, to be born into the tradition *and* be dramatically born again, the survey did distinguish between respondents brought up in Pentecostal or evangelical households and those who came from other traditions or none. In the church as a whole, religious upbringing had no effect on the way respondents answered the question about Jesus' return. But it did make a difference for *white* church members, albeit not a dramatic one: 74 percent of Caucasian ten-year millenarians were brought up outside the evangelical or Pentecostal tradition, compared to a figure of 65 percent for Caucasians in general. The explanation may lie in the status of Pentecostalism in Britain, Australia, New Zealand, and South Africa, the countries of origin of most white KT members. It does not represent the natural religious allegiance of middle-class white people in these societies; those who convert to it have crossed a significant cultural barrier.

Szubin's observations may be relevant here: the challenge of mastering a new religious culture could lead some converts to express belief in an imminent Second Coming as a way of compensating for previous unfamiliarity with apocalyptic ideas.

Participation in Ministry

So far, we have been looking at demographic variables such as sex, ethnicity, age, and education whose effect on millennial belief, however profound, is likely to be indirect. Now we move on to independent variables that signify religious commitment and immersion in a religious subculture. The effect of such factors on belief, while not always easy to measure, is likely to be much more direct, since it is often the subculture that communicated the belief in the first place and now provides its plausibility structure.

According to Peter Berger, ideas which the wider society regards as deviant often require a sectarian structure to sustain them ([1967] 1969: 45–51), and the applicability of this to millenarianism is obvious. In modern society, anyone who attempts to date the return of Jesus is regarded as eccentric—it is "a mark of marginality, a step beyond the boundaries of public discourse" (O'Leary 1994: 132). We might therefore expect those who did so in the questionnaire to be deeply committed to the group or the subculture that legitimates such an activity. We might even hypothesize that, since society regards ten-year millenarianism as more deviant than fifty-year millenarianism and non-speculation as not deviant at all, we should expect ten-year millenarians to be the group most immersed in Pentecostalism, non-speculators the least immersed, and fifty-year millenarians somewhere in between.

One way of testing this hypothesis is by finding out how people actively involved in the Kensington Temple community—the 469 "ministers" who include office staff, musicians, stewards, part-time preachers, street evangelists, and the church leadership—answered the question about the Second Coming. Table 6.4 sets out the responses of ministers and non-ministers.

There is no real support here for the idea that ten-year millenarians must by virtue of the intensity of their apocalyptic expectation be the most immersed in the Pentecostal subculture. Ministers, like everyone else, were overwhelmingly non-speculators: we can discount the one percentage point separating them from other church members in their support for ten-year millenarianism, and although they were more likely to favor the fifty-year option, the gap is not very large. The picture changes, however, when we distinguish between men and women ministers. For women, being in the ministry made little difference to responses on this question: levels of belief were very close to the average for women generally. Men in ministry, on the other hand, were slightly less likely to be ten-year millenarians than men outside the ministry but considerably more likely to be fifty-year millenarians: 16 percent of them chose this option, compared to 10 percent of the other men. So the 5 percent gap between ministers' and non-ministers' levels of belief in fifty-year millenarianism was produced almost entirely by men.

TABLE 6.4. Responses of ministers and non-ministers to the question about the return of Jesus

	Ministers (%)	Non-ministers (%)	Whole church (%)
10-year return	9	8	8
50-year return	12	8	9
Not our place to speculate	72	73	73
No response	8	10	10
Total	100	100	100
	(n = 469)	(n = 2,502)	(n = 2,973)

Note: Chi square test: p = 0.691; reject null hypothesis (p < 0.05): no.

If we narrow our sample even further, we find that 38 percent of Caucasian male ministers were fifty-year millenarians—the highest level we have encountered so far, and nearly four times the percentage of African male ministers who believed the same thing. Admittedly, by this stage the numbers are small: we are talking about 8 out of 21 Caucasians and 7 out of 54 Africans. The significance of the statistic lies in the fact that white male ministers occupy most of the important positions of authority at Kensington Temple. The 21 male Caucasian ministers included some of Colin Dye's closest associates, though the senior pastor himself did not complete the questionnaire. At least one of Dye's inner circle opted for fifty-year millenarianism; in addition, Andrew Kenworthy, former principal of the Bible college, told me that he would have made the same choice if he had been in London when the questionnaire was administered. But *not one* male Caucasian in KT ministry opted for the return of Jesus within ten years.

A similar picture emerges if we choose another indicator of commitment: past or present membership of the International Bible Institute of London. Once again, we find an above-average level of support for fifty-year millenarianism (14 percent) but not for the ten-year variety (8 percent). In this respect, Bible college students and alumni were like young church members, graduate church members, and men in ministry: they slightly favored the longer-term millenarian option but not the more imminent one.

Conspiracy Belief

Judged by the interviews, conspiracy theories often functioned as an alternative to, or a milder version of, doomsday millenarianism. The survey, which included statements about the euro and supermarket barcodes, gives us a clearer idea of how the two forms of millenarianism related to each other. We have already seen that 38 percent of all respondents agreed that the single currency was a sign of the Antichrist, while 27 percent thought barcodes were Satanic. If we treat conspiracy belief as an independent variable, we suddenly find significant gaps opening up between people who speculated about the Second Coming and those who chose not to. As table 6.5 shows, 60 percent of ten-

TABLE 6.5. How church members with different views about the return of Jesus responded to the statement "The move towards a single European Currency is a sign of the Antichrist"

	Agree	Disagree	Neither	No response	Total
10-year return (%)	60	9	26	5	100 (n = 247)
50-year return (%)	53	11	34	3	100 (n = 264)
Not our place to speculate (%)	35	15	45	5	100 (n = 2,169)
No response (%)	23	9	34	33	100 (n = 293)
Whole church (%)	38	14	41	7	100 (n = 2,973)

Note: Chi square test: p = 0.000; reject null hypothesis (p < 0.05): yes.

"Neither" signifies "neither agree nor disagree."

year millenarians assented to the statement about the euro, as opposed to 53 percent of fifty-year millenarians and 35 percent of non-speculators. Thirty-three percent of ten-year millenarians agreed with the barcodes statement, compared to 28 percent of fifty-year millenarians and 27 percent of non-speculators, a gentler gradient than for the euro statement, but in the same direction. Looking at the figures the other way round, conspiracy believers were only slightly more likely to be ten- or fifty-year millenarians—further evidence that, within the church, predictive millenarianism was generally considered to be a more deviant option than conspiracy theory.

The survey also asked respondents to indicate which popular prophecy authors and broadcasters they had encountered, and here the evidence is unambiguous. Forty percent of ten-year millenarians had read or listened to Barry Smith, as opposed to 29 percent of fifty-year millenarians and 22 percent of non-speculators. There is clear support here for the proposition that prophecy material plays a crucial role in making apocalyptic beliefs plausible.

Creationism

Alongside the conspiracy statements in the questionnaire was the following assertion: "The world was created in seven 24-hour days, just like the Bible says." Sixty percent of respondents agreed with this statement; presumably the total would have been higher if the question had not taken the hard-line Creationist position that the days of creation were exactly as long as normal days (see Pennock 1999). (The Kensington Temple position on the subject was summed up by John Starr as follows: "People might not call themselves Creationists, but if you were to use the word 'evolution' it wouldn't go down very well.") The real point of putting this statement in the questionnaire was to see whether belief in the return of Christ corresponded to Creationism, which is often regarded as an indicator of "fundamentalism" (i.e., adherence to a strictly literal interpretation of Scripture). The interview data suggested that there might be such a correlation: not only did several prophecy believers stress their rejection of evolution, but the two interviewees who were most skeptical about the End Times, Will Napier and Jim Saunders, also made it clear that they did not reject the theory of evolution. In the event, the survey results were broadly compatible with this hypothesis: 67 percent of ten-year millenarians, 64 percent of fifty-year millenarians, and 62 percent of non-speculators agreed with the Creation statement.[7] Again, note the pattern in which ten-year millenarians were most likely to agree with another "high-tension" statement of belief, non-speculators were least likely to agree with it, and fifty-year millenarians were somewhere in the middle. The survey also showed that people who assented to either of the two conspiracy statements were slightly more likely to be Creationists. On closer inspection, however, respondents who said they *disagreed* with the euro and barcodes statements were also more likely to be Creationists, a finding that underlines the dangers of generalizing about the fundamentalist mindset.

Conclusion

To what extent do the survey results reinforce the tentative findings of the interview data? My impression after talking to a small number of millenarians was that conversion, subcultural immersion, and individual psychology were important factors in molding their apocalyptic worldview. The questionnaire could tell us little about the psychology of the people who answered it, but it did produce a small but intriguing piece of evidence to support the conversion thesis: white church members born outside the Pentecostal or evangelical community were more likely to express belief in the imminent return of Christ than those brought up in it.

The evidence pointing to the significance of subcultural immersion was more substantial. Consumption of apocalyptic books and videotapes, for example, was a much better clue to the likelihood of someone holding millenarian beliefs than any demographic factors; acceptance of apocalyptic conspiracy theories was also an important clue. One might almost say that, rather than being produced by deep-seated social predispositions, millenarianism at Kensington Temple was "caused" by other expressions of millenarianism. As this study has stressed again and again, the apocalyptic argument is constantly threatened by disconfirmation, and there is evidence to suggest that some church members, having initially been won over by it, eventually found it less persuasive. For those who remained committed to an apocalyptic framework, however, it appears that being "into the End Times" was, like being born again, "an ongoing existential project, not a state acquired once for all" (Corten and Marshall-Fratani 2001: 7). It required frequent infusions of new analysis—in the shape of Barry Smith's latest book or other products of the prophecy subculture. On the whole, the most intense millenarians, who expected the Second

Coming within the decade, were the most likely to assent to the statements about the single currency and barcodes; those who expected Jesus within fifty years were less likely to agree, but still more so than non-speculators. The same pattern is observable in responses to the Creationist statement. On this evidence, predictive millenarianism may be an indicator of an all-round commitment to high-tension doctrines; but it is important to bear in mind that, at Kensington Temple at any rate, this commitment was primarily rhetorical, so we must be careful not to portray these people as dangerous fanatics.

One of the most striking survey findings was that 38 percent of white male ministers—the pool from which the church leadership emerges—were fifty-year millenarians. This finding, coupled with slightly raised levels of support for this option among graduates, young people, and Bible college alumni, raises an interesting possibility. In chapter 2, we discussed the conflict between, on the one hand, deviant, high-tension or "strict" doctrines that enact a high price from believers but also produce commensurate rewards, and, on the other hand, a process of accommodation or routinization that reduces uncomfortable tension with society but also eats away at cultural distinctiveness (see Iannaccone 1997; Swenson 1999; Stark and Finke 2000). Different groups will reach their own decisions about the optimum level of strictness—and, *within* groups, people will reach different points of balance. The survey suggests that, for certain enthusiastic young people, Bible college alumni and university graduates, and especially for those who were eligible to become leaders, expectation of Christ's return within fifty years offered just the right degree of tension with the surrounding environment. The risk it entailed was a small one: for, while people who predict the Second Coming within a decade are quite likely to be humiliated in front of those to whom they made the prediction, the cost of being proved wrong about the fifty-year option will, by definition, be deferred for half a century. For some respondents, the fifty- and ten-year alternatives represented the difference between a full-blooded (but sensibly cautious) commitment to the doctrine of the Second Coming and the foolhardiness associated with "prophecy nuts." It came as no surprise to discover that Bruce Atkinson, whose lectures on the End Times trod such a fine line between boldness and caution, was a fifty-year millenarian.

7

The Year 2000

This chapter examines the special importance that Western society, Pentecostal Christianity, and Kensington Temple attached to the dawn of the third Christian millennium. It begins with the historical background, showing how 2000 gradually became the focus of secular and religious visions of the future. But, as the 1990s unfolded, it became clear that much of the anticipation of 2000 was unrealistic; various schemes associated with it had to be abandoned. Born-again Christians, in particular, had nurtured ambitions to "win the world for Christ" by the end of the millennium; these became progressively more modest as the deadline approached.

Kensington Temple provides a case study in this trajectory of disappointment. For years, Colin Dye's Restorationist imagery had encouraged church members to believe that a last great wave of the Holy Spirit would coincide with the dawn of the calendar millennium. The church drew up a plan to plant 2,000 church groups in London by the end of the year 2000. This scheme was abandoned in 1999, at which point only 25 percent of the target had been reached; the next year, KT was forced to move out of its Tabernacle headquarters. This experience had some of the qualities of an apocalyptic drama: a build-up of expectation was followed by disappointment and, on the part of the authorities, some frantic ideological work. The chapter also examines worshippers' private interpretations of 2000, which were characterized by the ambiguity that marked their eschatological beliefs. In October 1999, over a quarter of census respondents agreed that the year 2000 marked "the beginning of the End." Yet nearly everyone I spoke to dismissed the media's inflated expectations of 2000, and many interviewees insisted that it was "just a date."

The Calendar Millennium: Secular and Sacred Perspectives

Historical Background

The measurement of time is inextricably bound up with religious belief and the pragmatic ordering of everyday affairs. In primitive societies and early civilizations, the calendar symbolized the integration of sacred and secular spheres. "Almost everywhere in the long development of human societies, priests were the first specialists in active timing," wrote Norbert Elias (1993: 53). In societies as different as imperial Babylon and the Mayan city-states of Central America, religious professionals regulated the calendar in accordance with the sacred significance of numbers themselves; yet their expertise had implications for the most prosaic areas of social activity. In the ancient Middle East and in Eastern religions, concepts of time were essentially cyclical, inspired by the rhythm of the seasons; but the Hebrews gradually evolved an understanding of history that was both cyclical and linear. Their cycle of six days of activity to one day of rest was expanded into the concept of jubilee, in which every 50th year—following seven "weeks" of seven years each—was the moment for bringing human affairs into line with sacred time, by remitting debts and freeing slaves (Campion 1994: 149). Jewish culture, borrowing from Zoroastrianism, also developed the literary genre of apocalypse, in which the sacred timeline came to an abrupt and miraculous end (Schmithals [1973] 1975; Cohn 1993). It bequeathed this to Christianity, along with the notion that the whole of history could be encompassed in a Great Week consisting of six 1,000-year days and a 1,000-year Sabbath. This structure was adopted by many early Christian thinkers, who identified the Millennium of the Book of Revelation as the last of the seven "days," and it is still influential in conservative evangelical Christianity: books proposing versions of it were on sale at Kensington Temple in the 1990s.

Any attempt to fit human history into a teleological structure raises questions about when, precisely, the End will be reached. Typically, apocalyptic believers perform calculations involving the calendar of their own society. In early medieval Christianity, calculators used the Jewish-inspired Anno Mundi (AM) system, which stretched back to a Creation a few thousand years in the past. As Richard Landes (1988) has demonstrated, the Western Church twice abandoned AM counts as they inched toward the highly charged year 6000, dawn of the millennial Sabbath: the first time, the Church pushed forward the date of Creation by a few centuries, initiating a new AM count; and, when this moved toward 6000, they switched to the little-known Anno Domini (AD) calendar, which was dated from Christ's birth and had reached only its eighth century. We can infer from this that religious leaders were already worried by the potential of calendar anniversaries to inflame apocalyptic expectations. In these two cases, the expectations were pegged to a specific theory; but we must also take into account the possibility that "round number" dates are powerful enough in themselves to create the sort of anticipation that worries the authorities.

There is insufficient evidence for us to reach a firm conclusion about apocalyptic expectation and the year A.D. 1000. Although the concept of a thousand bears a heavy symbolic weight in Zoroastrian, Hebrew, and Greek literature (Miller 1987: 13), and although the Millennium derived from the Book of Revelation lasts for 1,000 years, there was no strong tradition in the early Church that Christ would return in the year 1000. Nineteenth-century accounts of lords and peasants kneeling together at the dawn of the new millennium, waiting in terror for Doomsday, are romantic fabrications: the consensus among modern historians is that 1000 was a year like any other, and that most people in Christendom would not even have been aware of its arrival (Schwartz 1990; Thompson 1996). However, according to Landes (1997), this insistence on 1000 as a non-event is based on too literal a reading of the evidence: he suggests that contemporary reports of miracles, peace rallies, and pilgrimages point to intense apocalyptic expectation clustered around the anniversaries of Christ's birth and resurrection in 1000 and 1033. He concludes that, while it was in the interests of the ecclesiastical authorities to play down these anniversaries, their appeal would have proved irresistible to a population that was constantly being reminded of the imminence of the Last Judgment. The question is unlikely to be settled. We should note, however, that the romantic legend of the year 1000 survived its twentieth-century debunking: it appeared in unreconstructed form in several popular books published in the 1990s,[1] and it was quite common to hear people say that the society-wide panic that gripped Christendom in the 990s would be reproduced in the run-up to 2000.

Occasionally it was also claimed that the eschatological tensions tended to rise at the end of centuries as well as millennia; there is, however, very little evidence for this. The concept of centuries did not fully evolve until after the Reformation (Schwartz 1990), and the first mass end-of-century celebrations, in 1899–1900, were no more apocalyptic in tone than the average New Year's Eve. According to the historian Arndt Brendecke (1998), the century has never been an important eschatological category in Christian culture. He argues that "centenarianism," a secular celebration of society's achievements, has a completely different social function from millenarianism, an expression of religious hopes and fears, which might be inspired by calendrical round numbers but is by no means dependent on it. But the year 2000 was in a special category. With its approach, secular centenarians and some millenarians found their gaze fixed on the same horizon, because the date that the secular world was preparing to celebrate possessed an apocalyptic significance of its own—indeed, a more substantial one than the year 1000. This significance was partly derived from a particular application of the concept of the Great Week. Hugh Latimer, the Protestant Bishop of Oxford executed during the reign of Queen Mary, wrote in 1552: "The world was ordained to endure, as all learned men affirm, 6,000 years. Now of that number there be passed 5,552 years, so that there is no more left but 448" (quoted in Jeffrey [1988] 1997: 178). Latimer was working on the assumption that the world was created in 4000 B.C., which would place the Second Coming in 2000. A century later, Archbishop Ussher dated the Creation to 4004 B.C., a calculation accepted by the Church of England until the nineteenth century; this modest adjustment produced a Second Coming (or, in some versions, the Rapture) in 1996. One of the attractions of this model, irrespective of the precise date of Creation, was its symmetry. It could be divided into three 2,000-year segments: from the Creation to Moses, from Moses to Jesus, and from Jesus to the End.

By the late nineteenth century, such anticipation had largely been superseded by secular visions of 2000. These did not envisage the dawn of Christ's kingdom, but they were scarcely less apocalyptic in their desire to associate the calendar millennium with an ideal society. As Hillel Schwartz notes, the year 2000 became "the site of Edward Bellamy's co-operative utopia, William Morris's socialist revolution, Winnifred H Cooley's feminist welfare state, Friedrich E Blitz's universally deployed nature cure, and Edward Berwick's vegetarian farmer's paradise" (1990: 269). In the twentieth century, 2000 formed the backdrop to innumerable science-fiction fantasies and optimistic or pessimistic predictions: the millennial year was variously associated with galactic warfare, ecological devastation, and the ending of world poverty. These visions combined millenarian and centenarian impulses, and, together with the reappearance of explicitly apocalyptic ideas about the return of Christ in or close to 2000, ensured that the anniversary itself would create a uniquely poignant mixture of expectations.

Trajectory of Disappointment

In this section I suggest that the secular and sacred experiences of 2000 followed a similar trajectory of expectation and disappointment. The crucial point is one that most commentators failed to grasp at the time: that the hopes for the anniversary, apocalyptic and non-apocalyptic, peaked some years *before* it happened, and had already been scaled down by the end of the 1990s.

One scholar who did understand this was Michael Erard, then a Ph.D. candidate in the English department of the University of Texas at Austin, who in 1997 published an essay entitled "Millennium, Texas" based on interviews with residents of the small town of Alpine. He wrote:

> The year 2000 is now close, and conceivably so. That fact . . . influences how people think and talk about the end of the millennium, and it is the reason why, as 2000 approaches, the various fevers and fervours will cool, not intensify. . . . In all cases [i.e., for all his interviewees], 2000, while still a chronological and historical limit, no longer constituted "the future" for people living in 1995, because it was too close, too visible, to wear well with their hopes and fears. The year 2000, around the corner, falls inside the range of plans for individual lives. It is just another kind of tomorrow, in its more quotidian sense as a unit of the absolutely unknowable. (1997: 281)

Erard's observation is reminiscent of the distinction we considered in chapter 2 between two types of future: the long term (*le futur*) and the short term (*l'avenir*). For centuries, the year 2000 was synonymous with the exotic, far-off future; indeed, the notion of 2000 as a utopian or dystopic landscape survived into the 1990s—the Hollywood film *Strange Days* (1995), set in 1999, depicted a society transformed by bizarre technology. But, inevitably, the increasing proximity of the deadline brought 2000 closer to the reality of everyday life. In both secular and religious spheres, we might say that excitement reached a peak when the millennium was distant enough to retain its futuristic aura but near enough to be imagined in plausible detail. There was, of course, no single moment when this was true for everyone: as early as the late 1960s, an influential volume of essays edited by the sociologist Daniel Bell (1968) argued that the world of the year 2000 had in crucial respects already arrived. But, for many commentators, the late 1980s and early 1990s were years in which predictions about life at 2000 could be simultaneously exciting and believable. To offer just one example, a book called *Achieving Peace by the Year 2000*, by a senior official of the International Monetary Fund, argued in 1988 that international treaties, UN peacekeepers, and sanctions could achieve a war-free world by the magic deadline (Huddleston [1988] 1992). The fall of the Berlin Wall in 1989 seemed to justify such optimism; and the new mood was given intellectual expression by the publication in 1989 of Francis Fukuyama's *The End of History*, which suggested that ideological conflicts had become obsolete. By 1992–93, however, recession and ethnic cleansing made such optimism seem misplaced, and Fukuyama's essay was already being held up as an example of failed prophecy.

It would be wrong to suggest that the expectations of people in the West rose during the 1980s and then fell uniformly in the next decade. There was talk of *fin de siècle* anxiety in the early 1990s, but most of that could be attributed to the economic downturn; significantly, in the boom years that followed there were fewer media references to Pre-Millennial Tension, despite the increasing closeness of the deadline. On the other hand, memories of the recession were fresh enough to rule out a mood of sustained exhilaration. For most people, December 31, 1999 was essentially New Year's Eve on a grander scale than usual, an enjoyable experience perhaps tinged with regret that a long-anticipated moment had come and gone in an instant. The real trajectory of disappointment tended to affect leaders and institutions who had been seduced by the deadline into rhetorical excess and unrealistic aims.

In Britain, the clearest illustration of this dynamic was the Millennium Dome at Greenwich, the most ambitious millennial project undertaken anywhere. This giant fabric-covered structure, the size of fifteen Albert Halls, was intended to surpass the Great Exhibition and the Festival of Britain. It would be not just a showcase of technology, but a glimpse of the future and a voyage of discovery into the human mind and body. Early suggestions for its contents included a hollow humanoid figure bigger than the Statue of Liberty; a replica of a British seaside resort, complete with sun, sand, and fish and chips; and Dreamscape, a boat journey "floating along a river of dreams through environments intended to surprise, excite and entertain, setting minds free in a way that only dreams can achieve" (Thompson 1999a: 328). By 1998, however, it was already clear that the project was running out of time, money, and ideas; there was no consensus about what the Dome was for, or what should go in it, until it was too late to build anything sufficiently impressive to appeal to jaded late twentieth century tastes. In effect, the project's organizers had made a series of charismatic claims that they were unable to substantiate. The Dome's "zones," when they opened in January 2000, were far more cheaply constructed than, say, the Disney World attractions familiar to millions of tourists; visitor numbers remained depressingly low all year.

One thing the Millennium Dome revealed was the weak and divided state of British Christianity. The "Spirit Zone" section of the exhibition was visibly the result of an unhappy compromise between Christians and other faiths. An account of its genesis by Stephen Lynas, Millennium Officer for Churches Together in England (2001), underlines the wider context of the Churches' failure to come to terms with the anniversary itself: a plan to distribute candles to the entire population of England, to be lit just before midnight on New Year's Eve, was beset by logistical difficulties and never caught the popular imagination. At the root of the problem was the fact that, while the mainstream Churches were vaguely conscious of "owning" the year 2000, they could not agree on how to assert their ownership. Moreover, their own expectations of the year 2000, never great, had collapsed long before the Dome was built: various programs of evangelization launched in the early 1990s had produced negligible results. I had a number of conversations with Anglican churchmen about the year 2000 during the late 1990s and was struck by how vigorously they distanced themselves from it. They were eager to stress the artificiality of the anniversary; one diocesan bishop said he had every intention of being asleep in bed by the time midnight struck. Spokesmen for the Roman Catholic Church in England and Wales sounded much the same note and seemed uneasy with the Pope's quasi-apocalyptic insistence that the Great Jubilee of 2000 was an important milestone in the life of the Church (see John Paul II 1996).

Evangelical Responses

In contrast, for many born-again Christians the year 2000 was a genuinely thrilling prospect when they first began to think about it in the late 1980s. It might be useful to imagine a spectrum of evangelical attitudes to the approaching anniversary. At the non-apocalyptic end were skeptics for whom 2000 was a purely human construction—roughly the position of liberal churchmen. At the apocalyptic end were those who, subscribing to the 6,000-year thesis, expected the Rapture or the physical return of Christ in or around 2000. In the absence of survey data, it is not possible to say where the average church member was located on this spectrum; but most pastors and evangelists who pronounced on the subject were ranged somewhere in the middle. While rejecting date-setting prophecies, they did not see the calendar millennium as meaningless. On the contrary, they initially treated 2000 as a deadline for extravagant schemes to win the world for Christ. These schemes were implicitly apocalyptic in character, since they were based in the "Great Commission" of

Matthew's Gospel: "The Gospel will be preached throughout the whole world, as a testimony to the nations; and then the end will come" (Matt. 24: 14). Reaching out to the unchurched therefore assumed the awesome significance of an act that would help bring on the Second Coming. But, as the impossible scale of the task sank in, the Great Commission rhetoric was toned down. Between 1988 and 2000, the center of evangelical gravity moved along the spectrum to a point where most preachers attached little importance to the calendar millennium; even opportunistic date-setters abandoned their predictions in good time.

The number of evangelical predictions of the end of the world in 2000 was always very small, though one might not have gathered this from the media coverage. The first edition of Grant Jeffrey's *Armageddon: Appointment with Destiny* (1988) remains the fullest statement by a well-known evangelist of the arguments for the return of Christ in or around the millennial year. In chapter 5 of this study we encountered one of Jeffrey's calculations, involving the Book of Hosea; in fact, there were seven charts in his book, each employing different arithmetic and biblical verses, but all arriving at a probable date of 2000 for the reappearance of the Messiah. Jeffrey cited the early Christian writer Lactantius in support of a 6,000-year span of human history, aligning the start of the fifth millennium with the birth of Christ (173). He did, however, allow himself some leeway, by stressing that "these are only interpretations and not prophetic revelations" (194)—and, interestingly, he took advantage of this room for maneuver when he revised the book nine years later.

In the 1997 edition of *Armageddon: Appointment with Destiny*, all the time charts had disappeared. Lactantius and Latimer were quoted, but Jeffrey's own calculations no longer converged on the year 2000. Instead, he wrote: "It is unfortunate, but perhaps providential, that changes in the calendar make it impossible to calculate with precision when the two thousand year period [between the First and Second Comings] will end, except to note that it must occur in our generation" (1997: 223). It is not hard to account for this change of emphasis. By 1997 the claim that Jesus would return in 2000 invited swift disconfirmation: indeed, from a Darbyite perspective it was already disproved, since there was no time left for the seven-year Tribulation. Therefore, when he revised his book, Jeffrey retreated from predictive millenarianism into less costly explanatory rhetoric: the new edition offered an expanded list of signs of the times, including the fall of the Soviet Union and the Middle East peace process. He may also have taken into account the generally reduced appetite for date-setting in fundamentalist circles since the embarrassment of Whisenant's *88 Reasons Why the Rapture Will Be in 1988*, which had been read by millions. Arguably, predictive millenarianism in general reached a peak in the late 1980s, not only on the born-again Christian fringes but in the New Age movement: the Harmonic Convergence of 1987, which was supposed to usher in a new global consciousness, was identified by some enthusiasts as the Second Coming of the Christ.[2]

In more cautious evangelical circles, meanwhile, missionary fervor also peaked in the late 1980s and early 1990s and dissipated as prophecies failed or were abandoned as unrealistic. In 1989, 300 senior Pentecostal and Charismatic pastors and church growth experts met in Singapore to plan A.D. 2000, a global initiative to "reach," if not to convert, the world's 1.3 billion non-Christians by the end of the twentieth century. There was a precedent for this idea, though not an encouraging one. In 1888 Protestant missionaries had drawn up a scheme to evangelize the world by 1900 that ran out of steam long before the deadline was reached (Gary 1989: 35). The leaders of A.D. 2000 were determined not to suffer the same fate, but their project was marred by theological differences and the difficulty of agreeing on goals. There was some talk of doubling the numerical size of Christianity by the year 2000 (Braun 1992: 153) and of finally penetrating that least fertile of mission fields, the Muslim world. But many participants were convinced from the outset that such aims were unrealistic, and the movement's eventual mission statement, "A Church for Every People and the Gospel for Every Person by the Year 2000," was deliberately vague: although the small print talked about planting a church in every unreached "ethno-linguistic group," the precise meaning of this term was unclear (Thompson 1996: 157).

Reading between the lines of the A.D. 2000 literature, it is obvious that some of the movement's leaders did expect the return of Christ to happen in the early years of the twenty-first century. Ralph Winter, founder of the U.S. Centre for World Evangelism, admitted in 1995 that, although the return of Christ was "off limits" in official A.D. 2000 documents, many supporters were discussing it behind the scenes—and rightly so, in his opinion. He criticized those pastors who ignored the eschatological dimension of the project. The day of Christ's return would be a surprise, he wrote; but "an expectant mother is not completely in the dark about the time of the birth, since there are many signs leading up to it" (Winter 1995). As the anniversary approached, however, such arguments were heard less and less frequently. By the late 1990s, the A.D. 2000 movement had fragmented. Evangelical Christians moved from specific goals toward more general, disconfirmation-proof prophecies of revival. The dawn of the long-anticipated year was an anti-climax: the rallies and marches held at Pentecost 2000 were far more modest events than originally envisaged.

In Britain, there was a distinct sense of unfulfilled hopes. In the late 1980s, British Charismatics had fallen under the spell of Restorationist prophets who had forecast an outbreak of revival in the British Isles (Smail, Walker, and Wright 1995). There was embarrassment when this did not happen, and an evangelistic drive by classic Pentecostals intended to win 250,000 souls for Christ reached only 10 percent of its target (Thompson 1996: 165). The mass swooning and uncontrollable laughter of the Toronto Blessing in 1994–95 revived eschatological hopes: "We could be on the brink of the greatest revival in the history of the Church, the revival that precedes the return of Christ," said one leading Baptist (141). Some commentators suggested that the Blessing could be an outbreak of end-of-millennium madness; but, if so, the fever was over well before the actual millennium, leaving few traces in the form of conversions (Bruce 2002: 173). Pentecostals were not surprised: they felt that the Toronto Blessing was a Charismatic phenomenon, and, although it did have some influence on them, they preferred to take their cue from Pentecostal revival movements in America (Poloma 1999)—which, in turn, fizzled out.

By the late 1990s, few British evangelicals or Pentecostals reposed any great hopes in the year 2000. Nor was there much sense of the Pre-Millennial Tension that the media talked up at the time. There was some concern about Y2K, the "Millennium Bug" that, left untreated, might cause computers to crash on the dot of midnight on December 31, 1999. In America, the Y2K panic, fuelled by books with titles such as *Time Bomb 2000*, filtered through to the fundamentalist community via the survivalist fringe: prophecy conferences in 1997 and 1998 presented the sudden unraveling of global networks as God's judgment on a blasphemous world (Thompson 1999a: 336–7). By 1999, however, most churches had satisfied themselves that the crisis would be of modest proportions, thanks to preventative measures, and this was certainly the case in Britain, which had never really bought into the panic.

In July 2000 I interviewed the Rev. Paul Wallis, the Assemblies of God pastor quoted in the previous chapter. He made an interesting comment: "In the years running up to 2000, I didn't come across a single Christian who was terribly interested in the date. But I did come across a lot of non-believers who were slightly anxious and asked me what Christianity taught about the year 2000." The obvious explanation for this lack of interest is that Wallis's Christian friends knew something that the non-Christians did not: that, although freelance prophets have speculated about it, orthodox Christianity has never taught anything much about the year 2000. Another possible explanation is that born-again Christians had already considered, and been forced to reject, an apocalyptic interpretation of the calendar change. As I have tried to show, evangelical hopes for the anniversary were progressively scaled down in tandem with a number of high-profile secular ambitions, as the date drifted from *le futur* to *l'avenir*. The experience of Kensington Temple offers an illustration of this sequence.

The Millennium at Kensington Temple

The Public Dimension: 2,000 by 2000

By the time I began my fieldwork, in 1997–98, members of the Kensington Temple ministry team were stressing that 2000 had no intrinsic significance, though they conceded that some Christians took an apocalyptic view of it. Andrew Kenworthy and Will Napier were introduced to me as the church spokesmen who could answer my questions on the subject. Kenworthy told me:

> There are lots of cross-currents in our church and in Pentecostalism generally. For some people, the year 2000 comes right in the middle of the Tribulation, worked out from 4004 BC and the Trib beginning in 1996.[3] Someone might be simultaneously affiliated to KT and be a follower of Morris Cerullo, who doesn't talk much about what will

happen after 2000. . . . But for us, the date is a good target. Human psychology shows that if people have a finite amount of time they work harder.

Napier was positively scathing about the alignment of the year 2000 with the Second Coming. He said it was the sort of idea that appealed to "people who are weird or superspiritual or what the Americans call flaky," though he added: "Personally, I have never heard anyone I know seriously propose that Jesus will come back because it's the year 2000." We should bear in mind that Kenworthy and Napier were hardly typical Elim pastors. They were both former Anglicans who, even after joining KT, were uncomfortable with what they saw as the more eccentric claims of their adopted tradition, especially in relation to the End Times. Under normal circumstances, they found it difficult to distinguish between legitimate and illegitimate prophecy rhetoric. But the identification of 2000 with Doomsday was an obviously silly notion that could be safely dismissed: it served as a useful marker of theological deviance—and deviant people.

Bruce Atkinson, in contrast, felt more at home in the world of prophecy belief than either Kenworthy or Napier. But, despite this, he was determined not to be associated with date-setting. In his "End Times Truths" lectures of 1997, he suggested that millennial fever was the Devil's way of diverting attention from the imminent Second Coming, by reducing the subject to a joke:

> The Devil doesn't want this message to be preached, because it's sooner than it ever was. He wants us to stay in slumber, to say: "Oh yes, millennial fever. Of course, when it gets to the year 2000, if any church is going to start talking about Jesus' return, it's going to be that old Kensington Temple. And if any of those preachers get millennial fever, it's going to be Bruce Atkinson. Let's face it, he's an extremist, and he's using this millennial thing to push a doctrine. He'll be naming that date next." No, I won't be naming the date next. But I'm telling you, Jesus is coming, it's sooner than you think.

In fact, as I gradually came to realize, the basic approach of Kensington Temple toward 2000 was both pragmatic and, despite protestations to the contrary, implicitly apocalyptic. Colin Dye's pronouncements during the 1990s left his listeners in no doubt that the building of the London City Church network was in some sense a preparation for the return of Christ to claim his bride. At the heart of this enterprise lay a plan to found 2,000 LCC groups—churches, ministries, and fellowships—by the end of the year 2000. Therefore, although the calendar millennium possessed no intrinsic sacred significance, it stimulated apocalyptic hopes, just as it did for the A.D. 2000 movement (with which KT was loosely associated). Dye outlined the vision in a book entitled *It's Time to Grow: Kick-Starting a Church into Growth*:

Our vision at Kensington Temple is to become a fully functioning city church by the end of the decade—and to do this we need to be a network of 2,000 churches and groups. We believe that God gave us this vision through a mixture of prayer, discussion, realistic assessment of our situation, and an inspired off-the-cuff comment by a trusted and highly respected leader. It is a big vision, but it is realistic. Why, if each of our churches planted one new church a year, we would have 3,000 churches by the end of the year 2000! (1997b: 83)

By this stage, Dye was describing himself as "apostolic leader" of the London City Church, and his senior staff as "apostolic overseers." Kensington Temple was living through "the most exciting period yet in church history," he wrote; Jesus was re-establishing a biblical church, a "mature bride" for whom he would return (1997b: 36). This is the language of Restorationism, not classic Pentecostalism. As we saw in chapter 3, many Pentecostal churches in the 1980s and 1990s espoused the belief that the early Church was being restored in all its apostolic purity, but on an immeasurably greater scale, in time for the return of Jesus (Walker 1989; Hunt 2001b). This vision of the worldwide triumph of the Church was, however, hard to square with the traditional pessimism of Pentecostal eschatology. The solution for the new Pentecostal Restorationists was to envisage a future in which the activities of God and the Devil both grew in intensity: to use a favorite phrase of Dye's, "things will get better and better and worse and worse."

Where did these ideas come from? The leading exponent of this style of Restorationist eschatology was the American "prophet-apostle" Bill Hamon, who had preached at Kensington Temple and influenced Dye's thinking about the End Times. In a 1997 book entitled *Apostles, Prophets and the Coming Moves of God* (1997), Hamon presented the return of Christ as the culmination of an accelerating 500-year purification of the Church:

Restorational movements since AD 1500 have accelerated in their frequency of occurrence from three hundred years to one hundred to fifty to every ten years during the last half of the 20th century. . . . The Protestant Movement prepared the way for the Holiness Movement, the Pentecostal for the Latter Rain Restoration, the Charismatic Renewal and Faith Movement for the present Prophetic Movement, which is now preparing the way for the Apostolic Movement, which will in turn prepare the way for the Saints Movement, which enables the saints of the Most High to fulfil Daniel 2: 44; 7: 18, 22, 27; and Revelation 11: 15; 1: 5–6; 5: 9–10. (1997: 19)

In other words, the apostolic order was due to be restored *at the turn of the millennium*, after which the End Times drama would begin.[4] But, unlike the sponsors of A.D. 2000, Hamon did not attempt to predict the dimensions of the revival.

It is difficult to say precisely what influence his theory had on Kensington

Temple. Metin Tilki, pastor of the Covent Garden satellite, told me that he took his eschatology wholesale from *Angels, Prophets and the Coming Moves of God*; Tim Bradshaw, who expected the Second Coming in his lifetime, said that apostolic gifts were being restored to the Church in the order established by Hamon. On the other hand, Dye himself never endorsed Hamon's detailed timetable, and, while it is true that he predicted revival around the time of the millennium, the connection with the calendar was to an extent unavoidable: it was difficult for anyone predicting imminent moves of the Holy Spirit from the vantage point of the 1990s *not* to locate them rhetorically "at the end of this century" or "in the new millennium." A sermon preached by Dye in February 1999 shows how careful he was to distinguish between legitimate hopes of an end-of-millennium Restoration and illegitimate date-setting. He began by saying:

> I stand amongst you as a prophetic person today. Over the last ten, fifteen years I have given myself sacrificially, given 110 percent, that at the close of this decade, the close of this century, and the close of this millennium, we would see the fulfillment of everything that God has spoken to us. . . . All across the world, men and women are being raised up by the thousand. God wants to see a global harvest before Jesus returns, a new level of apostolic anointing, so that we will be lifted up to the faith realms of early Christianity. . . . God wants to restore to the Church the things that we have lost: a mighty Spirit-filled apostolic move will sweep the nations of Europe—a revival of apostolic doctrine and the purity of the apostolic word as we prepare to celebrate the 2000th anniversary of Christ's birth.

But, almost in the same breath, he added a qualification:

> Jesus was born in the reign of Caesar Augustus, who died in 4 B.C., so before you get too carried away with the millennium celebrations— you've missed it! It was in 1996.[5] It is *about* 2,000 years since Jesus came, *about* 2,000 years since the Resurrection, since Pentecost.

We might draw an analogy here between Dye's approach to the end of the millennium and that of Pope John Paul II, who also presented the anniversary as a moment of historic spiritual transformation without ever really explaining why God had chosen this particular time (Thompson 1996). The Pope, like Dye, tried to harness the energy created by anticipation of the calendar change for programs of evangelization. The difference, apart from the obvious one of scale, was that the Catholic Decade of Evangelization was safely vague about its objectives; Kensington Temple, in contrast, had effectively been bounced into adopting an unrealistic goal by a single chance remark.

According to Dye, 2,000 by 2000 grew out of "an inspired off-the-cuff comment" by a respected leader (1997b: 83). The leader was Wynne Lewis who, at some stage in the early 1990s, overheard the Kensington Temple ministerial staff planning to plant 200 churches by the year 2000. He is reported to have said, in a comment that entered KT folklore: "Two hundred? Why not make it two *thousand*?" When I began my fieldwork, this story was related to me as an example of how the will of the Holy Spirit could be revealed by a chance remark. Later, it was presented as a piece of hyperbole that led to a disastrously ill-conceived project. From the moment the goal was adopted, there were people in the ministry who felt that it was unattainable: planting 2,000 churches was unprecedented in British church history. According to one former pastor:

> We tried redefining things, so that instead of 2,000 churches it be-
> came 2,000 "groups." We already had 500 groups across the net-
> work, so that was a start. You might call it creative accounting. But
> we couldn't get anywhere close. I think the problem was that, after
> years of sustained growth, KT had reached a state of equilibrium.
> There was still talk of expansion, but I don't think there was much
> real growth by the middle of the 1990s.

In other words, Dye had committed the church to an extremely ambitious program of expansion at a time when KT had stopped growing (thanks, in part, to the increased competition for worshippers from London's new Nigerian churches). The Tabernacle building in Acton, with its warehouse-sized audi-torium, was supposed to accommodate 4,000 people at Sunday evening serv-ices (Hywel-Davies 1998: 176–77). The reality was different, says the former pastor:

> I admire Colin's guts for taking on the Tabernacle, but it never ful-
> filled its potential. As soon as we moved there [in 1997], we lost that
> feeling of services packed to capacity. We were getting 800, 1,000,
> maybe 1,200 people, but it no longer felt full. We had these huge
> black curtains that we would pull across in order to hide the empty
> space. We tried to get all the satellite churches to attend every week,
> but they didn't.

As the 1990s progressed, there was mounting anxiety among the Ken-sington Temple staff about the slowing rate of growth. But it was not until a rally or "convocation" of the London City Church network on October 2, 1998 that those worries were made public. Kensington Temple had hired Wembley Arena for the meeting, entitled "Grace for the City"; it was the first time for five years that the whole church network had come together. Around 6,000 people were present, which looked impressive, though many galleries had been closed off to maximize the impact of the crowd. Colin Dye seemed disappointed by the turnout; but within an hour he had worked up the audience to a pitch of excitement. The music was belted out at terrific volume, and became more intense and ecstatic as the evening wore on, prompting young worshippers to jump up and down like punk rockers.

Dye's speech began with a description of a vision—strictly speaking, a "mental impression"—that he had experienced seven years earlier. In it, he was shown an angel holding a bowl as wide as the (circular) M25 motorway outside London. "I knew about the bowls of God's wrath in the Book of Revelation, and I thought: we're done for, we're finished," he said. But the bowls did not contain wrath; they poured out "liquid glory," which the angel proceeded to splash over the city. Dye's voice dropped and, over the rumbling of an electric organ, he explained that Londoners urgently needed to repent of their sins—otherwise the promised revival would not happen.

> We are approaching the end of this century. The time is now. Don't hold on to your sin—your sin is blocking the revival. . . . Why is that angel not yet allowed to pour out God's grace upon this city? What is blocking him? You are blocking him. God is raising up a citywide church, a network of hundreds and thousands of churches and ministries and groups and families who are united as one body. But we have a long way to go. The Lord showed me that we need to be 2,000 by the year 2000, and there are now 800 churches and ministries and groups linked together as one body. We have 1,200 to go in the next year and a half or so. The foundation was laid well, but in recent weeks and months the building has stopped and discouragement has set in, an intimidation, a spiritual intimidation straight from the pit of hell, and we mustn't give in to it . . .

> Now I'm going to tell you the rest of the vision. I saw the face of the Lord. . . . The Lord showed me that there are seven other angels gathering around the city. These are not angels of mercy—please, nobody move! I will not be able to share this: I'm on a knife edge right now. Not angels of grace but angels of judgment. I wanted to see. I asked God, and the moment he gave me just a tiny sight I said [yelling] I can't see! Take it away! It's too terrible! The judgment has already begun. Only one thing can stop it: if my people will humble themselves and seek my face and turn from their wicked ways, and even then we will not be able to avert the judgment in its fullness.

> He showed me three signs of his judgment that are coming . . . Fire is coming to this city. It shall strike in the City of London, in the heart of the corrupt financial institutions—I would not be personally surprised if it was one of the financial buildings themselves. . . . Then there will be a judgment concerning the water of the city. It will affect our water supply and sewage. God is saying the stench of the city has reached his nostrils. And then there will be a major incident related to a bridge, and consequent traffic disaster. God says: this city traffics in sin . . . if we pray, God's mercy will soften the effects, but they will still be there for the discerning.

This is a textbook example of the radicalization of charisma, in which a charismatic leader abandons the striving for security that lies at the heart of routinization (Csordas 1997: 101). In his speech, Dye presented 2,000 by 2000 as a divinely ordained goal revealed to him personally, rather than to Wynne Lewis, and inserted it into an apocalyptic vision replete with imagery from the Book of Revelation. Yet he chose to unveil this fresh symbolism at a time when, by his own admission, the project had already run into trouble. It is not the task of the sociologist to comment on the authenticity of the vision of the angels (which in any case took a form closer to pure thought than to an apparition), but we can still observe that even Dye had rarely taken on such a degree of risk. The terms in which he spoke about 2,000 by 2000 left little room for maneuver. Admittedly, one could interpret the vision of the wrathful angels as a preparation for failure (and here Dye did allow room for the non-fulfillment of prophecy: he said that the punishment would be averted or modified if enough people repented). But he left his audience in no doubt as to his heavy personal investment in 2,000 by 2000.

The historian Albert Baumgarten (2000: x–xi) uses an image from gambling to explain the moment when apocalyptic prophets deliberately increase millennial expectations. A player "ups the ante" when he increases the amount bet, forcing everyone who wishes to stay in the game to increase their wagers as well. Millennial movements up the ante when they make their members accept new risks that will increase solidarity and loyalty, perhaps in response to previous minor disconfirmations. This is a fair description of what Dye was doing at the Grace for the City rally—or trying to do. Observing members of the audience after the meeting, I suspected that some of them had not raised their own wagers: they seemed skeptical of Dye's claims. I talked to Jonah, a young Londoner who worked as a receptionist for a mobile phone company. When I asked him about the vision, he laughed and said Colin was "a bit of a showman"; he was not sure how seriously to take "the stuff about the angels." On the train back to central London, I overheard one middle-aged member of a satellite church say to his friends: "I could do with one of those bowls for the washing up." This unexpected irreverence made me reflect that audiences bestow charisma on leaders rather than the other way round. From a distance, the worshippers at the rally could have been mistaken for willing receptacles of ideology. Close up, it was by no means clear that they had absorbed the quasi-apocalyptic narrative that Dye had just constructed around a faltering program of church growth. If, as Csordas maintains, the locus of charisma lies in the interactions of participants (1997: 139), then something was missing from this encounter: a sense that the audience had truly engaged with Dye's demands. I felt that I had witnessed a demonstration of the fragility of charismatic authority.

By March 1999, when I had lunch with Colin Dye in his office at Kensington Temple, he had decided that 2,000 by 2000 would have to be abandoned in its present form. I asked him whether he was confident of reaching the target, and he replied that no, he was not, which was why he had made so few references to it in recent sermons. He admitted that growth had slowed down and added that he was not prepared to boost the total simply by defining groups of three or four people as a church. I was surprised by how casually he dismissed the project; but he was obviously still optimistic that the turn of the century would herald the worldwide restoration of apostolic faith. On Easter Monday, April 5, 1999, Kensington Temple staged its "Revival Healing Meeting" in the Albert Hall; the circular hall was filled almost up to the top tier, mostly with Afro-Caribbean worshippers. Dye's mood was upbeat, and he had good news to announce. God had told him that, following the announcement of his impending judgment at the Wembley rally, he had decided to show mercy to his people. I suggested in my field notes that "some sort of storm has passed"; to return to the gambling analogy, KT's senior pastor had decided to lower the stakes.

The subject of 2,000 by 2000 was now dropped from the everyday rhetoric of the community; but it could not be swept under the carpet completely. In the January 2000 issue of *Revival Times*, Dye explained what had gone wrong:

> We set ourselves the target of 2,000 churches, fellowships and min-
> istries by the year 2000. It looks as if we will fall short, having
> reached only 25 percent of that goal.[6] The hold-up has been the lack
> of mature leaders willing to die to their own desires and personal
> plans in order to serve the corporate vision of the London City
> Church. Also, there has been a failure to mobilise the members of
> LCC into effective discipleship. Despite years of preaching, prophe-
> sying and praying, there is still a basic unwillingness among the or-
> dinary attenders of the London City Church to get involved in the
> serious business of reaching the lost and discipling them into the
> body of Christ.

As Csordas points out, the radicalization of charisma is usually presented as a sacred process, while retreat from radicalization tends to be attributed to human error (1997: 130). In this case, it seems to be attributed to anyone *but* Dye, and we are faced (not for the first time) with the possibility that he had manipulated religious ideology to disguise his own failure. It is difficult to make a judgment about this, but what we can certainly observe is that—in his actions, if not in his words—Dye recognized that with 2,000 by 2000 he had taken a step too far. His attempts to blame others notwithstanding, he showed an instinctive grasp of the limits of his own charismatic authority. According to Csordas, the radicalization of charisma can create "a kind of centrifugal force that results in the spin-off of those unwilling to follow the tightening spiral of charisma" (1997: 130). The years from 1991 to 1999 had witnessed a steady inflation of Dye's claims, which seem to have peaked rather later than those of Pentecostal Christianity as a whole; but now he was unable to conceal the threat of approaching disconfirmation. The 2,000 by 2000 project placed an unacceptable strain on his charismatic authority and threatened to spin off large numbers of unconvinced worshippers, perhaps into other churches; it was clearly unworkable, and so this particular investment had to be written off.

Aftermath: The Loss of the Tabernacle and the Jezebel Spirit

The calendar change itself passed uneventfully at Kensington Temple—as it probably would have anyway, given that hopes for miraculous growth had focused on the end of 2000, not its beginning. There had been a brief flurry of anxiety about the Millennium Bug, but that was over long before New Year's Eve. The mood of the church in January 2000 was not noticeably different from that of a few months earlier. By the spring of that year, however, it had darkened considerably in response to an unexpected setback.

The November 1999 issue of *Revival Times* had unveiled a program called "Building the London City Church Tabernacle of Glory." If every LCC member bought a "Tabernacle brick" for £250, then the church could buy the Acton warehouse after the lease expired in 2000. "We are going to see the Lord move in miraculous power and financial provision," predicted Dye. Instead, disaster struck. Kensington Temple did not have enough money to buy the building and was outbid on the renewal of the lease. At Easter, it was forced to vacate the building, which housed its auditorium, administrative headquarters, and Bible college. Accounting for this failure required more concentrated ideological work than the collapse of 2,000 by 2000. The message went out that God wanted Kensington Temple to "re-dig the wells" by returning to Notting Hill Gate; but my impression from talking to worshippers was that this explanation rang hollow. A junior member of the ministry team told me:

> I have to be careful what I say, but I feel we started organizing funds too late, making appeals for donations too close to the time we had to move out. There's a place for good planning in God's work. People didn't catch the vision. We shouldn't have lost the Tabernacle, because we've had to come back to this place, which is quite small . . . God wanted us to re-dig the apostolic well here—that was what was being said from the pulpit. But we lost our headquarters, a great facility. I believe that God wants us to participate in the plans that he has for us, and that through negligence we can forfeit a specific part of that plan.

In February 2000 Dye withdrew from preaching engagements and began a 40-day fast, a gesture that was widely interpreted as a response to the shock of the loss of the Tabernacle. In the April issue of *Revival Times*, he reported that during the fast he received "some wonderful promises and reassurances about my life and ministry"—but also "some surprising revelations concerning the unseen powers that are controlling London." Dye identified these powers as the Jezebel spirit, named after the wicked consort of Ahab in the First Book of Kings who encouraged the worship of Baal. In a book of seminar notes entitled *Satan Unmasked* (later turned into a paperback book), Dye wrote that, during his time of reflection, God had shown him that this spirit had taken control of his life, making him feel "confused, frustrated and, to a large extent, burnt out" (2000: 7). The origins of this malign force lay in the Devil's temp-

tation of Eve, though Dye stressed that men and women were equally susceptible to it. The Jezebel spirit had taken control of the arts, commerce, religion,
philosophy, and politics; it lay behind pornography, homosexuality, adultery,
drug addiction, and organized crime (9). Fortunately, Christians could defeat
it with weapons of spiritual warfare—but these would not become truly effective until they renounced their sins. The cover of *Satan Unmasked*, reminiscent
of a 1970s horror film, showed a broken mask with the face of a handsome
blond young man and, behind it, a glowering black-browed villain, also male.
The concept of the Jezebel spirit was not invented by Dye, and he himself had
warned church members about it some years earlier (Hywel-Davies 1998: 170–
72). But the sudden elaboration of the concept bore the hallmark of the ideological work that follows prophetic disappointment. Where human fallibility
had been sufficient to account for the collapse of 2,000 by 2000, the loss of
the Tabernacle required a full-scale theodicy involving the clash of divine and
Satanic powers.

The summer of 2000 brought an interesting postscript to the prophecies
of divine punishment that Dye issued at the 1998 Grace for the City rally. On
June 1, 2000, an IRA splinter group exploded a bomb under Hammersmith
Bridge in London; no one was killed or injured, but it caused severe traffic
problems. Dye immediately claimed that this was a fulfillment of his prediction
of "a major incident related to a bridge, and consequent traffic disaster." The
fact that no one was killed showed that God had softened his judgment, just
as Dye had said he might. What I found interesting about this claim was the
mixed response it drew from the Kensington Temple audience. Some interviewees accepted it without question: Maureen Archer, for example, said that
God would not mislead the senior pastor, and took it as further confirmation
of his anointed status. But there were also reports that some members of the
ministry team were unconvinced. One pastor felt that Dye was "trying it on,"
and told friends that the episode helped him make up his mind to leave KT
and found his own congregation. It appears that, coming so soon after various
setbacks, this particular prophetic claim drew too heavily on Dye's depleted
charismatic capital.

It is only fair to add that, by late 2000, Dye's morale had improved: he
threw the church into a new cell group initiative, G-12, imported from Colom-
bia. That story lies beyond the scope of this study. But, despite this new excitement, there was still an impression that Kensington Temple's size and
ambitions had contracted slightly since the late 1990s, when it believed it
formed the spearhead of a religious revival that would transform London. The
relation of the calendar to these changes is indirect rather than causal, but it
should certainly be taken into account. Before 2000, the magnetic pull of the
anniversary sharpened KT's sense of direction and (as it turned out) led its
pastors into some unrealistic goal-setting. The timing of the Tabernacle fiasco
was coincidental; but it did give a flavor of millennial disappointment to the
beginning of the twenty-first century. For years, the church had been hinting
that 2000 would be the moment when God's promises would be fulfilled with
a new intensity. There had been no preparation for the possibility that it would

bring a public humiliation. It is hardly surprising, therefore, that some people reacted to the loss of the Tabernacle with the sort of bewilderment associated with millenarian believers when prophecy fails. One keen young Bible student told me that the setback had been sent by God as a trial and would help KT distinguish between fair-weather friends and Christians who were really committed to revival. But, even as he spoke, it was obvious that he was struggling with this explanation, and within a few months he had moved on to another church.

Individual Attitudes to the Year 2000

We have discussed at some length the reluctance of rank and file members of Kensington Temple to talk about the Second Coming of Christ; they were even less willing to engage in discussion about the year 2000. I had originally intended to build this study around their ideas about the anniversary, comparing them to those of other congregations, but it soon became obvious that there would be relatively little raw material to analyze. The most common response to a question about 2000 was a statement along the lines of "It's only a date." Many people knew that the 2,000th anniversary of Jesus' birth had probably already passed. As Tom Rayner put it:

> The millennium is very important to the world, for whom it is 2,000 years from Christ. Therefore we should use it. We should get the focus back on Jesus. However, the millennium is, if anything, a red herring. It's unlikely that Jesus was born on 25 December in the year 1, so if we were looking at a proper bi-millennium we've passed it anyway.

Sophie Kempff, the German woman who had dismissed apocalyptic theories about the European Union, was equally adamant that 2000 was just a date: "Nothing will change in the year 2000. It's not special, it's normal. Some people expect change, but that's not the case for me." But note the reference to "some people." There was a recognition that *other* people were excited about the date, namely the media and those apocalyptic fanatics who were expecting Jesus to come back in 2000. The latter were spoken about in terms very similar to "prophecy nuts"—the difference being that, while everyone knew church members who were obsessed by the End Times, no one could point me in the direction of anyone who thought Christ would return on the stroke of midnight, December 31, 1999. The closest I came to this belief was a second-hand report from an elderly West Indian man called Lionel, who told me in June 1999 that he had a friend who was wandering around church meetings announcing that Jesus was coming back that September. This friend had apparently picked up the idea from a preacher who had visited KT (he did not know who) and had shifted his estimate at least once; he was unemployed, but not worried about this because it gave him time to evangelize. "I take it all with more than a pinch of salt," said Lionel with a smile. "I don't know whether

Christ is coming back in 1999, 2000, after the millennium. Naming a year is one thing, but when he narrows it down to a month I'm not convinced."

It would be a mistake, however, to assume that just because church members rejected the notion of 2000 as a deadline for the Second Coming, the date therefore possessed no eschatological resonances at all. Amelia, a 21-year-old business student from Nigeria whom I met at a Tabernacle party in March 1999, said the year 2000 was important because it was 2,000 years since Jesus was born and also because it was a sign of the End: "It's getting closer to the time Jesus Christ will come. It's like your 50th birthday approaching. You keep saying to yourself, it's getting closer and closer." Silvia, the Brazilian Bible college student, said that her ideas about the millennium had changed: "For me, a few years ago, 2000 was a really scary thing, but now I am living it. I do believe that London City Church is in God's heart for this generation at this time. We are not here by chance. For me, the year 2000 will be more a time of harvest and the Church will arise in mission." There is a strong hint here of a shift from *le futur* to *l'avenir*: the long-term future proves a natural backdrop for scary or utopian images, whereas the short-term future—and 2000 was by this stage less than six months away—is something that one already partly inhabits. And it is worth remembering that Silvia had already said something similar about the Second Coming. As a child growing up in a Pentecostal household, she had been afraid of the coming apocalypse, but her anxiety receded as her confidence in God grew. Moving to London in her early twenties, she came under the influence of Dye's Restorationist theology, in which the horrors of the Tribulation were juxtaposed with a vast End Times harvest associated with the year 2000.

Silvia's comments confirmed my general impression that ways of thinking about the Second Coming and the year 2000 were related to each other. Church members who were "into the End Times" were more likely to feel that the calendar millennium meant something, even if they were not sure what that something meant. When asked what 2000 meant for her, Sarah Kim—who looked forward to being Raptured within a few years—replied:

> It makes me a little bit frightened because many people are not
> saved, such as my own family. And I will be a little bit frightened to
> meet God face to face. But I don't think 2000 is going to be the
> End. Personally, I hope that it will make people wake up a little bit.
> But the media makes a big thing out of it, to make money. To me
> it's another year, though deep down I'm a bit frightened.

Metin Tilki told me in June 1999:

> From a world perspective, it's a big marketing hype, a lot of people
> will make a lot of money out of it. From a Christian perspective, it's
> insignificant to me, completely. But I think that God is so sovereign
> that he will do something before the year 2000. I just sense that
> God is never mocked. Something will happen, I don't know what.

For both Sarah and Metin, therefore, the millennial transition evoked confused feelings: although they recognized that it was in many respects a manufactured event, without any direct religious significance, it still had the power to evoke subliminal fears and hopes. Their remarks suggested that, behind the protestations that 2000 was "just a date," there might be a greater degree of eschatological anticipation than I had at first suspected.

The KT census of October 1999 offered an opportunity to find out more. On the last page of the form, alongside the questions about the Second Coming and conspiracies, I added the statement: "The year 2000 is an important date, marking the beginning of the End." To my surprise, 26 percent of all respondents—25 percent of men and 27 percent of women—agreed with it. This figure included 27 percent of Africans and 22 percent of Caucasians, which was again unexpected, given the lower proportion of Africans willing to predict the return of Christ. Overall, however, there was some evidence to suggest that anticipation of the Second Coming intensified apocalyptic interpretations of the calendar change. Forty-nine percent of ten-year millenarians thought 2000 was the beginning of the End, as opposed to 35 percent of fifty-year-millenarians and 24 percent of non-speculators. This gradient is in the direction one would expect, though it is puzzling that just over half of all the respondents who believed that Jesus would return by 2010 at the latest did not think that the turn of the millennium was significant. There was also evidence that ideas about 2000 and conspiracy were linked: 41 percent of believers in the euro conspiracy and 47 percent of believers in Satanic barcodes assented to the statement. Participation in the KT ministry made little difference, however.

The relatively high level of positive responses was hard to square with the reluctance of most interviewees to talk about 2000 as the beginning of the End, and with the fact that, by October 1999, Colin Dye was no longer presenting 2000 as an important date in the life of the church. I was keen to find out whether willingness to assent to the statement would survive into the year 2000. There was no possibility of a full-scale longitudinal survey, but in July 2000 I was able to put the same statement to 68 first-year Bible college students, now back in the Notting Hill church. A total of 19 (27 percent) agreed with it, which matched the percentage for both the whole church (26 percent) and the Bible college students and alumni (27 percent) in the October survey. So, whatever ideas were conveyed by the responses, they did not appear to be affected by passing through the calendrical deadline.

I returned to Kensington Temple at the beginning of 2003 to find the cell group system well established, the Bible college replaced by a part-time school of ministry, and the church once again on the verge of revival. "We are on the threshold of a great outpouring of the Holy Spirit. God is already moving in apostolic power within our cities and across the nations of the earth," wrote Dye in the February issue of *Revival Times*. I interviewed some church members and was not surprised to discover, given the traditionally high turnover, that few of them had belonged to the congregation in 1999–2000. We have already encountered Jason Robinson's theory that the significance of the calendar millennium was revealed on September 11 the following year. For all the other interviewees, however, the date seems to have meant very little, before or after the anniversary. "I don't know what to say about it—2000, 2001, 2002, they're all just dates," said Bill, a middle-aged businessman. "Maybe 1999 was a big thing for some people, but not for me." Daniel, a young man from Nairobi now working as a London bus driver, told me:

> Dates don't really matter, because Jesus told us that it was not for us to worry about the times and seasons. Some people were worried about the Millennium Bug, but that was a scientific problem—nothing to do with religion. It was a transition into a new millennium, and in a way that was exciting, but it didn't mean anything for Christians.

Sanjay, a Londoner from an Indian background, said he had not been a believer when 2000 dawned: "I can't tell you what it was like from a Christian perspective, because I wasn't saved in those days. It was just an excuse for a drink with my mates. I got drunk, went home, and thought: is that it? What a let-down." Then he produced an observation that neatly encapsulated the reservations of ordinary Pentecostalists about the prophecy subculture: "As for Christians, there might have been some people thinking about the Second Coming in 2000, but to be honest with you I don't think real, committed, born-again Christians worry about that mystical stuff. We don't worry about dates—because we're ready for him whenever he comes."

Emmanuel Johnson laughed when I raised the subject of 2000: "There was all that talk in America about the end of the world at the millennium, but it's 2003 now—and, hey, we're still here."

Conclusion

With the benefit of hindsight, almost everything written about the turn of the millennium during the 1990s seems to have exaggerated its importance. Academic commentators were as guilty of this as religious leaders. A collection of articles entitled *The Year 2000: Essays on the End* (Strozier and Flynn 1997) contained a memorably over-the-top piece entitled "Hysteresis of the Millennium" by Jean Baudrillard, which suggested that history had been sent into reverse as it approached "the terror of the year 2000." Next to it was an essay by Sandra Schanzer on "The Impending Computer Crisis of the Year 2000," which argued that it might already be too late (in 1997) to avert technological disaster. A similar volume entitled *Calling Time: Religion and Change at the Turn of the Millennium* (Percy 2000a), consisting of essays submitted in 1999, also overestimated the significance of the moment. One contributor, the Anglican theologian Michael Sadgrove, described the millennium as "a 'singularity' in the flow of time, an interruption of 'ordinary' time by a historical moment that is already 'pulling' us into orbit in fascinating and perhaps sinister ways" (2000: 78). There was also an essay by me arguing that the dawn of 2000 would be the first nearly universal experience in human history, one which, by distorting our understanding of time, would increase our feeling of powerlessness in the face of mortality (Thompson 2000: 123–24). I pointed out that the calendar change was what philosophers call a pseudo-event, without causal preconditions or consequences (Gell [1992] 1996: 161). The shift from 1999 to 2000 would occur instantaneously, unlike a real event occupying time and space; therefore it was both elusive and inescapable.

Looking back, I still think that the status of the transition as a pseudo-event is important, and that it helps explain why its reverberations were so limited. By insisting that 2000 was "just a date," members of Kensington Temple recognized the intangibility of the millennial moment. The Decade of Evangelism, the Millennium Dome, the hand on the clock pointing to twelve, the row of three zeros on newspaper mastheads: none of these was the thing itself, but merely a sign or token of the phenomenon that—carelessly glossing over the distinction between calendar unit and anniversary—we called "the millennium." The arrival of the year 2000 could signify nothing or anything. It could be endowed with apocalyptic, theological, philosophical, sociological, technological, political, and artistic significance, but the one thing it would never receive was an authoritative definition. Some Christian writers bravely tried to nail down its meaning: Sadgrove (2000) wrote of it as a *kairos* moment for Christianity that demanded serious theological work, enabling the Church to reach out to a complex, postmodern world. Yet there was little sign of such work being done. With the exception of Pope John Paul II, who never really communicated his millennial enthusiasm to his own Church, no mainstream Christian leader seemed very interested in 2000, and for a good reason: most of them instinctively realized that there was no Christian narrative of the millennium that churchgoers, let alone secular society, would find convincing. And, in any case, as practitioners of routinized religion, they were risk-averse; the calendar millennium held most appeal for those who aspired to charismatic authority and were prepared to take the gambles that this entailed.

For decades, if not centuries, 2000 was synonymous with the future. To talk authoritatively about it was therefore to claim some knowledge of the future, or at least the ability to anticipate it intelligently. In the late twentieth century, some visionaries portrayed 2000 as a threshold for the operation of supernatural power, while secular commentators—academics, scientists, market analysts, and politicians—made forecasts or emphasized the attainability of various goals. In practice, sacred and secular interpretations of 2000 were difficult to separate from each other. Pentecostalists tried to quicken the action of the Holy Spirit by devising action plans such as A.D. 2000; scientists issued predictions about the millennium that drew heavily on the resources of their imaginations and on the quasi-priestly status of their profession. In the 1990s, 2000 was sometimes described as "the year by which," a phrase that captures the charismatic essence of the rhetoric associated with the millennium. Predictions and promises lie at the heart of charismatic claims, which are translated into authority when an audience accepts them; but that authority can quickly crumble when the claims are invalidated. In this respect, those who attempted to harness the power of 2000 faced the same threat of disconfirmation as Weber's prophets or war leaders: things could so easily go wrong. The experience of millennial scholars after 2000 offered an ironic demonstration of this danger: the final conference of the Center for Millennial Studies at Boston University in November 2002 called for sustained ideological work to explain why academic predictions of apocalyptic fever and technological collapse had not come true. Colin Dye, too, had to execute some deft maneuvers to extricate himself from 2,000 by 2000; he left it rather late in the day, and his authority suffered real damage when this was followed by the loss of the Tabernacle, but one thing that never deserted him was his sense that charisma works best when routinization and radicalization are properly balanced. Risk management remains an essential part of his strategy for Kensington Temple. Dye's listeners may not have consciously realized that they were in the position of granting or withholding authority, but there was nothing automatic about their reception of his ideas. One of the questions facing them was: "Do we believe what Colin is telling us about God's plan for the year 2000?" The answer for many people was that they did not; otherwise Kensington Temple would have moved beyond 25 percent of its target. This was partly because Dye, at Wynne Lewis's prompting, had set the hurdle too high, but partly for deeper reasons to do with the loss of overarching meaning in modern society. Peter Berger's "heretical imperative" attacked narratives of 2000 with a vengeance: no plausibility structure was strong enough to sustain a single interpretation of the calendar millennium. Roman Catholics did not invest heavily in John Paul II's mystical understanding of 2000 as the beginning of a Christian springtime because to have done so they would have had to block out countless competing interpretations, many of which dismissed 2000 as an event, and surrender the freedom to make up their own minds about it. Pentecostal Christians were, on the whole, equally confused. The leaders of their community, having initially embraced over-ambitious schemes to evangelize all the nations by 2000, spent much of the 1990s backing away from them. And so, as my fieldwork at Kensington Temple suggests, most rank and file believers sought refuge in toned-down rhetoric colored by the ambiguities of common sense: 2000 was exciting, but not as exciting as the media pretended; the anniversary of Jesus' birth but not the exact anniversary; a milestone in history but just a date; a sign of the End but not the End itself.

8

Conclusions

This final chapter is divided into two sections. The first examines the wider lessons to be drawn from the study of millenarianism at Kensington Temple. It emphasizes the dangers of generalizing about the beliefs of conservative evangelical Christians, which are more varied than the popular image of the constituency suggests; moreover, there are unexplored parallels between their working out in practice and trends in secular society. The second section argues that, although the Problem of the End has manifested itself throughout the history of millenarianism, it is becoming more acute. The marginalization of apocalyptic doctrine at Kensington Temple reflects the way millenarian and other religious beliefs are being undermined by the fragmentation of plausibility structures in modernity; it is an aspect of secularization.

Kensington Temple: Perspectives and Parallels

When I began my fieldwork, I did not expect to discover that Kensington Temple was a hotbed of millenarianism. Even so, I was surprised by the circumscribed and tentative nature of its members' apocalyptic beliefs. As Bryan Wilson's (1961) account of the early Elim Pentecostals shows, KT has a substantial apocalyptic heritage; moreover, much of the literature on the wider conservative evangelical tradition implies that belief in the End Times is central to its appeal (see, for example, Ammerman 1987; Wills 1990; Strozier 1994). In particular, Charles Strozier's interviewees, who included Pentecostalists, spoke passionately about the coming apocalypse and its relevance to their daily lives. Given the closeness of the year

2000, I expected to encounter at least a similar level of intensity. Instead, almost from the first interview, it was clear that my study of millenarianism at Kensington Temple would be centered around what people did *not* believe— or, bearing in mind the difficulty of measuring belief, what they did not say and do. For a time, it was mildly depressing to focus on a negative; gradually, however, I came to see, like Sherlock Holmes, that the fact that the dog did not bark in the night time was a curious incident. Why would members of a religious movement founded amid expectation of an imminent Second Coming show so little interest in this prospect at a time of supposedly heightened apocalyptic sensibilities?

The basic answer is that they found that millenarian ideas, in their raw form, could not easily be reconciled with the dictates of common sense. And so, using their subjective rationality, they worked on these ideas until cognitive dissonance was minimized. In the process, apocalyptic theology did not disappear: I met no one for whom the concept of the End Times meant nothing, and many of those people who put it to the back of their minds would, *if asked*, produce a mild rhetorical expression of apocalyptic belief. There were also a few individuals who embraced millenarian or conspiracy ideas that had the effect of increasing the tension between themselves and their surroundings. But, on the whole, ideological work on millenarianism was intended to reconcile it with the reality of everyday life, thereby lowering subcultural deviance. In this, Kensington Temple was a microcosm of forces observable in the Pentecostal and evangelical world. Church members' lack of interest in eschatology was entirely consistent with the downgrading of premillennialism within the Elim denomination; their lack of support for the unworkable 2,000 by 2000 project mirrored Pentecostalism's pragmatic abandonment of schemes to evangelize the whole world by the millennium; the stigmatization of worshippers such as Linda Symondson, who thought she had uncovered a papal conspiracy to send light rays through the ionosphere, reproduced on a small scale the marginalization of "conspiracy nuts" in born-again Christianity.

The general direction of the modifications of apocalyptic belief at Kensington Temple was toward routinization and the societal consensus. That said, the results did not have a uniform quality. People adopted all sorts of strategies for coming to terms with the problematic notion of the end of the world, and this lack of uniformity is in itself significant. One of the aims of this study has been to identify some of the gaps that open up when millenarian ideas are adjusted to fit circumstances. These gaps exist at the level of official ideology: between, for example, Elim's eschatology before and after 1994, when belief in a premillennial Second Coming was downgraded from policy to a mere option. They exist between official and unofficial formulations of prophecy belief (the latter often moving away from the societal consensus) and between apocalyptic doctrines before and after they have been subjected to private customization by the ordinary worshipper. But that customization, of course, is applied to doctrines of every sort by religious believers everywhere. And that brings us to one of the most important questions raised by this study. What does the practical modification of apocalyptic doctrines tell us about the social construction of religious ideas in general?

One of the things it tells us is that the way people work on high-tension beliefs is not very different from the way they work on less controversial religious propositions. They make rational choices that take into account costs and benefits; a crucial factor is the degree of social support available for a particular idea. Such calculations can create substantial variations of belief even within groups that have a reputation for ideological uniformity, such as cults. It was her fieldwork with a new religious movement, the Unification Church, that led Eileen Barker (1984: 84–89) to coin the terms *horizontal* and *vertical* variations of belief, referring to differences of emphasis produced respectively by a believer's personal background and his or her place in the group hierarchy. Other ethnographic studies, such as those by John Lofland on the Unification Church ([1966] 1977), David Van Zandt on the Children of God (1991) and Phillip Lucas on the Holy Order of MANS (1995), have also revealed the flexibility of ideology, lack of internal consensus, and importance of negotiation within high-tension groups. Yet, as Barker (1989: 10) and Wilson (1990: 68) have pointed out, the beliefs of cult and sect members are the subject of sweeping generalizations in the media. These generalizations often exaggerate the content of high-tension doctrines and seek to identify spurious similarities between quite different movements; above all, they assume that everyone within a particular group subscribes with same degree of intensity to the exotic doctrines with which the group has become publicly identified. This non-existent ideological uniformity is often ascribed to brainwashing or mind control; but there is no reliable evidence to suggest that such a thing is possible (Barker 1989: 17–19; Bainbridge 1997: 235). If brainwashing did exist, however, many controversial movements would cheerfully use it, because they know better than anyone that a consistent level of subcultural deviance is hard to sustain against the gravitational pull of the societal consensus. The authority of cult leaders is notoriously fragile, and the groups themselves often fissiparous and short-lived. The simple reason for this is that they make charismatic claims that impose a punishing load of ideological work if cognitive dissonance is to be avoided; for many of their members, the cost is too high. A detailed ideological snapshot of a cult or sect would probably reveal a significant proportion of its members wrestling with ideas that offended against their common sense rationality. There would be people pushing in opposite directions, toward and away from subcultural deviance; the outcome might not be predictable, but history suggests that careful routinization increases a group's chances of survival.

Conservative evangelical Christians are not usually classified as cult members, even by their opponents; they think of themselves as strongly anti-cult and they are often the source of dubious generalizations about new religious movements. Yet they themselves have been the victims of sweeping media assertions about their "fundamentalist" beliefs, which some psychologists have argued—on the slimmest of evidence—are pathological in origin (see Savage

2002). In the last twenty years, sociological studies of evangelical Christianity have challenged some of the more misleading stereotypes, distinguishing between the theological traditions within the constituency and charting some of the variations of belief that go with them (see Hunter 1983, 1987; Ammerman 1987; Poloma 1989; Percy 1996; Miller 1997; Smith 1998, 2000; Coleman 2000; D. Martin 2001). But the message that born-again Christians do not all believe the same thing, or indeed what their leaders wish them to believe, has not been successfully communicated to the secular world. There needs to be a sharper focus on the rationality of evangelical Christians and its consequence: the fragility of religious authority in a milieu in which, as Mary Jo Neitz (1987) observed of Charismatic Catholics, hypotheses are constantly being tested. At Kensington Temple, religious claims were subjected to continual evaluation by rank and file worshippers and frequently failed the test. The collective memory of the church was littered with failed, defunct, or only partially successful charismatic claims: the Group-Gather-Grow initiative; pamphlets warning of Y2K meltdown, still on sale in the bookshop long after the millennial moment; Dye's interpretation of the Hammersmith Bridge bomb; and, of course, 2,000 by 2000. The failure of these claims should not be seen as evidence of intellectual dishonesty on the part of the people making them; rather, it underlines Neitz's point that believers use their common sense to work out strategies, analyze consequences, and assess "the goodness of fit between an item and an explanation" (1987: 79).

Analysis of conservative evangelical Christianity usually concentrates on the features that distinguish it from the rest of the world; there is rarely a focus on similarities. But the longer I spent at Kensington Temple, the more I was struck by the parallels between KT and the secular world, and also between my findings and those of scholars working outside the field of religion. The following paragraphs suggest areas in which further research into these parallels could yield useful insights. The suggestions may seem only tangentially connected to the subject of millenarianism, but they arise out of my observations of the management of apocalyptic belief at KT:

i. There are similarities between Pentecostal churches such as Kensington Temple, and the charismatic systems of the political and business world. The calculation of risk is central to the operation of charismatic authority, and its growing importance in the global economy has lent a strongly charismatic flavor to the authority of many chief executives. In the unitary structures of Pentecostalism, the success of spiritual claims depends partly on sound management techniques and anticipation of market trends; religious and commercial risk are closely intertwined. Will Napier, after leaving Kensington Temple, was briefly involved in direct marketing: he was struck by the way speakers would speak of a great wave of sales just around the corner, so similar to Colin Dye's forecasts of imminent revival, and said he was uncomfortably aware of having left one network of dissonance-inviting claims only to become involved in another. The similarities between Charismatic religion and business activity have been noted by a number of scholars (see B. Martin 1998; Coleman 2000; Corten and Marshall-Fratani 2001; D. Martin 2001), but there is room for more ethnographic research, such as a comparative study of the calculation of risk in a Pentecostal and a commercial setting.

ii. The work of organizational theorists throws a useful light on the exercise of power in churches such as Kensington Temple. Taking their lead from Michel Foucault, many scholars see power as unstable, exercised and resisted within moving networks, incorporating discourses that themselves seek to exercise power (Clegg 1998: 30–31). Applying this perspective to evangelical Christianity, Martyn Percy (1996, 1998) uncovered messy, volatile, and sometimes abusive relationships in the Charismatic churches influenced by John Wimber. Many similar relationships exist at Kensington Temple, where patterns of granting and withholding charismatic authority cut across the top-down structure associated with the classic Pentecostal pastor and his audience. For Foucault, a characteristic of modern power relations was their open-ended quality (Cousins and Hussain 1984: 249). This quality is certainly to be found at Kensington Temple, where, although pastors occasionally wield authority in a coercive way, the structure of power is forever shifting in response to the threat of disconfirmation and the network of tiny authority-claims emanating from worshippers' personal prophecies and "words of knowledge."[1] To paraphrase Barker, we might say that authority is exercised horizontally as well as vertically.

iii. The sociology of deviance is dominated by the study of crime and the stigmatization of minority groups by society.[2] Less attention has been given to the way minority groups themselves construct measures of deviance that they apply to their membership. A number of interviewees at Kensington Temple branded their fellow worshippers as "flaky" or superspiritual, and there was a general acceptance of the identification of strange people with strange ideas; the language used was reminiscent of that employed by political activists to describe their own fringes. A comparative study of boundary maintenance in a religious movement and a political party, examining the concept of deviance as it was applied *within* the groups, could make a substantial contribution to our knowledge of the management of ideology. It would be interesting to discover whether either organization faced the paradox experienced by Kensington Temple: that the most committed group members are also the most susceptible to heterodox ideas that can create unhelpful tension with society.

iv. There is a trend in the field of rhetorical analyses away from treating statements of belief as evidence of deep-seated attitudes. Michael Billig, drawing on the work of Jonathan Potter and Margaret Wetherell (1987), argues that, instead of treating an inner mental state as the "reality" that needs to be studied, social psychologists should take as their starting point the use of attitudinal language (1991: 15). Such language often takes the form of an argument that is intended to achieve particular ends. Kenneth Burke, the father of modern rhetorical studies, analyzed rhetoric in terms of strategy ([1941] 1973: 297–300), a military metaphor that implies the deployment of rhetorical resources in a deliberate sequence (Bygrave 1993: 109). Stephen O'Leary (1994) has stripped away some of the mystique of millenarian discourse by revealing the logic that underpins its arguments, an approach that could successfully be applied to

many religious movements. Evangelical Christianity places a stronger emphasis than most traditions on rhetorical expressions of belief and, partly as a result
of this, suffers from the oversimplified representations of those beliefs in public life. Although there have been studies of the use of language in evangelical
and Charismatic groups (see Harding 1994; Johannesen 1994; Roelofs 1994;
Percy 1996; Csordas 1997), relatively little attention has been given to the
operation of rhetoric within these groups. This is regrettable because such
analysis would help us to understand the difference between what people say
they believe and what their actions imply they believe. To cite an example from
Kensington Temple, Debbie Mowbray and her friends told each other that
"Jesus is coming soon"; but this assertion had little effect on their daily routine
because it owed more to rhetorical convention than to conviction. This is not
to say that church members did not hold firm beliefs (though they tended not
to be millenarian ones); rather, we need to recognize that their expressions of
belief were often molded to fit argumentative strategies and, as such, were
influenced by all sorts of factors—including, in many cases, the calculation of
risk.

    v. Finally, cognitive science is providing support for the consensus in so-
cial psychology, rhetorical studies, and the sociology of knowledge that belief—
and therefore religion—is too complex a phenomenon to be reduced to
straightforward causes. The anthropologist Pascal Boyer ([2001] 2002) concludes that religious activities involve too many areas of the brain for there to
be any single cause, function, or definition of religion. As he puts it: "There is
no religious instinct, no *specific* inclination in the mind, no particular dispo-
sition for these concepts, no special religion centre in the brain, and religious
people are not different from non-religious ones in essential cognitive functions" (378). Even when we narrow down our frame of reference to millenarianism alone, Boyer's analysis is still relevant. Apocalyptic believers may exhibit
distinctive psychological traits (though that is very hard to prove empirically),
but there is no evidence to suggest that, in some fundamental way, they process
information differently from everyone else.

Secularization and the Problem of the End

We have considered some of the lessons that the management of millenarian
belief in one setting can teach us about similar or wider social processes. But
what does it tell us about millenarianism itself? Having accepted that apocalyptic ideas are considered alongside other dissonance-inducing charismatic
claims at Kensington Temple, we are still left wondering why they are judged
so harshly—why, in a movement with a millenarian pedigree, so many church
members rejected, overlooked, or drastically modified doctrines relating to the
imminent end of the world.

    The basic reason for this, I have argued, is that millenarian claims offend
against the common sense rationality of believers. But this assertion raises as
many questions as it answers. The Pentecostal world accepts many claims that,

in the eyes of secular observers, cannot withstand close examination. The heal-ing rallies held by Morris Cerullo in London in the early 1990s attracted so many allegations of fakery that Kensington Temple, which had sponsored them, was effectively disowned by the leaders of British evangelicalism (Schae-fer 1999). Yet they were hugely popular with the KT membership and helped to cement Colin Dye's position as Britain's paramount Pentecostal pastor. Why should worshippers exempt healing claims from detailed rational scrutiny while vigorously editing out what they regard as implausible millenarian claims from their private cosmologies? One relevant factor is Pentecostalism's ambiv-alent relationship with End Times theology, which it has borrowed from fun-damentalism and does not "own" in the way it does the theology of Charismatic healing (Prosser 1999; Poloma 2001). We should also remember that both the evangelical and the secular milieux in Britain are less influenced by apocalyptic tradition than their equivalents in the United States. But for a fuller explanation of the marginalization of apocalyptic belief in the church we need to go back to J. Gordon Melton's observation ([1985] 2000: 147), quoted in the Introduc-tion, that supposedly apocalyptic groups *in general* do not organize their daily lives around millennial prophecy—at least, not to the degree that critics and scholars assume they do.

The importance of this observation was brought home to me halfway through my fieldwork. In March 1999 I visited one of the Amazon outposts of the Israelites of the New Universal Covenant, a Peruvian syncretist sect whose founder, Ezequiel Ataucusi Gamonal, prophesied the imminent emer-gence of a millennial kingdom presided over by himself in the role of Jewish Messiah and Inca Emperor (Thompson 1999b, 2001b). Most of the ordinary members, however, seemed uninterested in and ignorant of the detail of Eze-kiel's apocalyptic timetable. Instead, they told me how they had turned their backs on alcohol, drugs, and crime, and discovered true joy in an ascetic life-style based on the Ten Commandments. The evasive quality of their replies to questions about the apocalypse—and especially those about 2000, whose es-chatological significance had once been considerable but was now played down—reminded me of the interviewees at Kensington Temple: despite huge differences in theology, demography, and geographical setting, members of both groups appeared to be marginalizing millenarian ideas in roughly the same way. The anthropologist Miguel Leatham (1997) encountered a similar situation at Nueva Jerusalén, an ostensibly millenarian colony of Catholic sec-tarians in Mexico. The peasants who joined the community were not attracted by the scenario outlined by its renegade priest founder, in which Pope Paul VI would soon emerge from imprisonment in the Vatican to usher in the end of the world. Their beliefs were orientated "not around doctrines, but around an economy of procurement of this worldly-benefits, such as improved health, amelioration of social relations and crop protection" (299).

If Melton is right, and Leatham's findings point to a more general orien-tation on the part of members of apocalyptic religions, we are faced with a difficult question. Does this pragmatic approach reflect a peculiarly modern sensibility, or is it foreshadowed in earlier movements? Making direct comparisons between past and present religious activity is a hazardous business: supporters and opponents of the secularization thesis are still fighting over records of church attendance from previous centuries in an attempt to prove or disprove that Western religiosity has gone into sharp decline.[3] The question about millenarianism takes us into similar territory: it asks, in effect, whether changes in the nature and expression of apocalyptic belief offer support for a version of the secularization thesis.

During the nineteenth and twentieth centuries, leading social theorists believed that religion would eventually disappear. Supporters of the secularization thesis no longer make this claim. Their main proposition is more modest: that "modernisation creates problems for religion" (Bruce 2002: 2). According to Bryan Wilson's statement of the thesis, the social significance of religion has declined as its functions have been taken over by non-religious agencies; there has been a gradual replacement of a specifically religious consciousness by "an empirical, rational, instrumental orientation" (1982: 149). There is a paradox here, namely that the religious doctrines whose impact has been weakened by rationalization were themselves the product of, and contributed to, the growth of the rational mindset that led to secularization. Peter Berger ([1967] 1969), developing Max Weber's theories, argued that the process began with the ancient Hebrews, whose one God was beyond the reach of magical manipulation and made primarily ethical demands of his followers. This incipient secularization was partly reversed by the devotional practices of Catholicism, but gathered pace again when Protestantism restored the concept of ethnical rationalization. Interestingly, millenarianism as a system first emerged among the ancient Jews and was given many of its modern distinguishing features by Protestants. It, too, bears some of the hallmarks of emerging rationality. The Jewish apocalyptic genre appealed to reason in a way that previous texts had not, presenting its readers with mathematical puzzles that did not require the intermediary services of priests. Much the same could be said of Protestant apocalyptic theorizing; dispensationalism, in particular, exhibited the thoroughly secular impulse to assemble a structure that could be "tested" by proof texts in the manner of a scientific model. And, in a broader sense, it has been argued by some scholars that the millenarian vision of a perfected world gave birth to the utopianism that lies behind the modern concept of progress (see Campion 1994; Bull 1995).

But, as I have tried to show, rationality also dismantled the credibility of millenarian teachings. The traces of hasty recalculation in the Book of Daniel (Hartman and Di Lella 1990: 419) imply that, from the beginning, the authors of the apocalyptic argument had to negotiate their way around the Problem of the End—the tendency of the discourse to subvert itself by prophesying things that did not happen. The crucial point is that this tendency was, and is, unavoidable. Far from being an accidental flaw in the construction of the apocalyptic argument, it constitutes one of its defining qualities. The typical apocalyptic statement does not confine itself to prophesying the End: it says, "The End is coming *and this is the proof.*" The demonstration is provided because the listener requires it, but there is no guarantee that he or she will be persuaded and stay persuaded. For that, a plausibility structure—a social base of people who accept the argument—must be built and sustained. It must be strong enough to withstand disconfirmation and reasonably extensive: one of the features of millenarianism is that it offers *collective* salvation, and if the number of the elect remains tiny, then the millenarian claim on which their status is based will be undermined.

As Berger points out ([1979] 1980), religious plausibility structures as a whole, let alone those that espouse a high-risk charismatic theology, are difficult to sustain in modern society. The fragmentation of meaning systems has created an expansion of choice in religion—the "heretical imperative." This expanded choice is not fatal to religion; it may even be the source of religious vitality.[4] But it does pose special problems for the maintenance of orthodoxy, both in mainstream Christianity and in Pentecostalism; and it has proved almost fatal for large-scale millenarianism in the industrialized West. The story of apocalyptic theology in Europe and, to a lesser extent, America, has been one of steadily shrinking plausibility structures: first for predictive millenarianism and then for the explanatory variety. As McIver's (1999) survey shows, the actual *volume* of millenarian literature has not diminished; what has changed is the influence it commands in Western society. Millennial disappointment has had a cumulative effect. The failure of the last large-scale outbreak of predictive prophecy belief in the West, that of the Millerites, has been seared into the historical memory; evangelical Christians are adamant that they will not make the same mistake again. The phenomenon of the "apocalyptic cult" is testimony not so much to the potency of millenarian ideas as to the hothouse conditions they require if they are to flourish in an unroutinized form—and, even then, the focus of cult members is likely to lie elsewhere.

Part of the modern challenge to apocalyptic belief is produced by technology: although the multiplication of sources of information makes it easier for the individual to construct a customized apocalyptic worldview, the same deluge of data tends to sweep away the consensus necessary for the credibility of prophecies of collective salvation. Part of the challenge is produced by the way we now think about ourselves. To return to an earlier question, there *is* a peculiarly modern mindset that is shared even by members of apocalyptic religions, though it derives ultimately from the exercise of a rationality that can be traced back at least as far as the Book of Daniel. The main characteristic of this new mindset is its individualism. As doctrinal plausibility structures collapse, and people become detached from traditional ties of place and kinship, the search for meaning is increasingly bound up with what Anthony Giddens (1991) has called "the reflexive project of the self." Personal experience becomes the test of authenticity, even (or perhaps especially) in high- or medium-tension religious movements. Members of Kensington Temple, the Israelites of the New Universal Covenant and Nueva Jerusalén are as thoroughly engaged in this project as conventional religious believers: they are more concerned with their own spiritual journey than with abstract doctrine.

This is not secularization as Max Weber envisaged it: he believed that creeping rationalization would eradicate precisely those "magical" elements in religion that thrive in modern Pentecostalism. But, as David Martin observes (1996: 42), many scholars, including Weber, have misconstrued the consequences of technical rationality. Charismatic religion reflects the relocation of religious experience from public life to the private sphere; and this itself is an aspect of secularization. James Davison Hunter has written about the "narcissism and hedonism" of modern evangelicalism, which finds expression as "a fixation on the potentiality of the human being 'under the lordship of Jesus Christ'" (1983: 97). Evangelical narcissism and Pentecostal "signs and wonders" are not secular in the sense that they involve the application of scientific rationality to religious claims. But they *are* secular in the sense that their small-scale miracles, though fragile in the face of empirical investigation, provide the quick, customized spiritual benefits that consumers demand in a choice-driven marketplace (Wilson 1996: 27).

Yet Weber's insights relating to society as a whole remain valid. The gravitational pull of the societal consensus is indeed eroding the doctrinal foundations of religious belief. In Hunter's opinion, even conservative evangelical Christians are now quietly edging away from teachings that the secular world considers preposterous or socially offensive, such as those relating to the eternal punishment of non-believers (1987: 40). Something similar is happening at Kensington Temple. As we noted at the beginning of this chapter, church members were far more receptive to certain high-tension claims, such as those relating to healing miracles or personal prophecy, than they were to others, such as those of millenarianism. This preference can be explained by secularization—or, to be more specific, by a particular pattern of secularization that has altered the balance of the costs and benefits of religion as it is perceived by believers. The worshippers I interviewed, most of whom were under 40, were profoundly aware of societal norms: they responded to them, even if they did not entirely subscribe to them. They were not afraid of subcultural deviance—but it helped if it was the right *kind* of deviance, one that did not conflict too dramatically with modern society's shared values. Thus, many of them were (subject to some rational scrutiny) happy to embrace Charismatic healing and personal "words of knowledge," apparently high-tension concepts that, in practice, resonated with the secular emphasis on healing, the body, and personal fulfillment. They were less enthusiastic about doctrines that incurred the extra expense of offending against the canons of liberal society. A number of interviewees distanced themselves from traditional Pentecostal attitudes toward women; there was little support for the historic anti-Catholicism of the Elim movement; and there was unease about the prospect of damnation for virtuous non-Christians.

As for millenarian theology, we have seen that, although many members of Kensington Temple drew on it as an occasional resource, a majority viewed it as dubious or unimportant. Arguably, at some fundamental level, they found it hard to reconcile with their own cognitive style, which was closer to that of their secular contemporaries than to that of old-fashioned sectarian Elimites—not least in its demand for immediate spiritual benefits. The theologian Douglas Davies has suggested that Charismatic Christianity abolishes deferred gratification: "An interest in personal salvation remains, but its realisation has been brought forward from the hereafter to the here and now" (1984: 144). Mille-narianism brings salvation forward to this side of the grave; but the reward, however imminent, is nevertheless delayed to some degree, and that runs counter to modern priorities. Moreover, for the average KT member, there was a more obvious consideration: the fact that, for the most part, other worship-pers were not millenarians and regarded "prophecy nuts" with suspicion. Apoc-alyptic teaching received little in the way of social reinforcement within the community; the lack of a plausibility structure was a cause as well as an effect of the lack of millenarian belief.

My conclusion, therefore, is that secularization weakens millenarianism in an even more direct way than it weakens other forms of religious consensus. The bewildering expansion of the spiritual supermarket, coupled with the an-cient susceptibility of apocalyptic prophecy to disconfirmation and the ever more rapid circulation of the information that disconfirms prophecies, makes it hard to envisage a large-scale outbreak of classic millenarian excitement in the West; we should certainly not be surprised that the year 2000 failed to produce one. This is not to say that apocalyptic ideas will disappear. In the developing world, millenarian movements may yet have a profound effect on their societies—and, in the case of the syncretist Falun Gong sect in China, are already doing so. In the West, however, the Christian millenarian tradition is likely to be banished to the sort of after-life suggested by the version of the secularization thesis put forward by the sociologist James Beckford. In Beck-ford's view, religion has come adrift from its former points of anchorage: in-stead of operating as a sacred canopy, it serves as a resource to which individ-uals and groups have recourse from time to time, one example being the surge of quasi-religious emotion after the death of Diana, Princess of Wales. At a time when institutional religion is in decline, the deregulation of religious symbols, meanings, and values has made it easier for secular society to exploit them (2001: 232). If the imagery of mainstream Christianity can be plundered in this way, so, too, can the Judeo-Christian narrative of the end of the world, with its unforgettable images of Antichrist, Rapture, Armageddon, and Last Judgment. Indeed, the "improvisational millennialism" described by Michael Barkun (2003)—the fantastic *bricolage* of apocalyptic conspiracy theories to be found on the Internet—suggests that these symbols are more malleable than ever before. But how much significance should we attach to this development? Ideological malleability does not lend itself to the construction of strong plau-sibility structures. In the final analysis, the elaboration of apocalyptic themes in cyberspace and popular culture is not evidence of a renewal of faith in millennial transformation; rather, it suggests that doctrines in which people once devoutly believed are becoming routinized into metaphor and entertain-ment.

Appendix

Methodology

This study has involved qualitative and quantitative techniques of data collection. The choice of Kensington Temple for my fieldwork came about by accident: one of my fellow students at the London School of Economics was a member of the church, and he invited one of its pastors, Larry Grant, to speak to a sociology of religion seminar. Grant agreed to approach Colin Dye about the possibility of my conducting interviews at KT, though it was several months before permission was granted in the summer of 1998. Dye remained an inaccessible figure—I had only one long conversation with him, and that was off the record—but his senior assistants, Will Napier and Andrew Kenworthy, cheerfully answered my questions and suggested further lines of inquiry. (It was a stroke of luck, from my point of view, that Napier then left the church and proceeded to give me an uncensored account of life behind the scenes at Kensington Temple.)

My choice of interviewees was dictated partly by considerations of access: Napier and Kenworthy both served as head of the Bible college during my fieldwork, and essentially threw open its doors to me. I approached other interviewees outside services, and paid regular visits to the bookshop, where many customers were happy to talk to me. With the exception of Ravi Holy, whose testimony has been on the Internet and therefore in the public domain, the names of all the ordinary worshippers and staff members in this study are pseudonyms; pastors appear under their real names, except for Ron and Sarah Tomlinson. Longer interviews were taped and shorter ones recorded in shorthand (I am a trained newspaper reporter). I also kept detailed field notes of the services I attended, and made extensive use of the tape recordings of sermons provided by the church. As I have explained, I was careful to include in my interview sample members of the different demographic groups represented in the church, but I was not in a position to structure it in a way that reflected the precise composition of this large and porous community.

Fortunately, Kensington Temple conducts a "census" of its membership every two years, and allowed me to insert questions into the 1999 survey. The 2,973 respondents included the vast majority of worshippers at KT and Tabernacle Sunday services during the month of October; many of these (it is impossible to say how many) also belonged to satellite churches. Staff at the Tabernacle were responsible for entering the responses onto a database, which they emailed to me in the spring of 2000. Multivariate analysis of the data was carried out using the Microsoft Excel program. The text of the questions added to page four of the questionnaire was as follows:

A. Place the following in order of importance in your personal faith (numbering them 1 to 5, with 1 as the most important and 5 as the least important): Evangelism; Spiritual Warfare; End Times; Bible Study; Gifts of the Holy Spirit; Prayer.

B. When do you think it likely that Jesus Christ will return? Within the next 10 years; within the next 50 years; not our place to speculate.

C. Have you read books or watched tapes by the following authors? Kenneth Hagin; Barry Smith; Hal Lindsey; R T Kendall; Grant Jeffrey.[1]

D. Do you agree with the following statements?

1. The move towards a single European Currency is a sign of the Antichrist (Agree / disagree / neither agree nor disagree).

2. The world was created in six 24-hour days, just like the Bible says (Agree / disagree / neither agree nor disagree).

3. Supermarket barcodes may contain hidden Satanic information (Agree / disagree / neither agree nor disagree).

4. The year 2000 is an important date, marking the beginning of the end (Agree / disagree / neither agree nor disagree).

Glossary

Antichrist: In the fundamentalist Christian tradition, a demonic figure who will rule the world, ushering in a terrible persecution of Christians before the Second Coming.

Apocalypse: The cataclysmic events leading to the end of the world; also the name given to an ancient literary genre containing complex metaphorical prophecies of the End.

Apocalypticism: In this study, a synonym for millenarianism.

Armageddon: The final battle between the forces of good and evil, in which the armies of Christ vanquish those of Satan.

Charismatic Christianity: A worldwide movement which teaches that the New Testament gifts of Pentecost, such as prophecy and speaking in tongues, have been restored to modern Christians. It is more middle-class than classic Pentecostalism and is represented in the mainstream denominations.

Dispensationalism: A fundamentalist Christian model of divine history made up of Biblical "dispensations", the last of which will culminate in the return of Christ.

End Times: In evangelical Christian tradition, the period from the beginning of the fulfillment of the Bible's eschatological prophecies until the dawn of the Millennium.

Millenarianism: Also known as millennialism, a belief in the imminent and usually violent end of the current world and the dawning of a perfect society on earth.

Millennium: In the fundamentalist Christian tradition, the thousand-year reign of Jesus and his saints that follows the defeat of Satan at Armageddon. With a lower case "m", the word can signify any post-apocalyptic new world. Also a calendar unit of a thousand years.

Pentecostalism: An international Christian movement based around the restoration of the gifts of Pentecost. Its theology is similar to that of Charismatic Christianity, but its character tends to be more fundamentalist, sectarian and millenarian.

Postmillennialism: The belief, held by relatively few evangelicals, that Jesus will return after the Millennium, loosely defined as a long period of Christian righteousness on earth.

Premillennialism: The belief, held by a majority of fundamentalist and conservative
evangelical Christians, that Jesus will return to earth to initiate the thousand-year
reign of the saints

Rapture: The premillennialist doctrine that all true Christians will rise into the air to
join Jesus before he returns to earth.

Restorationism: The belief, shared by some Pentecostals, that Jesus will restore the
Church to apostolic purity before his return to earth.

Tribulation: The seven-year tyranny of Antichrist. Conservative evangelicals are divided as to whether Christians will be raptured before or after this period; hence
the "pre-Trib" and "post-Trib" schools of thought.

Notes

1. Leon Festinger was the major author of the study, and I shall follow convention in referring to *When Prophecy Fails* by his name alone.

2. Yonina Talmon offers a slightly different definition that is also often quoted: millennial movements are "religious movements that expect imminent, total, ultimate, this-worldly salvation" (1966: 166). For a useful summary of the academic debates about millenarianism, see chapter 7 of Hamilton's *The Sociology of Religion* (1995).

3. Beckford also points out that neither the socialization process nor the routine meetings of the Witnesses offer opportunities for expressing resentment at the prevailing social order: "In fact, Jehovah's Witnesses accord less importance to scriptural references to this-worldly or other-worldly privilege than do the clergy of mainstream Christian churches and denominations" (1975: 156).

4. For a summary of the theoretical and methodological objections to Festinger's theory, see the Introduction by Jon R. Stone to the volume of essays he edited entitled *Expecting Armageddon: Essential Readings in Failed Prophecy*. Stone writes: "The strong criticisms levelled at the Festinger study—which has not been unlike an ocean liner that developed leaks after its first launch—have all but scuttled its reliability for predicting responses to failed prophecy." In almost all subsequent studies of failed millennial prophecy, proselytizing did not occur; in Stone's view, the evangelistic behavior of Festinger's flying saucer group "was indeed *peculiar* to that group: their response was counterintuitive but largely idiosyncratic" (2000: 23).

5. See, for example, Meissner's *Thy Kingdom Come* (1995), which explores the "underlying narcissistic dynamic" of millenarian belief; in his very brief discussion of Protestant premillennialism, Meissner writes that it suggests that millennialism "is not necessarily the preserve of rampant psychopathology" (237).

6. For example, Joseph Bettis wrote in a 1984 essay:

During the past two decades, millennialism has returned. The resurgence of evangelical Christianity . . . has been accompanied by a new interest in historical transformation. This interest has been considerably abetted by the heightened awareness of the proximity of nuclear holocaust. Any attempt to introduce millennial ideas into the contemporary theological debate must understand . . . the political power of millennial thought worldwide. The effort to avoid nuclear destruction cannot justify genocidal totalitarianism. (153–54)

I encountered a similar attitude at a conference of the Center for Millennial Studies at Boston University in 1997. This was the heyday of the Promise Keepers, a movement of evangelical Christian men who met in sports stadiums to declare their commitment to Christ. Several attendees at the conference warned of the "dangers" of the movement; it was even claimed, absurdly, that a charismatic leader might trigger anti-Semitic apocalyptic hysteria among the membership.

CHAPTER 2

1. For a critique of rational choice theory in religion, see the essay by Neitz and Mueser (1997), who suggest that economic categories such as "output" and "consumption" underestimate the complexity of religious production. They also point out that, in contrast to the economic marketplace, the producers and consumers of religion tend to be the same people.

2. Max Weber, in *The Methodology of the Social Sciences*, came close to setting out a concept of subjective rationality. He wrote that an individual "weighs and chooses from among the values involved according to his own conscience and his personal view of the world" (1949: 53). The phrase "subjective rationality" was coined by Herbert Simon (1982) to convey the complexity of human decision-making in situations where goals conflict, perfect satisfactions can never be obtained, and available options are limited. For a discussion of its application to the sociology of religion, see Stark and Finke's *Acts of Faith* (2000: 37).

3. Bryan Wilson, in *The Social Dimensions of Sectarianism*, makes the following observation:

Denominationalisation—the loosening rigour; the loss of the sense of dissent and protest; the reduction of distance from other Christians; and the muting of claims that the sect's distinctive teachings are necessary for salvation—is a current that exerts some pressure on all contemporary movements. But some resist better than others. A sect's original stance may facilitate or impede the denominationalising process. Where there are practises and teachings that stand in sharp contrast with those of mainstream Christianity, these may act as insulating devices. (1990: 109)

Wilson describes the Methodists and Disciples of Christ as sects that have become denominationalized, unlike the Brethren, Hutterites, and Jehovah's Witnesses.

4. Nachman Ben-Yehuda, in *Deviance and Moral Boundaries* ([1985] 1987: 3), writes: "Defining deviance has always been a problem. With the exception of the general statement that deviance involves violation of norms, a satisfactory solution to the problem has apparently not yet been found."

5. Nicholas Campion's book *The Great Year: Astrology, Millenarianism and History in the Western Tradition* provides an authoritative comparative analysis of models of time. Drawing on the work of Eliade and Popper, Campion locates the roots of both millenarianism and historicist schemes such as Marxism in ancient myths about time based on the sequence of the seasons and the movement of the night sky. "All theories that assume a greater purpose underlying historical change are intimately bound up with concepts of order in nature and the cosmos: if nature has an order, runs the argument, then so does history," he writes. "From this simple assumption it follows that if this order can be understood, then history's purpose will become clear, and once its purpose it revealed, the future can be predicted" (1994: 8–9).

6. For a sense of the awesome explanatory range of prophecy literature, see Tom McIver's *The End of the World: An Annotated Bibliography*, which contains brief descriptions of more than 3,000 publications from the Book of Enoch to books warning of computer meltdown in the year 2000. All the major conflicts in Western history have been subjected to apocalyptic analysis, together with many less obvious phenomena: one fourteenth-century Islamic text argues that "the prevalence of tall buildings" is a sign of the End (1999: 31).

7. The difference between *l'avenir* and *le futur* was explored by Pierre Bourdieu in his writing about the Algerian Kabyle, for whom the short-term future could be planned for but the long-term future "belongs to God" (1963: 61–62). For a further discussion of the distinction, see Alfred Gell's *The Anthropology of Time* ([1992] 1996: 288).

8. This dynamic can be illustrated by an example of prophecy literature written during the Clinton administration. In 1996 the Christian Zionist author Marvin Byers published a book entitled *Yasser Arafat—An Apocalyptic Character?* that named the PLO chairman as the satanic "little horn" in Daniel. In making such an explicit identification, however, Byers faced the threat of empirical disconfirmation, and in anticipation of it he prepared several escape routes for himself. He acknowledged that the situation in the Middle East might improve instead of moving toward apocalyptic crisis, and he devoted two pages to the possibility that Arafat might die before fulfilling his prophetic role, explaining that the role of little horn could be transferred to his successor as head of the PLO (1996: 222–23); he also added an Introduction taking into account developments in Israel since he finished the original manuscript. Significantly, the tone of Byers's book and many similar texts is notably defensive; this is testimony to the ridicule and criticism that apocalyptic analysis of current events has always attracted, thanks to its tendency to issue incorrect forecasts and its often convoluted attempts to uncover the identity of living people in the pages of Scripture.

9. Detailed accounts of the formation of deviant cosmologies can be found in a volume edited by Jeffrey Kaplan and Heléne Lööw entitled *The Cultic Milieu: Oppositional Subcultures in an Age of Globalization*, which includes essays on occult National Socialism, neo-Shamanism, and the apocalyptic Satanism of Gothic rock music. Kaplan and Lööw argue (2002: 3) that the exchange of heterodox ideas in the anti-globalization movement of the late 1990s perfectly illustrates the circulation of proscribed knowledge described by Campbell a quarter of a century earlier.

10. Michael Barkun uses the phrase "stigmatized knowledge" to convey the full range of ideas circulating in the cultic milieu. He defines such knowledge as consisting of "claims to truth that the claimants regard as verified despite the marginalisation of those claims by the institutions that conventionally distinguish between

knowledge and error—universities, communities of scientific researchers and the like" (2003: 43). In other words, rejection by the societal consensus is a qualification for the special status of certain truth claims.

11. For example, the Mormons early on turned their back on the occult and Masonic elements in Joseph Smith's theology and banned polygamy (Barrett 2001: 157). The Seventh-day Adventists have distanced themselves from the colorful statements of their prophet, Ellen G. White, who claimed to have made out-of-body visits to other planets (Reavis 1995: 95; Barrett 2001: 171). The Church of Scientology has reduced the importance of magic in its programs (Stark and Bainbridge 1985: 263–83) and no longer insists on the literal truth of L. Ron Hubbard's science fiction-influenced cosmology. The Holy Order of MANS, a Christian order which sprang up in hippie San Francisco, purged itself of the theosophical and New Age elements in its teachings and embraced Eastern Orthodoxy (Lucas 1995). Such changes can be ascribed in part to the gravitational pull of societal norms that we noted earlier: it is difficult—and often not worth the effort—to preserve the plausibility of beliefs or practices that offer easy targets for critics in the outside world.

12. It is difficult to produce a simple definition of gnosticism, originally a complex early Christian heresy with roots in paganism and esoteric Judaism. Perhaps its most important feature was its emphasis on the intrinsic corruption of the created world and the need to free the soul from its material environment; these doctrines were typically secret and sometimes expressed in occult rites (Cross and Livingstone 1997: 683–85). For a discussion of the shared features of gnosticism and apocalypticism, see "The New Science of Politics" by Eric Voegelin ([1952] 1999); *The Apocalyptic Movement: Introduction and Interpretation* by Walter Schmithals ([1973] 1975); and *Prophecy and Gnosis: Apocalypticism in the Wake of the Lutheran Reformation* by Robin Bruce Barnes (1988).

CHAPTER 3

1. There can be no authoritative figure for the number of Pentecostalists in the world, since where the boundaries of the movement lie is a matter of opinion. Everything depends on whether the total includes Charismatic Christians from non-Pentecostal denominations and indigenous churches. David Martin argues that "broadly understood, Pentecostalism includes one in eight of the Christian 'constituency' of nearly two billion [i.e., 250 million] . . . and one in 25 of the global population" (2001:1). Hunt, Hamilton, and Walter, after attempting to identify the characteristics of Pentecostalism, conclude that "the movement is evolving so rapidly that it is not entirely clear whether these distinctive hallmarks still hold" (1997: 2).

2. In this study, "Charismatic" with a capital "C" refers exclusively to the exercise of the New Testament gifts of the Spirit; it normally applies to Christians outside the classic Pentecostal denominations. The use of the word with a lower-case "c" refers to the Weberian concept of charisma.

3. Branham had announced that a great miracle evangelization campaign would begin on January 25, 1966. But he died as a result of a car accident on Christmas Day, 1965, so his followers had his body embalmed and refrigerated to allow him to rise from the dead a month later (Hollenweger 1972: 354–55).

4. Although some Roman Catholics describe themselves as Pentecostalists, this label is potentially misleading. "Pentecostal" in a Catholic context is usually a syno-

nym for Charismatic. Certainly, so-called Catholic Pentecostalists have far more in common with middle-class Protestant Charismatics than they do with the classic Pentecostal denominations, which historically have been strongly anti-Catholic.

5. Spittler's essay, entitled *Are Pentecostals and Charismatics Fundamentalists?*, provides a useful summary of the arguments for and against the use of the label. He concludes that Pentecostals cannot be described as fundamentalists per se, but that they often "think and act like fundamentalists." He also points out that a majority of American Pentecostals would probably be happy to describe themselves as fundamentalists. The situation in Britain is different: many members of Kensington Temple associate the word "fundamentalist" with redneck Americans and refuse to apply it to themselves.

6. Barr, whose book about fundamentalism is marred by his inability to conceal his distaste for his subject, has this to say about dispensationalism's approach to disparate texts:

> The whole dispensationalist framework is in a certain mad way an attempt to cope with problems and facts that were being dealt with by critical study at the same time in a completely different mental world. Dispensationalism gives some sort of recognition, however distorted, to the fact that what Jesus says is not the same as what Paul says, that the gospels have a different theological role from the epistles, and that the idea of the kingdom of God does not easily fit into the customary structures of Christian doctrine. (1977: 198)

7. I am aware that the use of the word "subculture" here might be seen as contentious. Christian prophecy enthusiasts are usually members of the broader subculture of conservative evangelical Christianity, so perhaps it would be more accurate—if pedantic—to speak of a "sub-subculture."

8. Harding (1994: 66) writes that

> the heterogeneity, instability and partiality of dispensational narrative framings of current events undermine the absolute "futurism" of Bible prophecies. Everyone "knows for certain" that no Bible prophecy can be fulfilled before the Rapture. But what if events scheduled to occur after the Rapture seem to occur before it? Much of the variation in dispensational discourse revolves around questions such as these.

9. For example, Lindsey asserts that the feet of the returning Jesus will first touch the earth where they left it, on the Mount of Olives. This will cause the mountain to split in two, creating a crevice running from the Dead Sea to the Mediterranean. Lindsey adds: "It was reported to me that an oil company doing seismic studies of this area in quest of oil discovered a gigantic fault running east and west precisely through the Mount of Olives. The fault is so severe that it could split at any time. It is awaiting 'the foot' " ([1970] 1971: 174). This marshalling of small pieces of data is typical of the prophecy genre: it suggests that secular corroboration plays a crucial role in validating supernatural claims, just as it does in the case of Pentecostal faith healers who produce doctors' affidavits as evidence of cures.

10. The folklorist Robert Glenn Howard, who monitors Christian apocalyptic websites, writes that the people posting to them tend to adopt one of two conflicting modes of argumentation: appeals to "truth as known through individual experience," and appeals to "truth as pursued through pluralistic negotiation" (1999: 4). Howard

sees these modes as opposite ends of a spectrum. At the "revealed" end, a website called AlphathroughOmega.com predicts that the Rapture will occur after the Great Tribulation. This is a familiar, if minority, evangelical scenario—but the website's owners, a computer technician called Gene and his wife Susan, support it with an appeal to divine knowledge that has been granted to them. Gene is "not interested in exploring the possibility that he might be wrong because his knowledge is the result of direct experience with God" (6). At the "negotiated" end of the spectrum, meanwhile, is ldolphin.org, a popular End Times site run by Lambert Dolphin, a retired American physicist. This presents a standard dispensationalist scenario; there are no risky predictions, and Dolphin respectfully "compares notes" with other evangelical authorities. Howard adds that most End Times debaters on the Internet lie somewhere in the middle of the spectrum. This conclusion is consonant with the history of millennial belief, which suggests that it is difficult to introduce or interpret any authoritative prophecy without making some sort of claim to charismatic authority.

11. André Droogers (2001: 48) argues that Pentecostals have a special capacity for "the paradoxical combination of opposite characteristics." He cites the contrast between, on the one hand, a long-term, apocalyptic view of history, and, on the other, the use of Pentecostal gifts to solve problems in the short term. Other examples include the vigorous participation of believers in a secular world they profess to despise, and, in Pentecostal services, "the simultaneous presence of spontaneity and control, or of individual expression and social conformity." In short, it seems possible that Pentecostals have a greater tolerance for contradiction than more regimented religious traditions, and this has obvious implications for the present study.

CHAPTER 4

1. Roy Wallis (1984: 111–18) described the Jeffreys case as an example of "charismatic displacement," in which "institutionalisation proceeds without clear recognition by the charismatic leader of what is occurring, until [it is] too late for him effectively to reverse the situation."

2. The entry for British Israelism in the *Oxford Dictionary of the Christian Church* gives a flavor of the low regard in which the movement was held by the theological establishment: "The theory that the British people is ultimately descended from the ten Israelite tribes which were taken captive into Assyria c.721 BC, and thereafter wholly disappeared from Hebrew history. It was often found in conjunction with pronounced imperialist views; and though the numbers and influence of those who defend it are small, they often hold it with a persistence and enthusiasm which refuse to give a dispassionate consideration to objections urged against it. The theory meets with no support from serious ethnologists or archaeologists" (Cross and Livingstone 1997: 239). The implication of this statement is that British Israelism should not be taken seriously because its claims can be empirically disproved.

3. This dynamic is far from unique: one loose parallel might be with Pope John Paul II, who, to the dismay of proponents of a sophisticated, routinized Catholicism, publicly embraced some of the apocalyptic claims associated with the Portuguese shrine of Fatima.

4. Simon Coleman, in his ethnographic study of the Word of Life Church, describes its pastor, Ulf Ekman, in terms that could also apply to Colin Dye. He writes that Ekman, referred to as "Ulf" even by people who have never met him, is per-

ceived by group members to be the inspiration for most church projects, and that this perception is reinforced by organizational structures. He adds: "Even disillusioned adherents have described in interviews the sense of dread they have felt in leaving the group: the fact that they were required to have a personal meeting with Ekman in order to withdraw membership was often perceived as a major hurdle in the decision to leave" (2000: 97). Similarly, former KT staff have told me that the worst part of leaving the organization was breaking the news to Dye.

5. There are, in fact, several hundred Latin American worshippers at KT, but they presumably chose to represent themselves as Caucasian rather than Hispanic.

6. The shortage of marriageable Christian men is a persistent topic of conversation among women at KT; during my time there I heard a number of stories about good-looking young pastors being pursued by several women at the same time.

7. Kensington Temple lent prominent support to the American evangelist Morris Cerullo during his controversial Missions to London in the 1990s. Advertisements for the meetings claimed that the blind would see and the crippled walk again as a result of Cerullo's healing ministry; but his "cures" were ridiculed by the secular media, and many evangelical Christians expressed unease at his methods. Eventually the Evangelical Alliance disowned Cerullo, at which point Colin Dye took Kensington Temple out of the Alliance in protest. For an account of the controversy, see Schaefer (1999). Howard (1997) devotes a chapter to attacking Cerullo.

8. See also Sara Savage's essay "A Psychology of Fundamentalism" (2002), much of which is applicable to Pentecostalism. Savage concludes that there is little evidence to suggest that fundamentalists as a whole lack cognitive complexity, though this may be true of highly committed fundamentalists who resolve any doubts they might have by avoiding disconfirming information.

CHAPTER 5

1. *Welcome to Kensington Temple*, published by Kensington Temple, London City House, PO Box 9161, London W3 6GS, 1999 (address obsolete since the move from the Tabernacle).

2. Holy Trinity Brompton, or "HTB," is a successful Anglican Charismatic church in South Kensington, London, that enthusiastically embraced Wimberite "signs and wonders" during the 1990s.

3. The Kissinger/Antichrist link surfaced as early as 1972 in a tract by Julian E. Williams, *Henry Kissinger—Mystery Man of Power*. Two years later it was picked up by the best-selling prophecy author Salem Kirban, in *Kissinger: Man of Peace?* (1974). Doug Clark, in his 1975 book *Amazing Prophecies of the 70's—It's Super K!* further elaborates on the idea, as does Frank Allnutt's *Kissinger: Man of Destiny?* (1976). As recently as 1997, the prophecy website www.lasttrumpetministries.org implied that Kissinger was involved in a plan to make Jerusalem the headquarters of world religion headed by the Pope. But such references are increasingly rare: as Oropeza notes, "now that the Nixon years are long behind us, the Kissinger–Antichrist connection is getting old, and so is Kissinger" (1994: 151).

4. It is fairly safe to infer, from the greater prominence of apocalyptic themes in Elim literature of the mid-twentieth century, that they also featured more often in ser-

mons then than they do now. Even so, it is possible that, even then, Pentecostalism was less apocalyptic in practice than its reputation suggested. The anthropologist Malcolm Calley, in his 1965 study of West Indian Pentecostal sects in Britain, wrote that millennial doctrine "appears to be more significant as an ideological sanction for the maintenance of separation from the world than as a principle governing [church members'] day-to-day operation." He also reported that "not once has the second resurrection or the thousand years' reign of Christ been the subject of a sermon or testimony at a service I have attended" (1965: 69).

5. The American author Rebecca Brown, MD, is the author or co-author of several books arguing that Christians are under greater assault from Satan than they realize. See, for example, *Unbroken Curses: Hidden Source of Trouble in the Christian's Life*, which argues that even household pets can be attacked by demonic curses (1995: 108).

6. "But of that day and that hour no one knows, not even the angels of heaven, nor the son, but only the Father" (Mark 13:32; Matt. 24:36). Geza Vermes ([2000] 2001: 203) writes that this text "flatly contradicts" all the warnings Jesus is supposed to have given in his eschatological discourse of Mark 13, Matt. 24, and Luke 21.

7. Aleister Crowley (1875–1947), English occult writer and magician who liked to be known as "the great beast" and "the wickedest man alive."

8. Holy's memoir was still posted at www.RaviHoly.com at the time of writing (April 2003).

9. For a discussion of the place of the "Illuminatus" books in conspiracy circles, see *Conspiracy Theories, Secrecy and Power in American Culture* by Mark Fenster (1999). Fenster says that Wilson and his co-author Robert Shea are by no means conventional conspiracy theorists:

> In fact, their trilogy is an extensive parody of the fear of conspiracy . . . a subversion of conspiracy theory through parodic humour and excess. As conspiracy folds into conspiracy and it becomes increasingly difficult to identify the political orientations and goals of groups and individual characters . . . the trilogy emerges as an anarchic treatise about a world in which conspiracies have run amok. (203)

10. The point of this well-known saying is that someone living in accordance with God's will need not worry about an imminent apocalypse. Whether Luther actually said it is not known: it has also been attributed to medieval rabbis and to John Wesley. Many references to it on the Internet ascribe it to Dr. Martin Luther King Jr.

11. The basis for this claim is the suggestion in Dan. 9:2 that "seventy days" actually means seventy years, by which calculation "seventy weeks" (490 days) would equal 490 years. See Boyer 1992: 29.

CHAPTER 6

1. As Dan Cohn-Sherbok notes in his study of the phenomenon, many Messianic Jews are convinced premillennialists who believe that the Antichrist will soon plunge mankind into the Great Tribulation. During this time, "crises will occur for the Jewish people and the rest of humanity, including floods, famines, earthquakes

and disease . . . both traditional Jews and Christians will be persecuted and killed"
(2000: 172). This is what Maureen meant when she talked about "what would happen to the Jews." But this is not a specifically Messianic Jewish prophecy: it is the
standard fundamentalist Christian understanding of the role of the Jews in the End
Times, which paradoxically honors and inflicts untold suffering on the (unconverted)
people of Israel.

2. Maureen's identification of a divine day with 1,000 years appears first in the
Second Epistle of Peter, written in the second century A.D., which says that "with the
Lord one day is as a thousand years, and a thousand years as one day" (2 Peter 3:8);
this is a reworking of Psalm 90, verse 4: "For a thousand years in thy sight are but as
yesterday when it is past." Early Christian authorities such as Irenaeus combined this
idea with the Jewish tradition of a Great Week to produce a structure of history consisting of six 1,000-year days followed by the sabbatical Millennium prophesied in the
Book of Revelation (Campion 1994: 324). Maureen made use of the day = 1,000
years equation but combined it instead with the 24-hour clock. When I interviewed
her, she was not sure where her inspiration came from; the most likely explanation is
that she was taught about the Second Epistle of Peter in Bible college but learned
how to work on the information from Jeffrey.

3. Maureen was right to say that the company abandoned its logo a few years
ago but wrong about the goat's head: the logo showed a face on a crescent moon
looking at 13 stars representing the original American states. The rumor that this contained Satanic symbolism surfaced in fundamentalist circles around 1980; within a
few years it had become more elaborate, alleging that Procter & Gamble had made a
pact with the Devil and given a share of the company's profits to the Church of Satan.
The company was eventually forced to employ four staff members to reply to the 500
complaints it was receiving every day. In 1985 it removed the logo from all its products, but the rumors continued. According to the sociologist Jeffrey Victor, "research
sponsored by the company found that the rumours were transmitted primarily through
informal communication networks beyond the reach of lawsuits: through flyers given
out in churches and shopping centres and by word-of-mouth conversation. The persistence of the Procter & Gamble Satanism rumour stories demonstrates the power of
the fundamentalist communication network in American society" (1993: 14).

4. See, for example, Dean R. Hoge's study of religious change among American
Catholics, which found that the attitudes of converts were "closer to the doctrinal
teachings of the Church" than those of other active Catholics, and that religion was
more important in their lives (1981: 42).

5. We know from numerous historical accounts that the young children of apocalyptic believers can be just as carried away by millennial fear or enthusiasm as new
converts. The young Edmund Gosse, author of *Father and Son* ([1907] 1965), shared
all the convictions of his Plymouth Brethren father, and more: "I proposed at the end
of the summer holidays that I should stay home [from boarding school]. 'What is the
use of my going to school? Let me be with you when we rise to meet the Lord in the
air!' To this my father sharply and firmly replied that it was our duty to carry out our
usual avocations to the last, for we knew not the moment of His coming" (1965:
208–9).

6. According to Eileen Barker (1984: 36), the expertise of social scientists is confined to empirical reality. They cannot assess non-empirical claims that are incapable of being refuted. Maureen's claim that Jesus was speaking to her comes into this category.

7. The total of those who assented to the Creationism statement in the whole church—60 percent—is lower than these figures because it includes respondents who did not answer the question about the return of Christ.

CHAPTER 7

1. For example, *Millennium Prophecies* by Stephen Skinner (1994: 69) made the following claims, none of which is supported by the historical record: "December [999] saw fanaticism reach new heights. . . . Bands of flagellants roamed the countryside; mobs called for the execution of supposed sorcerers or unpopular burghers, and even some farm animals were freed to roam through the towns, giving a slightly surreal air to the proceedings."

2. Jose Arguelles, chief proponent of the Harmonic Convergence, described it as "the return of Quetzalcoatl. But the elimination of Armageddon as well. To some it may even be as another Pentecost and second coming of the Christ. Amidst spectacle, celebration, and urgency, the old mental house will dissolve, activating the return of long-dormant archetypal memories and impressions" (1987: 169–70).

3. It is interesting to compare this position with that of Jeffrey (1988). It accepts Ussher's Creation date of 4004 B.C. rather than Jeffrey's 4000 B.C., but actually produces a later Second Coming, since it envisages 6,000 years between the Creation and the Tribulation rather than the *parousia*. Kenworthy was not sure where he had heard this theory; I did not encounter it anywhere. If he came across it before 1996, then possibly it involved a pre-Tribulation Rapture; but it is more likely that its supporters took a post-Trib view and thought that the persecution of the Church had begun in 1996.

4. Hamon prophesies a war that will bring about an effective theocracy: "Unless a tremendous revival happens within these nations [China and the Islamic world], a great war between East and West will take place around the turn of this century. . . . The end result will be the exaltation of the righteous nations, while the wicked nations are subdued and come under the rule of the righteous" (21).

5. In fact, it was Herod the Great, not Augustus, who died in 4 B.C. Matthew dates Jesus' birth to the period of Herod's death, which is why most scholars believe that Jesus was born between four and seven years before the notional start of the A.D. calendar. E. P. Sanders ([1993] 1995: 11–12) points out that the sixth-century founder of the calendar, Dionysius Exiguus, did not know when Herod died. Luke (3:1) tells us that John the Baptist began preaching in the 15th year of Tiberius, in A.D. 29. He also says (3:23) that Jesus was about 30 years old when he began his ministry. Dionysius probably calculated that Jesus began his ministry a year after John, making him 30 in the year we now refer to as A.D. 30.

6. Twenty-five percent of the total is 500 groups, rather than the 800 Dye had spoken about at Grace for the City; it seems reasonable to ask what had happened to the other 300. According to a former pastor, the 800 total included every cell group

in the LCC network. Later, however, it became clear that even "creative accounting" would not produce the desired result, and it looks as if Dye went back to a stricter method of counting that reduced the total to 500.

CHAPTER 8

1. Percy (1996: 126), writing about Wimberite Charismatic churches, says that:

power and authority relationships are readily acknowledged, and understood to be necessary. Yet each believer also has a "personal" authority or power, just like Jesus, which can be exercised at will, only in relation to the Father. Thus, if Jesus possessed authority and power independent of human attribution, so can believers. Inevitably, this can lead to unrestrained individualism and particularity; believers can sometimes imagine that they are the centre of God's attention, at the expense of any wider commitments that divine power might have.

The same problem manifests itself at Kensington Temple, though the authority of the pastor in classic Pentecostalism, and the deference shown to him by many worshippers from the Third World, acts as a restraint on disruptive behavior.

2. For an overview, see the volume of essays entitled *Social Deviance: Readings in Theory and Research*, edited by Henry N. Pontell (2001).

3. Stark and Finke, in a chapter of their book *Acts of Faith* entitled "Secularization RIP," attack what they call "the myth of past piety." They maintain that religious participation in Western Europe was very low, centuries before the onset of modernization: therefore, "claims about a major decline in religious participation in Europe are based on a very exaggerated perceptions of past religiousness" (2000: 68). Bruce (2002: 58) replies that medieval and early modern people attended church in far greater numbers than their modern descendants, and even those who did not go to services exhibited a profoundly supernaturalist worldview. In my opinion, Bruce makes the stronger case.

4. Berger himself no longer believes that modernity will lead to religious decline: in an interview in 1997, he said that the argument that secularization and modernity go hand in hand had been proved "basically wrong" by the flourishing of religious faith in many parts of the world (1997: 974).

APPENDIX

1. Smith, Lindsey, and Jeffrey are leading prophecy authors, Hagin is a proponent of "health and wealth" theology, and Kendall is a leading British evangelical theologian; the last two are not regarded as End Times authors. The proportion of respondents who had read each author was as follows: Hagin 41 percent; Smith 23 percent; Kendall 22 percent; Jeffrey 15 percent; and Lindsey 9 percent. This might imply that Hagin's message of prosperity appeals to book-buyers more than the apocalyptic message of the prophecy authors, though other factors such as the number of titles stocked should be taken into account.

Bibliography

Abanes, Richard. 1998. *End-Time Visions: The Road to Armageddon?* New York and London: Four Walls Eight Windows.

Allnutt, Frank. 1976. *Kissinger: Man of Destiny?* Mission Viejo, Calif.: Allnutt Publications.

Alnor, William. 1989. *Soothsayers of the Second Advent.* Old Tappan, New Jersey: Revel.

Ammerman, Nancy Tatom. 1987. *Bible Believers: Fundamentalists in the Modern World.* New Brunswick and London: Rutgers University Press.

Andrews, Valerie, Robert Bosnak, and Karen Walter Goodwin Andrews, eds. 1987. *Facing Apocalypse.* Dallas: Spring Publications.

Appadurai, Arjun. 1997. *Modernity at Large: Cultural Dimensions of Globalization.* Minneapolis: University of Minnesota Press.

Arguelles, Jose. 1987. *The Mayan Factor: Path beyond Technology.* Santa Fe: Bear and Company.

Atkinson, Bruce. 1997. *End-Time Truths.* Series of six audiotapes. London: Dovewell Communications.

Augustine of Hippo. 1955. Letter 199, To Heysichius, On the End of the World. In *Writings of St Augustine,* Vol. 12. New York: Fathers of the Church, Inc.

———— 1972. *The City of God.* Trans. H. Bettenson. New York: Penguin Books.

Aune, David E. [1983] 1991. *Prophecy in Early Christianity and the Ancient Mediterranean World.* Grand Rapids, Mich.: Eerdmans.

Bainbridge, William Sims. 1997. *The Sociology of Religious Movements.* New York and London: Routledge.

Barker, Eileen. 1984. *The Making of a Moonie: Brainwashing or Choice?* Oxford: Basil Blackwell.

———— 1989. *New Religious Movements: A Practical Introduction.* London: Her Majesty's Stationery Office.

Barkun, Michael. 2003. *The Culture of Conspiracy: Apocalyptic Visions in Contemporary America*. Berkeley and Los Angeles: University of California Press.

Barnes, Robin Bruce. 1988. *Prophecy and Gnosis: Apocalypticism in the Wake of the Lutheran Reformation*. Stanford, Calif.: Stanford University Press.

Barr, James. 1977. *Fundamentalism*. London: SCM Press.

Barrett, David V. 2001. *The New Believers: Sects, "Cults" and Alternative Religions*. London: Cassell.

Baudrillard, Jean. 1997. Hysteresis of the Millennium. In *The Year 2000: Essays on the End*, ed. Charles B. Strozier and Michael Flynn. New York and London: New York University Press.

Baumgarten, Albert I., ed. 2000. Introduction to *Apocalyptic Time*. Leiden: Brill.

Becker, Howard S. [1963] 1997. *Outsiders: Studies in the Sociology of Deviance*. New York: Free Press.

———— 1998. *Tricks of the Trade: How to Think about Your Research While You're Doing It*. Chicago and London: University of Chicago Press.

Beckford, James A. 1975. *The Trumpet of Prophecy: A Sociological Study of Jehovah's Witnesses*. Oxford: Basil Blackwell.

———— 2001. Social Movements as Free-Floating Religious Phenomena. In *The Blackwell Companion to Sociology of Religion*, ed. Richard K. Fenn. Oxford: Blackwell.

Bell, Daniel, ed. 1968. *Toward the Year 2000: Work in Progress*. Boston: Houghton Mifflin.

Ben-Yehuda, Nachman. [1985] 1987. *Deviance and Moral Boundaries: Witchcraft, the Occult, Science Fiction, Deviant Sciences and Scientists*. Chicago and London: University of Chicago Press.

Berger, Bennett M. 1981. *The Survival of a Counterculture: Ideological Work and Everyday Life among Rural Communards*. Berkeley: University of California Press.

Berger, Peter L. [1967] 1969. *The Sacred Canopy: Elements of a Sociological Theory of Religion*. Garden City, N.Y.: Anchor Books.

———— [1979] 1980. *The Heretical Imperative: Contemporary Possibilities of Religious Affirmation*. London: Collins.

———— 1997. Epistemological Modesty: An Interview with Peter Berger. *Christian Century* 114 (October 14): 972–975

———— and Thomas Luckmann. [1966] 1971. *The Social Construction of Reality: A Treatise in the Sociology of Knowledge*. Harmondsworth, Middlesex: Penguin.

Bettis, Joseph. 1984. Millennialism and the Transformation of History. In *The Return of the Millennium*, ed. Joseph Bettis and S. K. Johannesen. Barrytown, N.Y.: International Religious Foundation.

Billig, Michael. 1991. *Ideology and Opinions: Studies in Rhetorical Psychology*. London: SAGE Publications.

Blumenberg, Hans. 1985. *Work on Myth*. Trans. Robert M. Wallace. Cambridge, Mass., and London: MIT Press.

Boal, Frederick W., Margaret C. Keane, and David N. Livingstone. 1997. *Them and Us? Attitudinal Variation among Churchgoers in Belfast*. Belfast: Institute of Irish Studies.

Bourdieu, Pierre. 1963. The Attitude of the Algerian Peasant towards Time. In *Mediterranean Countryman*, ed. Julian Pitt-Rivers. Paris: Recherches Mediterranéennes 1.

Bowker, John, ed. 1997. *The Oxford Dictionary of World Religions*. Oxford and New York: Oxford University Press.

Boyer, Pascal. [2001] 2002. *Religion Explained: The Human Instincts that Fashion Gods, Spirits and Ancestors*. London: Vintage.

Boyer, Paul. 1992. *When Time Shall be No More: Prophecy Belief in Modern American Culture*. Cambridge, Mass.: Belknap Press.

Braun, Willys. 1992. *Roots and Possible Fruits of AD 2000*. Kinshasa, Zaire: International Center of Evangelism.

Brendecke, Arndt. 1998. Is Centenarianism Replacing Millenarianism? Paper delivered at the annual conference of the Center for Millennial Studies, Boston University. November.

Brierley, Peter, ed. 1999. *UK Christian Handbook: Religious Trends 2000/2001 No. 2*. London: Christian Research.

Brown, Rebecca, and Daniel Yoder. 1995. *Unbroken Curses: Hidden Source of Trouble in the Christian's Life*. New Kensington, Penn.: Whitaker House.

Bruce, Steve. 2002. *God is Dead: Secularization in the West*. Oxford: Blackwell.

Bull, Malcolm. 1995. On Making Ends Meet. In *Apocalypse Theory and the Ends of the World*, ed. Malcolm Bull. Oxford: Blackwell.

Burke, Kenneth. [1941] 1973. *The Philosophy of Literary Form: Studies in Symbolic Action*, 3rd edn. Berkeley and Los Angeles: University of California Press.

Byers, Marvin. 1996. *Yasser Arafat—An Apocalyptic Character? An Urgent Call to the Nation of Israel and the Body of Christ*, 2nd edn. Miami: Hebron Press.

Bygrave, Stephen. 1993. *Kenneth Burke: Rhetoric and Ideology*. London and New York: Routledge.

Calley, Malcolm, J. C. 1965. *God's People: West Indian Pentecostal Sects in England*. Oxford: Oxford University Press.

Campbell, Colin. [1972] 2002. The Cult, the Cultic Milieu and Secularisation. In *The Cultic Milieu: Oppositional Subcultures in an Age of Globalization*, ed. Jeffrey Kaplan and Heléne Lööw. Walnut Creek, Calif.: Altamira Press.

Campion, Nicholas. 1994. *The Great Year: Astrology, Millenarianism and History in the Western Tradition*. London: Penguin Arkana.

Cantwell Smith, Wilfred. 1998. *Faith and Belief: The Difference between Them*. Oxford: Oneworld.

Carpenter, Joel A. 1997. *Revive Us Again: The Reawakening of American Fundamentalism*. New York and Oxford: Oxford University Press.

Chaves, Mark. 1998. Denominations as Dual Structures: An Organisational Analysis. In *Sacred Companies: Organisational Aspects of Religion and Religious Aspects of Organisations*, ed. N. J. Demerath et al. New York and Oxford: Oxford University Press.

Cho, Paul Yonggi. 1991. *Revelation: Visions of Our Ultimate Victory in Christ*. Milton Keynes, Buckinghamshire: Word Publishing.

Clark, Doug. 1975. *Amazing Prophecies of the 70's—It's Super K*. Orange, Calif.: Amazing Prophecy Center.

Clegg, Stewart. 1998. Foucault, Power and Organisations. In *Foucault, Management and Organization Theory*, ed. Alan McKinlay and Ken Starkey. London: SAGE Publications.

Cohn, Norman. 1993. *Cosmos, Chaos and the World to Come: The Ancient Roots of Apocalyptic Faith*. New Haven and London: Yale University Press.

——— [1957] 1993. *The Pursuit of the Millennium: Revolutionary Millenarians and Mystical Anarchists of the Middle Ages*, revised edn. London: Pimlico.

Cohn-Sherbok, Dan. 2000. *Messianic Judaism*. London and New York: Cassell.

Coleman, Simon. 2000. *The Globalization of Charismatic Christianity: Spreading the Gospel of Prosperity*. Cambridge: Cambridge University Press.

Corten, André, and Ruth Marshall-Fratani, eds. 2001. *From Babel to Pentecost: Transnational Pentecostalism in Africa and Latin America*. Bloomington and Indianapolis: Indiana University Press.

Cousins, Mark and Athar Hussein. 1984. *Michel Foucault*. New York: St Martin's Press.

Cox, Harvey. 1994. *Fire from Heaven: The Rise of Pentecostal Spirituality and the Reshaping of Religion in the Twenty-first Century*. Reading, Mass.: Addison-Wesley.

Craib, Ian. 1997. *Classical Social Theory*. Oxford: Oxford University Press.

Cross, F. L., and E. A. Livingstone, eds. 1997. *The Oxford Dictionary of the Christian Church*, 3rd edn. Oxford: Oxford University Press.

Csordas, Thomas J. 1997. *Language, Charisma and Creativity: The Ritual Life of a Religious Movement*. Berkeley: University of California Press.

Cuneo, Michael W. 1997. *The Smoke of Satan: Conservative and Traditionalist Dissent in Contemporary American Catholicism*. New York and Oxford: Oxford University Press.

Davies, Douglas J. 1984. *Meaning and Salvation in Religious Studies*. Leiden: Brill.

Douglas, Mary. 1973. *Natural Symbols: Explorations in Cosmology*, 2nd edn. London: Barrie and Jenkins.

Driscoll, James P. 1971. Transsexuals. In *Trans-Action* 8:28–37

Droogers, André. 2001. Globalization and Pentecostal Success. In *From Babel to Pentecost: Transnational Pentecostalism in Africa and Latin America*, ed. André Corten and Ruth Marshall-Fratani. Bloomington and Indianapolis: Indiana University Press.

Durkheim, Émile. 1915. *The Elementary Forms of the Religious Life*. London: George Allen & Unwin.

———— 1938. *The Rules of Sociological Method*. New York: Free Press.

Dye, Colin. 1997a. *Healing Anointing: Hope for a Hurting World*. London: Hodder and Stoughton.

———— 1997b. *It's Time to Grow: Kick-starting a Church into Growth*. Harpenden: Gazelle Books.

———— 2000. *Satan Unmasked: Overcoming the "Jezebel Spirit" at Work in Your Life*, seminar notes. London: Dovewell Publications.

Eisenstadt, Samuel N. 1968. *Max Weber on Charisma and Institution Building*. Chicago: University of Chicago Press.

Elias, Norbert. 1993. *Time: An Essay*. Oxford: Basil Blackwell.

Ellwood, Robert. 1992. How New Is the New Age? In *Perspectives on the New Age*, ed. James R. Lewis and J. Gordon Melton. Albany: State University of New York Press.

Erard, Michael. 1997. Millennium, Texas. In *The Year 2000: Essays on the End*, ed. Charles B. Strozier and Michael Flynn. New York and London: New York University Press.

Fenster, Mark. 1999. *Conspiracy Theories: Secrecy and Power in American Culture*. Minneapolis and London: University of Minnesota Press.

Festinger, Leon, Henry W. Riecken, and Stanley Schachter. [1956] 1964. *When Prophecy Fails: A Social and Psychological Study of a Modern Group that Predicted the Destruction of the World*. New York: Harper and Row.

Fukuyama, Francis. 1992. *The End of History and the Last Man*. New York: Free Press.

Fuller, Robert C. 1995. *Naming the Antichrist: The History of an American Obsession.* New York and Oxford: Oxford University Press.

Galanter, Marc. [1989] 1999. *Cults: Faith, Healing, and Coercion,* 2nd edn. New York and Oxford: Oxford University Press.

Garfinkel, Harold. 1967. *Studies in Ethnomethodology.* Englewood Cliffs, N.J.: Prentice Hall.

Gary, Jay. 1994. *The Star of 2000: Our Journey toward Hope.* Colorado Springs: Bimillennial Press.

————— and Olgy Gary, eds. 1989. *The Countdown Has Begun: The Story of the Global Consultation on AD 2000.* Rockville, Va.: AD 2000 Global Service Office.

Gell, Alfred. [1992] 1996. *The Anthropology of Time: Cultural Constructions of Temporal Maps and Images.* Oxford and Washington, D.C.: Berg.

Gerlach, Luther, and Virginia Hine. 1970. *People, Power and Chance.* Indianapolis, Ind.: Bobbs-Merrill.

Giddens, Anthony. 1991. *Modernity and Self-Identity: Self and Society in the Late Modern Age.* Cambridge: Polity Press.

Gifford, Paul. 1998. *African Christianity: Its Public Role.* London: Hurst and Company.

Gosse, Edmund. [1907] 1965. *Father and Son.* Boston: Houghton Mifflin.

Grenz, Stanley J. 1992. *The Millennial Maze: Sorting Out Evangelical Options.* Downers Grove, Ill.: Inter Varsity Press.

Gurr, Ted Robert. 1970. *Why Men Rebel.* Princeton, N.J.: Princeton University Press.

Hall, John R., with Philip D. Schuyler and Sylvaine Trinh. 2000. *Apocalypse Observed: Religious Movements and Violence in North America, Europe, and Japan.* London and New York: Routledge.

Hamilton, Malcolm B. 1995. *The Sociology of Religion: Theoretical and Comparative Perspectives.* London and New York: Routledge.

Hamon, Bill. 1997. *Apostles, Prophets and the Coming Moves of God: God's End-Time Plans for His Church and Planet Earth.* Santa Rosa Beach, Fla.: Christian International.

Hancock, Graham. 1998. *The Mars Mystery: The Secret Connection between Earth and the Red Planet.* London: Heinemann.

Harding, Susan. 1994. Imagining the Last Days: The Politics of Apocalyptic Language. In *Accounting for Fundamentalisms: The Dynamic Character of Movements (The Fundamentalism Project,* Vol. 4), ed. Martin E. Marty and R. Scott Appleby. Chicago and London: University of Chicago Press.

Hardyck, Jane Allyn, and Marcia Braden. 1962. "Prophecy Fails Again: A Report of a Failure to Replicate." *Journal of Abnormal and Social Psychology* 65, 2: 136–141.

Harrison, J. F. C. 1979. *The Second Coming: Popular Millenarianism 1780–1859.* London and Henley: Routledge & Kegan Paul.

Harrold, Francis B., and Raymond A. Eve. 1995. *Cult Archaeology and Creationism: Understanding Pseudoscientific Beliefs about the Past,* expanded edn. Iowa City: University of Iowa Press.

Hartman, Louis F., and Alexander A. Di Lella. 1990. Daniel. In *The New Jerome Biblical Commentary,* ed. Raymond E. Brown, Joseph A. Fitzmyer, and Roland E. Murphy. London and New York: Geoffrey Chapman.

Hexham, Irving, and Karla Poewe. 1997. *New Religions as Global Culture: Making the Human Sacred.* Boulder, Colo.: Westview.

Hill, Christopher. 1980. *Some Intellectual Consequences of the English Revolution.* Madison: University of Wisconsin Press.

Hill, Michael. 1973. *A Sociology of Religion*. London: Heinemann.

Hobsbawm, E. J. [1959] 1965. *Primitive Rebels: Studies in Archaic Forms of Social Movements in the 19th and 20th Centuries*. New York and London: W. W. Norton.

Hoftstadter, Richard. 1979. *The Paranoid Style in American Politics and Other Essays*. Chicago: Chicago University Press.

Hoge, Dean R. 1981. *Converts, Dropouts, Returnees: A Study of Religious Change among Catholics*. New York: Pilgrim Press.

Hollenweger, Walter. *The Pentecostals*. London: SCM Press.

Hornsby-Smith, Michael P. 1991. *Roman Catholic Beliefs in England: Customary Catholicism and Transformations of Religious Authority*. Cambridge: Cambridge University Press.

Howard, Robert Glenn. 1999. Negotiating Finality: Electro-Folk Rhetorics of Apocalypse. Paper delivered to the annual conference of the Center for Millennial Studies, Boston University. November.

Howard, Roland. 1997. *Charismania: When Christian Fundamentalism Goes Wrong*. London: Mowbray.

Huddleston, John. [1988] 1992. *Achieving Peace by the Year 2000*. Oxford: Oneworld.

Hunt, Stephen. 2000. The "New" Black Pentecostal Churches in Britain [1]. Paper presented at Cesnur 14th International Conference, Riga, Latvia. August.

———— ed. 2001a. *Christian Millenarianism: From the Early Church to Waco*. London: Hurst.

———— 2001b. The Rise, Fall and Return of Post-Millenarianism. In *Christian Millenarianism: From the Early Church to Waco*, ed. Stephen Hunt. London: Hurst.

———— Malcolm Hamilton and Tony Walter, eds. 1997. *Charismatic Christianity: Sociological Perspectives*. Basingstoke: Macmillan.

Hunter, James Davison. 1983. *American Evangelicalism: Conservative Religion and the Quandary of Modernity*. New Brunswick, N.J.: Rutgers University Press.

———— 1987. *Evangelicalism: The Coming Generation*. Chicago: University of Chicago Press.

Hywel-Davies, Jack. 1998. *The Kensington Temple Story*. Crowborough, East Sussex: Monarch Books.

Iannaccone, Laurence R. 1997. Rational Choice: Framework for the Scientific Study of Religion. In *Rational Choice Theory and Religion: Summary and Assessment*, ed. Lawrence A. Young. London and New York: Routledge.

James, William. [1902] 1985. *The Varieties of Religious Experience: A Study in Human Nature*. New York and London: Penguin Books.

Jeffrey, Grant R. [1988]. *Armageddon: Appointment with Destiny*. Toronto: Frontier Research Publications; revised and enlarged edn., 1997.

Jenkins, Richard. 1996. *Social Identity*. London and New York: Routledge.

Johannesen, Stanley. 1994. Third-Generation Pentecostal Language: Continuity and Change in Collective Perspective. In *Charismatic Christianity as Global Culture*, ed. Karla Poewe. Columbia: University of South Carolina Press.

John Paul II. 1996. *Agenda for the Third Millennium*. London: HarperCollins.

Kaplan, Jeffrey, and Heléne Lööw, eds. 2002. *The Cultic Milieu: Oppositional Subcultures in an Age of Globalization*. Walnut Creek, Calif.: Altamira Press.

Kay, William K. 2000a. *Pentecostals in Britain*. Carlisle: Paternoster Press.

———— 2000b. Pre-Millennial Tensions: What Pentecostal Ministers Look Forward to. In *Calling Time: Religion and Change at the Turn of the Millennium*, ed. Martyn Percy. Sheffield: Sheffield University Press.

Kelley, Dean M. 1972. *Why Conservative Churches Are Growing*. New York: Harper & Row.

Kirban, Salem. 1974. *Kissinger: Man of Peace?* Huntington Valley, Penn.: Salem Kirban, Inc.

LaHaye, Tim. 1992. *No Fear of the Storm*. Sisters, Ore.: Multnomah.

———— and Jerry B. Jenkins. 1995. *Left Behind: A Novel of the Earth's Last Days*. Wheaton, Ill.: Tyndale House.

Lamy, Philip. 1996. *Millennium Rage: Survivalists, White Supremacists, and the Doomsday Prophecy*. New York and London: Plenum Press.

Landes, Richard. 1988. Lest the Millennium Be Fulfilled: Apocalyptic Expectations and the Pattern of Western Chronography 100–800 CE. In *The Use and Abuse of Eschatology*, ed. V. Werbecke et al. Leuven: Leuven University Press.

———— 1997. The Apocalyptic Year 1000: Millennial Fever and the Origins of the Modern West. In *The Year 2000: Essays on the End*, ed. Charles B. Strozier and Michael Flynn. New York and London: New York University Press.

Lawson, Ronald. 1997. The Persistence of Apocalypticism within a Denominationalising Sect: The Apocalyptic Fringe Groups of Seventh-day Adventism. In *Millennium, Messiahs and Mayhem: Contemporary Apocalyptic Movements*, ed. Thomas Robbins and Susan J. Palmer. London and New York: Routledge.

Leatham, Miguel C. 1997. Rethinking Religious Decision-Making in Peasant Millenarianism: The Case of Nueva Jerusalén. *Journal of Contemporary Religion* 12 (3): 295–309.

Lerner, Robert, E. 1976. Medieval Prophecy and Religious Dissent. *Past and Present* 72: 3–24.

———— 1983. *The Powers of Prophecy: The Cedar of Lebanon Vision from the Mongol Onslaught to the Dawn of the Enlightenment*. Berkeley: University of California Press.

Lewis, James R. 1992. Approaches to the Study of the New Age Movement. In *Perspectives on the New Age*, ed. James R. Lewis and J. Gordon Melton. Albany: State University of New York Press.

Lindsey, Hal, with C. C. Carlson. [1970] 1971. *The Late Great Planet Earth*. London: Lakeland.

Lofland, John. [1966] 1977. *Doomsday Cult: A Study of Conversion, Proselytization, and Maintenance of Faith*, enlarged edn. New York: Irvington.

Lofland, John and Rodney Stark. 1965. "Becoming a World-Saver: A theory of conversion to a deviant perspective." *American Sociological Review* 30: 862–74.

Lucas, Phillip C. 1992. The New Age Movement and the Pentecostal/Charismatic Revival: Distinct Yet Parallel Phases of a Fourth Great Awakening? In *Perspectives on the New Age*, ed. James R. Lewis and J. Gordon Melton. Albany: State University of New York Press.

———— 1995. *The Odyssey of a New Religion: The Holy Order of MANS from New Age to Orthodoxy*. Bloomington and Indianapolis: Indiana University Press.

Luckmann, Thomas. 1970. *The Invisible Religion: The Problem of Religion in Modern Society*. London: Collier-Macmillan.

Luhrmann, T. M. 1989. *Persuasions of the Witch's Craft: Ritual Magic and Witchcraft in Present-Day England*. Oxford: Basil Blackwell.

Lynas, Stephen. 2001. *Challenging Time: The Churches' Millennium Experience*. London: Churches Together in England.

Malinowski, Bronislaw. [1925] 1992. *Magic, Science and Religion*. Prospect Heights, Ill.: Waveland Press.

Marsden, George M. 1995. *Fundamentalism and American Culture: The Shaping of Twentieth-Century Evangelicalism 1870–1925.* New York and Oxford: Oxford University Press.

Martin, Bernice. 1998. From Pre- to Postmodernity in Latin America: The Case of Pentecostalism. In *Religion, Modernity and Postmodernity,* ed. Paul Heelas. Oxford: Blackwell.

Martin, David. 1990. *Tongues of Fire: The Explosion of Protestantism in Latin America.* Oxford: Blackwell.

———— 1996. Religion, Secularization and Post-Modernity: Lessons from the Latin American Case. In *Religion and Modernity: Modes of Co-existence,* ed. Pål Repstad. Oslo: Scandinavian University Press.

———— 2001. *Pentecostalism: The World Their Parish.* Oxford: Blackwell.

McCain, Robert Stacy. 2002. Misread Rapture. *Washington Times,* 24 January.

McCarthy, E. Doyle. 1996. *Knowledge as Culture: The New Sociology of Knowledge.* London and New York: Routledge.

McGinn, Bernard. 1994. *Antichrist: Two Thousand Years of the Human Fascination with Evil.* San Francisco: HarperSanFrancisco.

———— 1995. The End of the World and the Beginning of Christendom. In *Apocalypse Theory and the Ends of the World,* ed. Malcolm Bull. Oxford: Blackwell.

———— [1979] 1998. *Visions of the End: Apocalyptic Traditions in the Middle Ages.* New York: Columbia University Press.

McIver, Tom. 1999. *The End of the World: An Annotated Bibliography.* Jefferson, N.C., and London: McFarland.

Meissner, W. W. 1995. *Thy Kingdom Come: Psychoanalytic Perspectives on the Messiah and the Millennium.* Kansas City: Sheed & Ward.

Melton, J. Gordon. [1985] 2000. Spiritualization and Reaffirmation: What Really Happens When Prophecy Fails in *Expecting Armageddon: Essential Readings in Failed Prophecy,* ed. Jon R. Stone. London and New York: Routledge.

Merton, Robert. [1957] 1968. *Social Theory and Social Structure.* New York: Free Press.

Miller, David L. 1987. Chiliasm: Apocalyptic with a Thousand Faces. In *Facing Apocalypse,* ed. Valerie Andrews, Robert Bosnak, and Karen Walter Goodwin Andrews. Dallas: Spring Publications.

Miller, Donald E. 1997. *Reinventing American Protestantism: Christianity in the New Millennium.* Berkeley, Los Angeles, and London: University of California Press.

Mission for the Coming Days. 1990. Testimonies of Believers, Seoul. Typewritten documents in the files of Inform at the London School of Economics.

Neitz, Mary Jo. 1987. *Charisma and Community: A Study of Religious Commitment within the Charismatic Renewal.* New Brunswick and Oxford: Transaction Books.

———— and Peter R. Mueser. 1997. Economic Man and the Sociology of Religion: A Critique of the Rational Choice Approach. In *Rational Choice Theory and Religion: Summary and Assessment,* ed. Lawrence A. Young. London and New York: Routledge.

Niebuhr, H. Richard. [1929] 1957. *The Social Sources of Denominationalism.* Cleveland, Ohio: Meridian.

O'Dea, Thomas F. 1966. *The Sociology of Religion.* Englewood Cliffs, N.J.: Prentice Hall.

O'Leary, Stephen D. 1994. *Arguing the Apocalypse: A Theory of Millennial Rhetoric.* New York and Oxford: Oxford University Press.

———— and Michael McFarland. 1989. The Political Use of Mythic Discourse: Prophetic Interpretation in Pat Robertson's Presidential Campaign. *Quarterly Journal of Speech* 75: 433–452.

Oropeza, B. J. 1994. *99 Reasons Why No One Knows When Christ Will Return*. Downers Grove, Ill.: InterVarsity Press.

Pennock, Robert T. 1999. *Tower of Babel: The Evidence against the New Creationism*. Cambridge, Mass., and London: MIT Press.

Percy, Martyn. 1996. *Words, Wonders and Power: Understanding Contemporary Christian Fundamentalism and Revivalism*. London: SPCK.

———— 1998. *Power and the Church: Ecclesiology in an Age of Transition*. London: Cassell.

———— ed. 2000a. *Calling Time: Religion and Change at the Turn of the Millennium*. Sheffield: Sheffield University Press.

———— ed. 2000b. *Previous Convictions: Conversion in the Present Day*. London: SPCK.

———— 2001. Whose Time Is it Anyway? Evangelicals, the Millennium and Millenarianism. In *Christian Millenarianism: From the Early Church to Waco*, ed. Stephen Hunt. London: Hurst.

———— and Ian Jones, eds. 2002. *Fundamentalism: Church and Society*. London: SPCK.

Plummer, Ken. 1996. Symbolic Interactionism in the Twentieth Century: The Rise of Empirical Social Theory. In *The Blackwell Companion to Social Theory*, ed. Bryan S. Turner. Oxford: Blackwell.

Poewe, Karla, ed. 1994. *Charismatic Christianity as Global Culture*. Columbia: University of South Carolina Press.

Poloma, Margaret. 1989. *The Assemblies of God at the Crossroads*. Knoxville: University of Tennessee Press.

———— 1999. Pentecostalism at the Millennium: Renewal and Revival. Paper presented at the annual meeting of the Society for the Scientific Study of Religion, Boston. November.

———— 2001. The Millenarianism of the Pentecostal Movement. In *Christian Millenarianism: From the Early Church to Waco*, ed. Stephen Hunt. London: Hurst.

Pontell, Henry N. ed. 2001. *Social Deviance: Readings in Theory and Research*, 4th edn. Upper Saddle River, N.J.: Prentice Hall.

Potter, Jonathan, and Margaret Wetherell. 1987. *Discourse and Social Psychology: Beyond Attitudes and Behaviour*. London: SAGE Publications.

Prosser, Peter E. 1999. *Dispensationalist Eschatology and Its Influence on American and British Religious Movements*. Lewiston, N.Y.: Edwin Mellen Press.

Quinby, Lee. 1997. Coercive Purity: The Dangerous Promise of Apocalyptic Masculinity. In *The Year 2000: Essays on the End*, ed. Charles B. Strozier and Michael Flynn. New York and London: New York University Press.

Rambo, Lewis R. 1993. *Understanding Religious Conversion*. New Haven and London; Yale University Press.

Reavis, Dick J. 1995. *The Ashes of Waco: An Investigation*. New York: Simon & Schuster.

Robbins, Thomas, and Susan J. Palmer, eds. 1997. *Millennium, Messiahs and Mayhem: Contemporary Apocalyptic Movements*. London and New York: Routledge.

Roelofs, Gerard. 1994. Charismatic Christian Thought: Experience, Metonymy, and Routinization. In *Charismatic Christianity as Global Culture*, ed. Karla Poewe, Columbia: University of South Carolina Press.

Ryrie, Charles C. 1995. *Dispensationalism*. Chicago: Moody Press.

Sadgrove, Michael. 2000. A Threshold of Fear and Hope: Religion, Society and the Dawn of the Millennium. In *Calling Time: Religion and Change at the Turn of the Millennium*, ed. Martyn Percy. Sheffield: Sheffield University Press.

Sanders, E. P. [1993] 1995. *The Historical Figure of Jesus*. London: Penguin Books.

Savage, Sara. 2000. A Psychology of Conversion—From All Angles. In *Previous Convictions: Conversion in the Present Day*, ed. Martyn Percy. London: SPCK.

——— 2002. A Psychology of Fundamentalism: The Search for Inner Failings. In *Fundamentalism: Church and Society*, ed. Martyn Percy and Ian Jones. London: SPCK.

Schaefer, Nancy A. 1999. "Some Will See Miracles": The Reception of Morris Cerullo World Evangelism in Britain. *Journal of Contemporary Religion* 14(1): 111–126.

Schanzer, Sandra. 1997. The Impending Computer Crisis of the Year 2000. In *The Year 2000: Essays on the End*, ed. Charles B. Strozier and Michael Flynn. New York and London: New York University Press.

Schmalz, Mathew N. [1994] 2000. When Festinger Fails: Prophecy and the Watchtower. In *Expecting Armageddon: Essential Readings in Failed Prophecy*, ed. Jon R. Stone. London and New York: Routledge.

Schmithals, Walter. [1973] 1975. *The Apocalyptic Movement: Introduction and Interpretation*. Nashville, Tenn.: Abingdon Press.

Scholem, Gershom. [1971] 1995. *The Messianic Idea in Judaism and Other Essays on Jewish Spirituality*. New York: Schocken Books.

Schroeder, Ralph. 1992. *Max Weber and the Sociology of Culture*. London: SAGE Publications.

Schwartz, Hillel. 1987. Millenarianism: An Overview. In *The Encyclopaedia of Religion*, ed. Mircea Eliade, Vol. 9. London and New York: Macmillan.

——— 1990. *Century's End: A Cultural History of the Fin de Siècle from the 990s through the 1990s*, New York: Doubleday.

Scotland, Nigel. 1995. *Charismatics and the Next Millennium: Do They Have a Future?* London: Hodder and Stoughton.

Simmons, J. L. 1964. On Maintaining Deviant Belief Systems. *Social Problems* 11: 250–256.

Simon, Herbert A. 1982. *Models of Bounded Rationality*, Vol. 1. Cambridge, Mass.: MIT Press.

Singelenberg, Richard. [1989] 2000. "It Separated the Wheat from the Chaff": The "1975" Prophecy and Its Impact among Dutch Jehovah's Witnesses. In *Expecting Armageddon: Essential Readings in Failed Prophecy*, ed. Jon R. Stone. London and New York: Routledge.

Skidmore, William. 1979. *Theoretical Thinking in Sociology*, 2nd edn. Cambridge: Cambridge University Press.

Skinner, Stephen. 1994. *Millennium Prophecies*. London: Virgin.

Smail, Tom, Andrew Walker, and Nigel Wright, eds. 1995a. *Charismatic Renewal: The Search for a Theology*. London: SPCK.

——— 1995b. "Revelation Knowledge" and Knowledge of Revelation: The Faith Movement and the Question of Heresy. In *Charismatic Renewal: The Search for a Theology*, ed. Tom Smail, Andrew Walker and Nigel Wright. London: SPCK.

Smith, Barry R. 1996. *Better Than Nostradamus or The Secret World Takeover*. Marlborough, New Zealand: International Support Ministries.

Smith, Christian. 1998. *American Evangelicalism: Embattled and Thriving*. Chicago and London: Chicago University Press.

——— 2000. *Christian America? What Evangelicals Really Want*. Berkeley, Los Angeles, and London: University of California Press.

Spittler, Russell P. 1994. Are Pentecostals and Charismatics Fundamentalists? A Review of American Uses of These Categories. In *Charismatic Christianity as Global Culture,* ed. Karla Poewe. Columbia: University of South Carolina Press.

St Clair, Michael. 1992. *Millenarian Movements in Historical Context.* New York: Garland.

Stark, Rodney. 1992. How Sane People Talk to the Gods: A Rational Theory of Revelations. In *Innovation in Religious Traditions: Essays in the Interpretation of Religious Change,* ed. Michael A. Williams, Collett Cox, and Martin S. Jaffe. Berlin and New York: Mouton De Gruyter.

Stark, Rodney, and Roger Finke. 2000. *Acts of Faith: Explaining the Human Side of Religion.* Berkeley, Los Angeles, and London: University of California Press.

Stark, Rodney, and William Sims Bainbridge. 1985. *The Future of Religion: Secularisation, Revival and Cult Formation.* Berkeley: University of California Press.

Stone, Jon R., ed. 2000. *Expecting Armageddon: Essential Readings in Failed Prophecy.* London and New York: Routledge.

Strozier, Charles. 1994. *Apocalypse: On the Psychology of Fundamentalism in America.* Boston: Beacon Press.

———— and Michael Flynn, eds. 1997. *The Year 2000: Essays on the End.* New York and London: New York University Press.

Swenson, Donald S. 1999. *Society, Spirituality and the Sacred: A Social Scientific Introduction.* Peterborough, Ontario: Broadview Press.

Szubin, Adam Jacob. 2000. Why Lubavitch Wants the Messiah Now: Religious Immigration as a Cause of Millenarianism. In *Apocalyptic Time,* ed. Albert I. Baumgarten. Leiden: Brill.

Taithe, Bertrand, and Tim Thornton, eds. 1997. *Prophecy: The Power of Inspired Language in History 1300–2000.* Stroud: Sutton Publishing.

Talmon, Yonina. 1968. "Millenarism". *International Encyclopedia of the Social Sciences.* Vol. 10: 349–62.

Thomas, Keith. [1971] 1973. *Religion and the Decline of Magic: Studies in Popular Beliefs in Sixteenth- and Seventeenth-Century England.* London: Penguin.

Thompson, Damian. 1996. *The End of Time: Faith and Fear in the Shadow of the Millennium.* London: Sinclair-Stevenson; revised edn., Vintage, 1999a.

———— 1999b. Judgment Day in the Jungle. *Telegraph Magazine,* November 13.

———— 2000. Are you Suffering from PMT? The Impact of Millennial Time. In *Calling Time: Religion and Change at the Turn of the Millennium,* ed. Martyn Percy. Sheffield: Sheffield University Press.

———— 2001a. Fundamentally Wrong. *The Spectator,* September 29.

———— 2001b. A Peruvian Messiah and the Retreat from Apocalypse. In *Christian Millenarianism from the Early Church to Waco,* ed. Stephen Hunt. London: Hurst.

Van Zandt, David E. 1991. *Living in the Children of God.* Princeton, N.J.: Princeton University Press.

Vermes, Geza. [2000] 2001. *The Changing Face of Jesus.* London: Penguin Books.

Victor, Jeffrey S. 1993. *Satanic Panic: The Creation of a Contemporary Legend.* Chicago and La Salle, Ill.: Open Court.

Voegelin, Eric. [1952] 1999. The New Science of Politics (1952). In *Modernity Without Restraint: The Collected Works of Eric Voegelin,* Vol. 5. Columbia: University of Missouri Press.

Walker, Andrew. 1989. *Restoring the Kingdom: The Radical Christianity of the House Church Movement,* revised edn. London: Hodder and Stoughton.

———— 1995a. The Devil You Think You Know: Demonology and the Charismatic

Movement. In *Charismatic Renewal: The Search for a Theology*, ed. Tom Smail, Andrew Walker, and Nigel Wright. London: SPCK.

———— 1995b. Miracles, Strange Phenomena, and Holiness. In *Charismatic Renewal: The Search for a Theology*, ed. by Tom Smail, Andrew Walker, and Nigel Wright. London: SPCK.

———— 1995c. Notes from a Wayward Son. In *Charismatic Renewal: The Search for a Theology*, ed. Tom Smail, Andrew Walker, and Nigel Wright. London: SPCK.

Wallis, Roy. 1975. Reflections on When Prophecy Fails. *Zetetic Scholar* 4: 14–14.

———— 1984. *The Elementary Forms of the New Religious Life*. London: Routledge & Kegan Paul.

Weber, Max. 1949. *The Methodology of the Social Sciences*. New York: Free Press.

———— [1948] 1970. *From Max Weber: Essays in Sociology*, tran., ed., and with an Introduction by H. H. Gerth and C. Wright Mills. London: Routledge & Kegan Paul.

———— [1922] 1993. *The Sociology of Religion*. Boston: Beacon Press.

Weber, Timothy P. 1979. *Living in the Shadow of the Second Coming: American Premillennialism 1875–1925*. New York and Oxford: Oxford University Press.

Weiser, Neil. [1974] 2000. The Effects of Prophetic Disconfirmation of the Committed. In *Expecting Armageddon: Essential Readings in Failed Prophecy*, ed. Jon R. Stone. London and New York: Routledge.

Wessinger, Catherine. 1997. Millennialism with and without the Mayhem. In *Millennium, Messiahs and Mayhem: Contemporary Apocalyptic Movements*, ed. Thomas Robbins and Susan J. Palmer. London and New York: Routledge.

———— 2000. *How the Millennium Comes Violently: From Jonestown to Heaven's Gate*. New York: Seven Bridges Press.

Whisenant, Edgar. 1988. *88 Reasons Why the Rapture Could Be in 1988*. Nashville: World Bible Society.

Williams, Julian E. 1972. *Henry Kissinger—Mystery Man of Power*. Tulsa, Okla.: Christian Crusade Publications.

Wills, Garry. 1990. *Under God: Religion and American Politics*. New York: Simon and Schuster.

Wilson, Bryan R. 1961. *Sects and Society*. London: Heinemann.

———— 1966. *Religion in Secular Society: A Sociological Comment*. London: C. A. Watts & Co.

———— [1973] 1975. *Magic and the Millennium*. St Albans: Paladin.

———— 1982. *Religion in Sociological Perspective*. Oxford: Oxford University Press.

———— 1990. *The Social Dimensions of Sectarianism: Sects and New Religious Movements in Contemporary Society*. Oxford: Clarendon Press.

———— 1996. Toleration, Pluralism and Privatization. In *Religion and Modernity: Modes of Co-existence*, ed. Pål Repstad. Oslo: Scandinavian University Press.

Wilson, Robert Anton, with Robert Shea. [1975] 1988. *Illuminatus!* New York: Dell Books.

Winter, Ralph. 1995. Editorial in *Mission Frontiers*, bulletin of the US Center for World Mission, Pasadena, California, May/June.

Wojcik, Daniel. 1997. *The End of the World As We Know It: Faith, Fatalism and Apocalypse in America*. New York and London: New York University Press.

Worsley, Peter. 1957. *The Trumpet Shall Sound: A Study of "Cargo" Cults in Melanesia*. London: MacGibbon and Kee.

Wright, Nigel. 1995a. "The Rise of the Prophetic" in *Charismatic Renewal: The Search for a Theology*, ed. Tom Smail, Andrew Walker and Nigel Wright. London: SPCK.

———— 1995b. "The Theology and Methodology of 'Signs and Wonders' " in *Charismatic Renewal: The Search for a Theology,* ed. Tom Smail, Andrew Walker and Nigel Wright. London: SPCK.

Young, Lawrence A., ed. 1997. *Rational Choice Theory and Religion: Summary and Assessment.* London and New York: Routledge.

Index